The Transformative Value of EU Citizenship after Brexit

Christian Dadomo • Noëlle Quénivet

The Transformative Value of EU Citizenship after Brexit

palgrave
macmillan

Christian Dadomo
Bristol, UK

Noëlle Quénivet
Law School
University of the West of England
Bristol, UK

ISBN 978-3-032-20594-0 ISBN 978-3-032-20595-7 (eBook)
https://doi.org/10.1007/978-3-032-20595-7

This Palgrave Macmillan imprint is published by the registered company Springer Nature Switzerland AG.
The registered company address is: Gewerbestrasse 11, 6330 Cham, Switzerland

Preface

This book is the product of a reflection that began after the Brexit referendum, during which we participated in several workshops as EU Law lecturers. The aim of these workshops was to explore the potential implications of Brexit for EU citizens. At that time, there was considerable uncertainty surrounding the legal status and rights of EU citizens living in the UK. As such citizens, we found ourselves questioning the meaning of EU citizenship from a purely theoretical, legalistic, and political to an experiential perspective. This prompted us to think about the transformative value of EU citizenship, especially regarding the possible loss of rights for our EU fellow citizens ("concitoyens") in the UK. It is often when we are on the verge of losing something valued that we truly appreciate its importance, and EU citizenship is no exception.

While this concept has never been articulated in philosophical, political, and legal terms, delving back into the exegesis of EU citizenship, we rediscovered the transformative value that EU citizenship can have on EU citizens who have exercised their right to free movement within the EU territory.

We presented our reflections on the transformative value of EU citizenship at a conference aptly titled "Transformation of Citizenship", organised by the Institute of International Law and International Relations of the University of Graz and the UNI-ETC, Austria, which took place on 20–21 November 2018. Our paper was originally entitled *Assessing EU Citizenship Under the Myopic Lens of Brexit*.

Our original plan was to develop this conference paper into a full journal article. However, as time progressed, we realised that the scope of our research and writing exceeded the confines of an article. As a result, we submitted a book proposal to our current publisher. Although we may not have met the original deadline for submission, this delay ultimately allowed us to include a wealth of empirical research studies and official reports on the topic.

For disclosure, we acknowledge that in the process of writing this book, we used the following technologies and writing tools:

1. Grammarly (Premium version) was used to ensure no errors in spelling, grammar, and syntax were made. Yet, not all suggestions offered by Grammarly were accepted.
2. Zotero (free) was used as a reference management tool to organise sources and generate citations.
3. Google was used to translate a judgement in Dutch, a language that none of the authors is sufficiently fluent in. All other translations (French and German) are by the authors.

After using these tools, the authors double-checked the accuracy of the translations and references.

January 2026
Bristol, UK

Christian Dadomo
Noëlle Quénivet

Contents

Abbreviations

CJEU	Court of Justice of the European Union
DWP	Department for Work and Pensions
EC	European Community
EEA	European Economic Area
EEC	European Economic Community
ECHR	European Convention of Human Rights
ECJ	European Court of Justice
EU	European Union
EU27	European Union with 27 Member States
EU CFR	Charter of Fundamental Rights of the European Union
HMRC	His Majesty's Revenue & Customs
OJ	Official Journal (of the European Communities)
OJEU	Official Journal of the European Union
TEC	Treaty Establishing the European Community
TEEC	Treaty Establishing the European Economic Community
TEU	Treaty on European Union
TFEU	Treaty on the Functioning of the European Union
UK	United Kingdom of Great Britain and Northern Ireland
WA	Withdrawal Agreement

CHAPTER 1

Introduction

Abstract This chapter introduces the book, which examines the transformative value of EU citizenship through the prism of Brexit. Traditionally understood as a legal status conferring rights, EU citizenship has often been approached from a minimalist perspective focused on status and rights. Brexit, however, exposed its broader significance by highlighting what is lost when citizenship is removed. The authors argue that EU citizenship comprises a triad of status, rights, and practice (with practice following the exercise of free movement) that reveals its experiential and transformative dimensions. Drawing on a socio-legal methodology, the book explores how EU citizenship enables individuals to embed themselves in other Member States without formal integration. Using a doctrinal approach that focuses on the law and incorporates interdisciplinary insights, the study offers a novel conceptual framework and a long-term perspective on Brexit's impact, emphasising that EU citizenship is more than a juridical construct: it is a lived experience.

Keywords EU citizenship • Brexit • Legal status • Rights • Free movement • Citizenship • Nationality

In *Grzelczyk,* the Court of Justice of the European Union (CJEU) defined EU citizenship as a fundamental status that enables nationals of Member

C. Dadomo, N. Quénivet, *The Transformative Value of EU Citizenship after Brexit*,
https://doi.org/10.1007/978-3-032-20595-7_1

States to enjoy the same treatment in law (*Case C-184/99 Grzelczyk* 2001). Later, in *Zambrano,* the close correlation between this fundamental status and the enjoyment of substantive rights was highlighted (*Case C-34/09 Zambrano* 2011). Since then, scholars have sought to understand the implications of this status and its legal value.[1] They focused on what this status had brought to individuals in addition to their rights and obligations as nationals. They were, of course, underlining the additional gains and benefits. Yet, EU citizenship was never looked at from the other side of the scope.

Brexit has put into relief many of these previous academic debates: what if EU citizenship was lost or removed? What would this mean for former EU citizens and EU citizens in the country withdrawing from the EU? Which rights and freedoms would they lose? In *Wightman*, the CJEU recognised that the withdrawal of a Member State from the EU would have "considerable impact on the rights of all Union citizens" (*Case C-621/18 Wightman* 2018, ¶ 64). Indeed, according to a 2020 report, an estimated 3.5 to 4.1 million EU citizens and their family members (Specialised Committee on Citizens' Rights 2020, 10) and 1 million UK nationals and their family members in the EU27[2] were impacted. For individuals, "citizenship and its associated rights are often taken for granted or unrecognised by [them] until they cease to exist or function as expected" (Ferbrache 2019, 83; Brahic and Lallement 2020, 14). Brexit has brought to the surface discussions about the legal value, or more generally, the worth of EU citizenship in contrast to (State) nationality, but this time from a completely different angle.

In its usual understanding, the concept of a "national" refers to the legal link between a State and an individual, to the effect that the individual belongs to a State by the application of domestic nationality laws. In contrast, the notion of citizenship relates more to an individual's local status, which is relevant at the domestic level (van den Berghe and Huber 1981, 758; Tassin 1994, 98). Accordingly, as Weiss stresses, nationality and citizenship are two sides of the same idea: State membership (Weiss 1979, 5). Whilst one is an external marker, the other is an internal one

[1] Among the key authors in the field are D. Kostakopoulou, J. Weiler, D. Kochenov, G. Davies, E. Spaventa, N. Nic Shuibhne, J. Shaw, S. Coutts, C. Barnard, E. Pataut, D. Thym, etc.

[2] This is the sum of those living in a Member State that has adopted a constitutive and declaratory system of registration (Specialised Committee on Citizens' Rights 2020, 10 and 12).

(Gamberale 1995, 635). Yet, nationality encompasses a broader pool of individuals than citizenship (see Blachèr 2000, 87), because, citizenship relates essentially to constitutional arrangements that enable a specific category of persons to participate in the life of a State/entity (Evans 1991, 198–99; Moura Ramos 1992, 39), and form the political subject (Closa 1992, 1138; Simon and Kovar 1993, 286). Citizenship denotes the possession of rights and duties of individuals (see van den Berghe and Huber 1981, 758) in relation to a political community (Vasiljević 2006, 116–17) to the effect that, as a concept, it "connects the ideas of legal status, identity, rights, and duties" (Newman 1996, 146; see Kiernan 1997, 323–25).

In this traditional dichotomy between nationality and citizenship,[3] EU citizenship inscribes itself as a citizenship. Literature on citizenship offers numerous definitions of the concept, most of them stressing two core aspects: status, usually defined as a set of rights and obligations, and identity, which expresses the affective dimension of membership in a community (see Kostakopoulou 1998, 396; Enjolras 2008, 495). A third aspect, that of participation (in political life), is sometimes included (Eder and Giesen 2003, 4). In other instances, the third aspect, in addition to status and rights, is that of identity (see Joppke 2007, 38). Or identity becomes the fourth (see Kostakopoulou 2007, 645).

In the EU context, Becker argues that there are three visions of European citizenship: legal-participatory, cultural identity-based, and constructive citizenship, the idea that a collective identity is created "out of shared and contested visions of citizenship itself" (Becker 2004, 140 and 143–45). The first vision emphasises the two aforementioned elements, *status* and *rights*, that are often combined under what is called the "minimalist approach" that focuses on the legal status and the rights conferred upon individuals. If "Europe must be close to its citizens" (*Tindemans Report—Report on European Union* 1975, 11–35), those citizens must feel some attachment to and loyalty towards the EU (Barber 2002, 246). Hence, the original focus was on the legal status of EU citizens, thereby highlighting a formal approach towards EU citizenship as a juridico-political institution. However, this attachment and loyalty to the EU cannot be fostered by a limited focus on citizens' status and rights alone. After all, it might be counterproductive to use a notion such as

[3] As Sredanovic notes, this understanding of the difference between nationality and citizenship is prevalent in some States but not all. In some States, the concept of nationality is linked to ethnicity, as recognised by the State (Sredanovic 2014, 47–48).

European citizenship if its direct benefits are unclear (van den Berghe and Huber 1981, 759). It must also be genuinely enjoyed, as it is in its *practice* that individuals could or might perceive their EU citizenship. The status and rights are more palpable in the lives of EU citizens who have exercised their right to free movement, as they are the everyday manifestation of EU citizenship. There is an even broader and more dynamic approach to EU citizenship that looks at the symbolism of EU citizenship (see Simon and Kovar 1993, 288) and more specifically at the solidarity between EU citizens that should inevitably create some form of common identity (*Tindemans Report—Report on European Union* 1975, 3), which could be seen as the fourth element of the concept of citizenship (Becker's third vision of EU citizenship of one created by citizens themselves). It is principally about reinforcing "in each individual the consciousness of their belonging not only to a nation but also to a much wider community" (Solbes Mira 1991, 170). Joppke also refers to citizenship as identity as "the behavioral aspects of individuals acting and conceiving of themselves as members of a collectivity [...] *or* the normative conceptions of such behavior imputed by the state" (Joppke 2007, 38). It is more aspirational and, though not necessarily, somehow inscribes itself within a vision of the EU as a polity in which a *European civitas* exists and thrives. Both the practical and the symbolic value of EU citizenship have been underscored by the CJEU. In this book, the authors adopt a more finely grained definition that comprises three related perspectives of citizenship: status, rights, and practice. As shown, status and rights are essential core aspects of EU citizenship, part of the so-called minimalist, legal-participatory vision of EU citizenship. Yet, as the authors will explain in this book, status and rights only reveal themselves when practised as part of the principle and right of free movement within the European Union, especially in relation to permanent residents. Hence, the authors view EU citizenship through the triad of status, rights, and practice.

At first sight, Brexit undergirded this minimalist approach to EU citizenship, as many discussions centred on the status and rights of EU citizens and the rights they would lose as a result of Brexit. After all, the European Union had enabled a shift in how EU nationals were viewed in other Member States: from foreigners (immigrants or temporary guests) to workers, residents, and then EU citizens. As some authors note, it was tempting to view Brexit as "a complete dismantlement of the EU legacy" (Juverdeanu 2025, 278). With Brexit, the pendulum could have swung back to viewing UK nationals in the EU who were EU citizens, and EU citizens in the UK, as foreigners again. Yet, the Withdrawal Agreement (Withdrawal Agreement 2020) has mitigated this outlook to some extent. Accordingly, Brexit has shown that EU citizenship has subtly, though fundamentally, changed how others (whether individuals, collective entities, or institutions) view EU citizens who have exercised their right to free movement, and how those citizens view themselves.

This book argues that Brexit highlights that the concept of EU citizenship is more than just a status and a bundle of rights (Worster 2018, 353). As Coutts states, "there is certainly more to Union citizenship than a naked market-driven, transnational citizenship denuded of any social or political dimension" (Coutts 2018, 246). It has a transformative value. The transformative value of EU citizenship can be understood as the process whereby, to para- and re-phrase *Zambrano,* EU citizens can genuinely and fully enjoy the rights granted to them under their fundamental status as EU citizens, ***and,*** the authors add, come to perceive themselves and are perceived as quasi-nationals. Nonetheless, it is claimed that this transformative value is essentially, though not exclusively, based on practice, that is, the exercise of the right to free movement of persons and this is more prominent for permanent residents, that is, those citizens who live for more than five years in a country different from the country of their nationality (Citizenship Directive 2024, art. 16(1)). EU citizenship is experiential as it makes EU nationals fully aware of their EU citizenship as truly additional[4] to their nationality (or national citizenship as referred to in Articles 9 TEU and 20(1) TFEU) ***and*** helps them "embed themselves"[5] in the society of any other Member State without any obligation to integrate.[6] Behind the legal façade of citizenship, the authors also try to uncover the EU person. Throughout the book, the authors' focus is on

[4] The distinction between EU citizenship "complementing" national citizenship (which was introduced by the Amsterdam Treaty) and EU citizenship being "additional" to national citizenship (introduced by the Lisbon Treaty) is very important and has been overlooked by commentators. To the authors' knowledge, only H. de Waele has rightly analysed this alteration in terminology and showed that it "substantially exceeds the cosmetic" (de Waele 2010, 322).

[5] In this book, the authors do not distinguish between the words "embed", "integrate", "incorporate", "anchor", or "belong" as colleagues in social sciences do. By "embed" the authors actually mean that individuals have grown strong links with the local structures and community and eventually become settled.

[6] To use a Heideggerian concept, this is the *Dasein* of EU citizenship: the uniqueness of being an EU citizen in that EU citizens concern themselves with being EU citizens and define their own being as EU citizens as they go along in everydayness.

permanent residents, those whose sustained practice of EU citizenship most vividly reveals its transformative value. It should be noted that whilst the word permanent is used under the Citizenship Directive (Citizenship Directive 2024, ch. IV) in relation to EU citizens, the word "long-term" is used in relation to third-country nationals who have resided legally and continuously in an EU Member State (Council Directive on Long-Term Resident Third-Country Nationals 2003, ch. II). Whilst the authors acknowledge that EU citizens do not form a monolithic group and that elements such as race, class, gender, and nationality affect their daily practices (Kulz 2023, 222; Davies and Carter 2025, 164), this book will only make references to these elements whenever appropriate. Moreover, the special status of Irish nationals that is covered by the Common Travel Area (GOV.UK 2026), that pre-dates the UK and Ireland's entry into the EU, is not examined in this book.

Brexit has exposed the transformative value of EU citizenship inasmuch as especially, but not only, those EU citizens who exercised their right to free movement have not only gained a much better understanding of (or even realised) the full value of EU citizenship but also considered ways to keep it. The wider, aspirational approach towards EU citizenship is no less visible in Brexit. It might therefore be contended that Brexit has revealed that EU citizenship goes beyond this minimalist approach that focuses solely on status and rights to a vision of EU citizenship with broader appeal because of its practice.

To support this research, this book uses a socio-legal methodology, which enables the authors to combine legal analysis with insights from the social sciences to understand law in its broader social, political, economic, and cultural context. Rather than viewing law as an isolated system of rules, it examines how law operates in practice, how individuals and institutions interact with it, how these rules govern and affect relations between individuals, and more generally, what the social consequences of these legal norms are. It is thus the most suited methodology as the authors can go beyond the law, that is, the *status* and the *rights* of EU citizenship, and understand how this status and rights are experienced, contested, and applied, that is, its *practice*, which are, in the authors' opinion, the three core aspects of EU citizenship that create the transformative value of EU citizenship. The method is doctrinal, that is, desk-based. The authors interpret various legal sources, specifically the treaties (TFEU (Lisbon) 2025; TEU (Lisbon) 2025), the Citizenship Directive (Citizenship Directive 2024), and pertinent case law. Additionally, the authors incorporate legal academic literature and scholarly works in other disciplines, particularly those grounded in empirical research methods (e.g., focus groups, surveys, interviews). This interdisciplinary perspective draws insights from political science, human geography, sociology, and anthropology, thereby allowing the authors to gain a more nuanced, granular understanding of how the law operates in practice. It is however noticeable that, as much literature has been devoted to the fate of EU citizens in the UK rather than UK nationals in the EU27, partially because of the numbers affected, the fact that UK nationals "are rarely considered as migrants" (Benson et al. 2022, 382) and the difficulty of carrying out empirical research spread across 27 States, this book tends to draw on more examples of the former compared to the latter.

The point of this book is not to rehash existing theories and perspectives on EU citizenship, which are more than adequately covered in legal literature, as this book will demonstrate in its references. Neither is it to provide a comprehensive examination of the protection of EU citizens under the Withdrawal Agreement and the specificity of each situation, which has already been addressed (see, e.g., Barnard et al. 2022; Peers 2021; Dougan 2020; Barnard et al. 2024). Rather, it seeks to explore EU citizenship through the prism of Brexit. Whilst Coutts has approached this from a legal perspective (Coutts 2018), the authors adopt a more holistic approach by including other disciplines. Moreover, the conceptual framework, the transformative value of EU citizenship presented in Chap. 3, is a novel contribution to understanding EU citizenship. Furthermore, most legal discussions about the impact of Brexit and EU citizenship took place over the four to five years following the referendum. The authors' work, however, is set 10 years after the referendum, offering them a chance to take a much longer view than most studies. Through a socio-legal approach, the originality of this work lies in the clear demonstration of the essence and existence of the transformative value of EU citizenship as experienced through the Brexit period and beyond.

This book begins in Chap. 2 by explaining the evolution of EU citizenship, stressing the link between *status* and *rights*. Chapter 3 starts by analysing the interrelationship of EU citizenship as a status, and EU Member States' nationality as two layers that are separate, albeit related, in law and intermingled in practice. It then moves on to explain how the three rights, that of residence, non-discrimination, and to vote and stand as a candidate in local elections, have created the "transformative value" of EU citizenship that is based on the triad of *status, rights,* and *practice*. In Chap. 4, the authors explore how Brexit challenged the fundamental status of EU citizenship. For this, two tests are used: first, whether EU citizenship can be revoked (thereby referring to the idea of layers) and second, how the EU and the UK have approached the issue of EU citizenship in their interactions and negotiations. Chapter 5 then evaluates the Withdrawal Agreement against the three elements of the transformative value of EU citizenship, that is, the right to residence, the principle of non-discrimination, and the right to vote and stand in local elections. Finally, Chap. 6 focuses on the emotions and actions of EU citizens, individually and collectively, in the wake of the referendum. By examining the pro-EU movements, the suggestion of associate EU citizenship and the rush towards British and EU passports, Chap. 6 further reveals the transformative value of EU citizenship.

References

Agreement on the Withdrawal of the United Kingdom of Great Britain and Northern Ireland from the European Union and the European Atomic Energy Community, OJ L 29/7. 2020. https://eur-lex.europa.eu/legal-content/EN/TXT/?uri=CELEX%3A02020W%2FTXT-20250430.

Barber, N. W. 2002. Citizenship, Nationalism and the European Union. *European Law Review* 27 (3): 241–259.

Barnard, Catherine, Sarah Fraser Butlin, and Fiona Costello. 2022. The Changing Status of European Union Nationals in the United Kingdom Following Brexit: The Lived Experience of the European Union Settlement Scheme. *Social & Legal Studies* 31 (3): 365–388. https://doi.org/10.1177/09646639211032337.

Barnard, Catherine, Fiona Costello, and Fraser Butlin. 2024. *Low-Paid EU Migrant Workers: The House, the Street, the Town*, Bristol Studies in Law and Social Justice. Bristol University Press.

Becker, Michael A. 2004. Managing Diversity in the European Union: Inclusive European Citizenship and Third-Country Nationals. *Yale Human Rights & Development Law Journal* 7:132–183.

Benson, Michaela, Nando Sigona, Elena Zambelli, and Catherine Craven. 2022. From the State of the Art to New Directions in Researching What Brexit Means for Migration and Migrants. *Migration Studies* 10 (2): 374–390. https://doi.org/10.1093/migration/mnac010.

Berghe, Guido van den, and Christian H. Huber. 1981. European Citizenship. In *Das Europa Der Zweiten Generation. Gedächtnisschrift Für Christophe Sasse*, ed. Roland Bieber and Dietmar Nickel II. N.P. Engel Verlag.

Blachèr, Philippe. 2000. Les aspects juridiques de la citoyenneté européenne. In *Vers une citoyenneté européenne*, ed. Lydie Pfander-Meny and Jean-Guy Lebeau. Canopé—CRDP de Dijon.

Brahic, Benedicte, and Maxime Lallement. 2020. From "Expats" to "Migrants": Strategies of Resilience Among French Movers in Post-Brexit Manchester. *Migration and Development* 9 (1): 8–24. https://doi.org/10.1080/21632324.2018.1503486.

Case C-184/99. 2001. Rudy Grzelczyk v. Centre Public d'aide Sociale d'Ottignies-Louvain-La-Neuve, ECLI:EU:C:2001:458 (ECJ).

Case C-34/09. 2011. Gerardo Ruiz Zambrano v. Office National de l'Emploi (ONEm), ECLI:EU:C:2011:124 (CJEU).

Case C-621/18. 2018. Andy Wightman and Others v. Secretary of State for Exiting the European Union, ECLI:EU:C:2018:999 (CJEU).

Closa, Carlos. 1992. The Concept of Citizenship in the Treaty on European Union. *Common Market Law Review* 29 (6): 1137–1169. https://doi.org/10.54648/cola1992065.

Consolidated Version of Treaty on European Union (Lisbon). 2025. http://data.europa.eu/eli/treaty/teu_2016/2025-03-15.

Consolidated Version of Treaty on the Functioning of the European Union (Lisbon). 2025. http://data.europa.eu/eli/treaty/tfeu_2016/2025-03-15.

Council Directive 2003/109/EC of 25 November 2003 Concerning the Status of Third-Country Nationals Who Are Long-Term Residents, OJ L16/44. 2003.

Coutts, Stephen. 2018. Citizens of Elsewhere, Everywhere and ... Nowhere? Rethinking Union Citizenship in Light of Brexit. *Northern Ireland Legal Quarterly* 69 (3): 231–247. https://doi.org/10.53386/nilq.v69i3.161.

Davies, Katherine, and Adam Carter. 2025. Living with Brexit: Families, Relationships and the Temporalities of Everyday Personal Life in "Brexit Britain". *The Sociological Review* 73 (1): 156–174. https://doi.org/10.1177/00380261241260112.

Directive 2004/38/EC of the European Parliament and the of the Council of 29 April 2004 on the Rights of Citizens of the Union and Their Family Members to Move and Reside Freely within the Territory of the Member States Amending Regulation (EEC) No 1612/68 and Repealing Directives 64/221/EEC, 68/360/EEC, 72/194/EEC, 73/148/EEC, 75/34/EEC, 75/35/EEC, 90/364/EEC, 90/365/EEC, and 93/96/EEC, OJ L158/77. 2024.

Dougan, Michael. 2020. So Long, Farewell, Auf Wiedersehen, Goodbye: The UK's Withdrawal Package. *Common Market Law Review* 57:631–704. https://doi.org/10.54648/cola2020689.

Eder, Klaus, and Bernhard Giesen, eds. 2003. *European Citizenship: Between National Legacies and Postnational Projects.* Oxford University Press.

Enjolras, Bernard. 2008. Two Hypotheses about the Emergence of a Post-National European Model of Citizenship. *Citizenship Studies* 12 (5): 495–505. https://doi.org/10.1080/13621020802337923.

Evans, Andrew. 1991. Nationality Law and European Integration. *European Law Review* 16 (3): 190–215.

Ferbrache, Fiona. 2019. Acts of European Citizenship: How Britons Resident in France Have Been Negotiating Post-Brexit Futures. *Geography* 104 (2): 81–88. https://doi.org/10.1080/00167487.2019.12094067.

Gamberale, Carlo. 1995. National Identities and Citizenship in the European Union. *European Public Law* 1 (4): 633–661. https://doi.org/10.54648/euro1995066.

GOV.UK. 2026. Common Travel Area: Rights of UK and Irish Citizens. January 1. https://www.gov.uk/government/publications/common-travel-area-guidance.

Joppke, Christian. 2007. Transformation of Citizenship: Status, Rights, Identity. *Citizenship Studies* 11 (1): 37–48. https://doi.org/10.1080/13621020601099831.

Juverdeanu, Cristina. 2025. Brexit and the EU Settlement Scheme: Continuity and Rupture with the European Union. *Journal of Contemporary European Studies* 33 (1): 278–293. https://doi.org/10.1080/14782804.2024.2372677.

Kiernan, Annabel K. 1997. Citizenship—The Real Democratic Deficit of the European Union? *Citizenship Studies* 1 (3): 323–334. https://doi.org/10.1080/13621029708420662.

Kostakopoulou, Dora. 1998. Nested Old and New Citizenships in the European Union: Bringing out the Complexity. *Columbia Journal of European Law* 5 (3): 389–413.

Kostakopoulou, Dora. 2007. European Union Citizenship: Writing the Future. *European Law Journal* 13 (5): 623–646. https://doi.org/10.1111/j.1468-0386.2007.00387.x.

Kulz, Christy. 2023. Spaces of the Local, Spaces of the Nation: Intersectional Bordering Practices in Post-Brexit Berlin. *European Urban and Regional Studies* 30 (3): 221–234. https://doi.org/10.1177/09697764221087644.

Moura Ramos, Rui Manuel. 1992. Les nouveaux aspects de la libre circulation des personnes: vers une citoyenneté européenne. *Boletim Da Faculdade de Direito* 68:17–57.

Newman, Michael. 1996. *Democracy, Sovereignty and the European Union*. 1st ed. St. Martin's Press.

Peers, Steve. 2021. The End—Or a New Beginning? The EU/UK Withdrawal Agreement. *Yearbook of European Law* 39 (March): 122–198. https://doi.org/10.1093/yel/yeaa010.

Simon, Denys, and Robert Kovar. 1993. La citoyenneté européenne. *Cahiers de Droit Européen* 3–4:285–316. https://doi.org/10.54648/COLA2004023.

Solbes Mira, P. 1991. La citoyenneté européenne. *Revue du Marché Commun de l'Union Européenne* 345:168–170.

Specialised Committee on Citizens' Rights. 2020. *Joint Report on the Implementation of Residence Rights under Part Two of the Withdrawal Agreement*. Specialised Committee on Citizens' Rights. https://commission.europa.eu/document/download/111c431d-3bee-44d4-935b-33c44d12167d_en?filename=joint_report_on_article_18_after_the_jc_meeting.pdf.

Sredanovic, Djordje. 2014. Quelle est la valeur de la nationalité/citoyenneté en Italie?: Résultats d'une recherche auprès des migrants et des ouvriers Italiens à Ferrare. *Migrations Société* 153–154 (3): 47–61. https://doi.org/10.3917/migra.153.0047.

Tassin, Etienne. 1994. Identités Nationales et Citoyenneté Politique. *Esprit* 198 (1): 97–111.

Tindemans Report—Report on European Union. 1975. Bulletin of the European Communities, Supplement 1/76. European Communities. https://www.cvce.eu/en/education/unit-content/-/unit/02bb76df-d066-4c08-a58a-d4686a3e68ff/63f5fca7-54ec-4792-8723-1e626324f9e3/Resources#284c9784-9bd2-472b-b704-ba4bb1f3122d_en&overlay; http://aei.pitt.edu/942/1/political_tindemans_report.pdf.

Vasiljević, Snježana. 2006. The Concept of European Citizenship. In *Croatian Accession to the European Union (Volume 4)—Challenges of Participation*, ed. K. Ott. Institute of Public Finance and Friedrich Ebert Stiftung. https://d-nb.info/1191058271/34.

Waele, Henri de. 2010. EU Citizenship: Revisiting Its Meaning, Place and Potential. *European Journal of Migration and Law* 12 (3): 319–336. https://doi.org/10.1163/157181610X520391.

Weiss, P. 1979. *Nationality and Statelessness in International Law*. 2nd ed. Brill.

Worster, William Thomas. 2018. Brexit and the International Law Prohibitions on the Loss of EU Citizenship. *International Organizations Law Review* 15 (2): 341–363. https://doi.org/10.1163/15723747-01502005.

CHAPTER 2

EU Citizenship: A Status as a Gateway to Rights

Abstract This chapter examines the evolution of EU citizenship from its origins in economic integration to its current status as a gateway to rights. Initially tied to the *homo economicus* and free movement provisions under the Treaty of Rome, rights were gradually extended beyond economic activity through directives and jurisprudence. The Maastricht Treaty formalised EU citizenship, introducing political and non-economic rights, while subsequent treaties and case law reinforced its autonomy from market-based status. Today, EU citizenship is recognised as the "fundamental status" of Member State nationals, underpinning free movement, the rights of residence, and the principle of non-discrimination.

Keywords EU citizenship • Free movement • Right of residence • Principle of non-discrimination • Brexit

2.1 Introduction

Citizenship at the national level is typically viewed as a status leading to rights and duties, that is, citizenship is the source of rights, it is the "right to have rights" (*Top v. Dulles* 1958). In contrast, at the EU level, it can be argued that the evolution of citizenship appears to have developed in the opposite direction. Indeed, EEC nationals were first granted specific rights

C. Dadomo, N. Quénivet, *The Transformative Value of EU Citizenship after Brexit*,
https://doi.org/10.1007/978-3-032-20595-7_2

(primarily relating to free movement and equal treatment and some social rights) by a range of provisions in the 1957 Treaty of Rome (TEEC (Rome) 1957) before being granted the status of EU citizens by the 1992 Treaty of Maastricht (TEU and TEC (Maastricht) 1992). Initially, rights were granted to those engaged in an economic activity, that is, the *homo economicus,* but were later expanded to encompass a wider category of individuals. This early form of citizenship, termed "mercantile citizenship", was abandoned for a fuller citizenship, a *status* as a gateway to *rights* (see Pataut 2018, 256; Kochenov 2013, 507), though it remains "one of the few—and possibly the only—examples of a polity based exclusively on rights as opposed to substantive notions of peoplehood" (Delanty 2007, 65; see also Pataut 2010; Bux and Maciejewski 2025).

2.2 From *Homo Economicus* to Rights Unrelated to Economic Activity

Initially, the rights of nationals of EEC Member States were not linked to EU citizenship as EU citizenship did not yet exist. After all, "[t]he Treaty [of Rome] [did] not safeguard the fundamental rights of the individuals affected by its application, nor [did] it recognise, even in an embryonic form, a constitutional right to European citizenship. Europe [could not] confer citizenship; this remain[ed] the prerogative of the Member States" (Mancini 1989, 596). At the inception of the now European Union, "[n]ationality [was] [...] used as a connecting factor for determining the beneficiaries of freedom of movement" (Evans 1991, 191). The concept of "national of a Member State" was included in Articles 52(1), 58, and 59 of the EEC Treaty, as well as in regulations and directives relating to workers (see Regulation (EEC) No 1612/68 1968, art. 1; Council Directive 68/360/EEC 1968, art. 1) and seemed to have been understood as individuals having the nationality of one of the Member States (van den Berghe and Huber 1981, 757; Edens and Patijn 1972, 323; Davis 2002, 131). Whilst the concept of "Community national" appeared in some legal literature (see Evans 1982, 1984, 688), the stress was primarily on the *homo economicus* who was granted rights commensurate to their economic activities, such as being workers or self-employed persons: "individuals were bearers of rights *qua* nationals of a Member State and *qua* economic agents" (Closa 1992, 1141–42). Remarkably, the European Court of Justice referred in 1986 to EEC citizen (*Case C-139-85 Kempf*

1986, ¶ 4), in 1988 to "Community citizens" (*Case 143/87 Stanton* 1988, ¶ 13), and in 1991 to "Community nationals" (*Case C-292/89 Antonissen* 1991, ¶¶ 9, 14 and 21).

According to the discrimination theory that clarifies the scope of the free movement provisions (see Spaventa 2004, 744–45), freedom of movement was granted to facilitate labour movement across borders and to preclude States from denying foreign nationals access to their territory (Olsen 2008, 46; Evans 1982, 497; see also Spaventa 2004, 763). Intra-European migration was integral to the policy of economic development, which was based on the liberalisation and harmonisation process within the common/single market (Dubucs and Mourlane 2017, 10). More crudely, "[i]ndividuals were seen merely as factors of production [...] to be put in the service of the construction of the internal market" (Coutts 2019, 243–44; see also Barnard and Butlin 2022; Elsmore and Starup 2007, 71). The rights of such nationals, including non-discrimination based on nationality (Article 18 TFEU (formerly Articles 12 TEC and 7 TEEC)) and the right of lawful residence in a different Member State, were intrinsically appurtenant to the economic status and value of individuals (Ramos 1992, 18–20) who had exercised their right to free movement (see Olsen 2008, 47; Barnard and Butlin 2022, 643). Hoogenboom adds that there was a trade-off as although the rights were claimed against individual Member States, rather than the E(E)C, individuals were contributing to the economy of such States (Hoogenboom 2015, 302). Originally, the "right of residence [...] was subject to the condition that the person concerned was carrying on an economic activity" (*Case C-413/99 Baumbast* 2002, ¶ 81). Yet, early on, the Court tempered the harshness of the rule by setting the threshold of an economic activity rather low. Not only did it state that the term "worker" was a European law concept (*Case 75/63 Unger* 1964), thereby giving the Court sole authority over its definition as States could not unilaterally alter this definition, but it also took a broad approach in defining a worker, encompassing, for example, activities performed by members of a religious community as part of the community's commercial activities (*Case 196/87 Steymann* 1988), as well as those performed by a person with mental disabilities as part of an economic and social programme set up in a work rehabilitation centre (*Case C-316/13 Fenoll* 2015). The only exclusions from the remit of "effective and genuine activities" (*Case 53/81 Levin* 1982, ¶¶ 17–18) were those that were "on such a small scale as to be regarded as purely marginal and ancillary" (*Case 53/81 Levin* 1982, ¶ 17).

Although granting family members of economically active migrants EU rights under former Regulation 1612/68 (Regulation (EEC) No 1612/68 1968) (now (Regulation (EU) No 492/2011 2011)) could be mistakenly viewed as a shift away from a *homo economicus* approach, it actually reinforced the idea that EU migrants' rights were primarily linked to or derived from the exercise of an economic activity (see Regulation (EEC) No 1612/68 1968, preamble ¶ 5; Regulation (EU) No 492/2011 2011, preamble ¶ 6; see also Ramos 1992, 27–28). Resultantly, the concept of a "*Marktbürger*" (Ipsen and Nicolaysen 1964, 340), "market citizenship" (see Barber 2002, 244; Shuibhne 2010, 1599), or "citizen-as-worker" (Meehan 1996, 101) emerged (see also Olsen 2008, 48; Kostakopoulou 1998, 641) even though some scholars saw in the original treaty "an incipient form of European citizenship" (Vignes 1961, 669–70; Plender 1976) which was, to some extent, bolstered by the Court's jurisprudence (Jacobs 2007, 593).

The right to move and reside freely within the territories of EC Member States was later expanded, under three separate EC Directives of 1990 (Directive 364/90/EEC 1990; Directive 90/365/EEC 1990; Directive 90/366/EEC Replaced by Directive 93/96/EEC 1993; see Elsmore and Starup 2007, 73–74), to those not exercising a professional activity (i.e., students and persons able to prove they had enough financial support) or no longer exercising a professional activity (the retired). This extension of free movement rights to non-economically active migrants had already been adumbrated by the European Commission in 1979 and 1980 (Proposal for Council Directive on Right of Residence 1979; Amended Proposal for Council Directive on Right of Residence 1980). The Court of Justice also in *Luisi and Carbone* (*Joined Cases 286/82 and 26/83 Luisi and Carbone* 1984, ¶ 10) and *Gravier* (*Case 293/83 Gravier* 1985; see Elsmore and Starup 2007, 73) accepted that non-economically active individuals, namely the recipients of a service and a student registered in an institution of higher art education respectively, could benefit from free movement rights. The adoption of the three above-mentioned Directives in 1990 was viewed as a "decisive step towards the recognition of a full European citizenship" (Blumann 1991, 288) in the sense that they removed that "formal link between enjoyment of freedom of movement and the desire to pursue an economic activity" (Evans 1991, 201). Kovar and Simon, however, note that these directives still link the right to reside to some form of economic status, whether past, current, or future (Simon and Kovar 1993, 296).

Whilst some EU citizens' rights still seemed to be dependent on being economically active (with the aforementioned extension), additional political rights were introduced in the Treaty of Maastricht in 1992, amending the treaty establishing the European Economic Community to establish the European Community:

- the right to vote and stand in local elections in the State of residence of the EU citizen (TEU and TEC (Maastricht) 1992, art. 8(b)(1); TFEU (Lisbon) 2025, art. 20(2)(b) and 22(1); EU CFR 2012, art. 40; Council Directive 94/80/EC 1994),
- the right to vote and stand in European Parliament elections in the State of residence of the EU citizen (TEU and TEC (Maastricht) 1992, art. 8(b)(2); TFEU (Lisbon) 2025, art. 20(2)(b) and 22(2); EU CFR 2012, art. 39; Council Directive 93/109/EC 1993),[1]
- the right to petition the European Parliament (TEU and TEC (Maastricht) 1992, art. 8(d); TFEU (Lisbon) 2025, art. 20(2)(d) and 24 second paragraph; EU CFR 2012, art. 44),
- the right to apply to the Ombudsman (TEU and TEC (Maastricht) 1992, art. 8(d); TFEU (Lisbon) 2025, art. 20(2)(d) and 24 third paragraph; EU CFR 2012, arts 41 and 43), and
- the right to protection by the diplomatic or consular authorities of any Member State in a third country (TEU and TEC (Maastricht) 1992, art. 8(c); TFEU (Lisbon) 2025, art. 20(2)(c) and 23 first paragraph; EU CFR 2012, art. 46; see Wouters et al. 2014).

Later, the Amsterdam Treaty expanded these rights by adding the right to access documents of the Union (TEC Amsterdam 1997, art. 255; TEU (Lisbon) 2025, art. 15(3); EU CFR 2012, art. 42) and the right to communicate with EU institutions and bodies in any EU official language (TEC Amsterdam 1997, art. 21 third paragraph; TFEU (Lisbon) 2025, art. 22(2)(d) and 24 fourth paragraph; EU CFR 2012, art. 41(4)).

Although these rights are related to the status of EU citizenship, it should be stressed that the concept of "special rights", in addition to those based solely on economic activity, was first introduced in the final communiqué issued at the European Summit held in Paris on 9 and 10 December 1974 (*Final Communiqué* 1974, para. 11). It was the first

[1] The right to vote in the European Parliament had already been granted to EU citizens in pre-Maastricht legislation.

instance where the term "citizen" was used instead of "national" in an EU document (*Final Communiqué* 1974, para. 11; see van den Berghe and Huber 1981, 761). The communiqué prompted the Commission to submit several reports, including the Nielsen report on "The Granting of Special Rights" (*Granting of Special Rights* 1975, 26–32), and ultimately led to the Tindemans report (European Commission 1975), the aim of the latter being to "strengthen the feeling of belonging to a single legal community" (Kostakopoulou 2018, 863). However, the first enlargement stymied these initial efforts (Maas 2021, 169). Later, the second Adonnino report of June 1985 suggested extending additional special rights, such as greater participation in the political process in the European Community, and granting the same rights as nationals to freedom of speech and assembly as well as consultation of citizens on transfrontier issues within the European Community to Community citizens (European Commission 1985, 19–20). Yet, it was the proposal from the Spanish government that galvanised the movement towards creating a "personal and indivisible status of nationals of the Member States" (Note of the Spanish delegation SN 3940/90 "The Road to European Citizenship" of 24 September 1990, as reproduced in Laursen and Vanhoonacker 1992, 328 (quote at 329)) in the form of EU citizenship. In the view of the Spanish government, this was a way to "eliminate the negative effects [...] accompanying the condition of foreigner for a citizen of a Member State in another Member State" (Document in Corbett, The Treaty of Maastricht, pp 156 ff as cited in Preuß 1998, 147). The principle of free movement thus resulted in the granting of rights typically reserved for nationals (see Stephanou 1991, 36), serving as a classic example of the spill-over effect theory.

2.3 EU Citizenship: The End of a Mercantile and Exclusively Mobile Citizenship?

EU citizenship was formally created under Article 8(1) of the Maastricht Treaty establishing the European Community (TEU and TEC (Maastricht) 1992). This status granted EU citizens rights delinked from their exercise of an economic activity (see Maas 2021, 169), albeit references were made in the TEC to restrictions imposed by the treaty and measures adopted to implement those rights (Article 8(2) and Article 8a(1) TEC Maastricht) (Closa 1992, 1161–62). Essentially, EU citizenship was made up of rights that already belonged to mobile citizens (i.e., primarily those related to economic activity or self-sufficiency) but were extended to all citizens along with additional rights (Simon and Kovar 1993, 295; Schönberger 2007, 75–76). Unlike previous treaty provisions, the introduction of Union citizenship "challenge[d] the existing migrant paradigm" (Spaventa 2008, 18) for Union citizens can exercise rights, such as the right to petition, the right to apply to the EU Ombudsman, the right of access to documents, the right to communicate with EU institutions in one of the official languages, and since the Treaty of Lisbon the right to sign a European Citizens' Initiative, both in the home State and abroad independently of the exercise of free movement. The rights of EU citizens were conferred upon those who stayed in their home country, thus putting an end to an exclusively mobile citizenship. As Advocate General Colomer stated, "[European Union citizenship] separates [freedom of movement] from its functional or instrumental elements (the link with an economic activity or attainment of the internal market) and raises it to the level of a *genuinely independent right inherent in the political status of the citizens of the Union*" (*Joined Cases C-65/95 and C-111/95 Shingara and Radiom* 1996, ¶ 34 (emphasis added)). Yet, at the time, as Kostakopoulou emphasised, "most scholars saw European citizenship as a purely decorative and symbolic institution, which added little new to the 'pre-Maastricht' regime of free movement rights" (Kostakopoulou 2007, 623–24; see More 2020, 459; Elsmore and Starup 2007, 58). It was "regarded in some quarters as a false prospectus" (Jacobs 2007, 592), "a pie in the sky" (Jessurun d'Oliveira 1995), "little more than a cynical exercise in public relations on the part of the High Contracting Parties" (Weiler 1996, 68). However, as time passed, those scholars were proven wrong as this new EU citizenship status was not only viewed as "enshrin[ing] *a right of a different kind, a true right of movement, stemming from the status as a citizen of the Union*, which is not subsidiary in relation to European unification, whether economic or not" (*Case C-378/97 Wijsenbeek (A.G.)* 1999, ¶ 85), but also as "becoming less a metaphor and more a 'source of rights'" (Reich and Harbacevica 2003, 615–16). As White stated, the rights derived from EU citizenship are "the right to be free from immigration control in all Member States" and "the right for all citizens of the Union to be treated equally with nationals of the host Member State when lawfully present in that Member State" (White 2005, 886; see Shaw 2007, 2550). In *Baumbast*, the European Court of Justice spelt out that "Article 18(1) TEC [now Article 21(1) TFEU] [had] conferred a right, for every citizen, to move and reside freely within the territory of the Member States" (*Case C-413/99 Baumbast* 2002, ¶ 81; see Kostakopoulou 2005, 253 and 257–59). This was a watershed in the Court's jurisprudence which attracted quite some criticism on the basis that the citizenship provisions were only aimed at creating a "market" citizenship (see Arestis 2010, 8–9). With *Baumbast,* as White explains, the "right to move and reside in the Member State of choice [became] a constitutional right flowing from the status of citizenship of the Union" (White 2005, 886). Furthermore, the provision also has direct effect as it is clear, precise, and unconditional (*Case C-413/99 Baumbast* 2002, ¶ 84). In fact, even an EU citizen who no longer enjoys a right of residence by virtue of their economic status has a lawful right of residence under Article 21(1) TFEU (though with limitations and restrictions) (*Case C-413/99 Baumbast* 2002, ¶ 94). In the case of *Zhu and Chen,* the EU citizen in question was a child who, naturally, could not be economically active (*Case C-200/02 Zhu and Chen* 2004). In *Martinez Sala,* after observing that "a national of a Member State lawfully residing in the territory of another Member State [...] comes within the scope *ratione personae* of the provisions of the Treaty on European citizenship" (*Case C-85/96 Sala* 1998, ¶ 61), the Court extended the application of the principle of equal treatment to all European citizens whether economically active or not (*Case C-85/96 Sala* 1998, ¶ 61). The Court's approach no doubt "strengthened the constitutional importance of European citizenship" to the effect that "the market citizenship template [was] superseded by an understanding of European citizenship that privileges citizen status over economic activity" (Kostakopoulou 2005, 233; see 2008, 289; Shaw 2007, 2551; and notably van den Brink 2019, 248–49). This gradual dissociation between EU citizenship and the economic status of the EU migrant, on the one hand, and the ever-closer association between the former and equal treatment, on the other hand, naturally culminated in the Court of Justice's assertion in *Grzelczyk* that "Union citizenship is destined to be the *fundamental status of nationals of the Member States*" (*Case C-184/99 Grzelczyk* 2001, ¶ 31 (emphasis added); *Case C-413/99 Baumbast* 2002, ¶ 82) which was repeated in various cases (*Case C-713/23 Cupriak-Trojan and Trojan* 2025, ¶ 40; *Case C-181/23 Citizenship by Investment* 2025, ¶ 92; *Case C-34/09 Zambrano* 2011, ¶ 41; *Case C-438/14 Bogendorff von Wolffersdorff* 2016, ¶ 29; *Case C-673/16 Coman* 2018, ¶ 30; *Case C-4/23 Mirin* 2024, ¶¶ 50–51; *Case C-490/20 V.M.A.* 2021, ¶ 41; *Case C-118/20 J.Y.* 2022, ¶¶ 38 and 58; *Case C-689/21 X* 2023, ¶¶ 29 and 38; *Case C-135/08 Rottman* 2010, ¶¶

55–56; *Case C-221/17 Tjebbes* 2019, ¶ 40). As Advocate General Maduro emphasised,

> [w]hen the Court describes Union citizenship as the "fundamental status" of nationals, it is not making a political statement; it refers to Union citizenship as a legal concept which goes hand in hand with specific rights for Union citizens. Principal among them is the right to enter and live in another Member State. (*Case C-524/06 Huber (A.G.)* 2008, ¶ 19)

The essence of this statement is that EU citizenship, as a status, is the basis of rights. As Garner adds, it has also become "the mission statement for the aspirational nature of Union citizenship" (Garner 2018, 124).

The Citizenship Directive supplements treaty provisions by detailing the rights of free movement and residence conferred upon EU citizens and their family members (see Dadomo and Quénivet 2020, ch. 20). As the Court noted in the *Ziebell* case, "[t]hat directive, far from pursuing a purely economic objective, aims to facilitate the exercise of the primary and individual right to move and reside freely within the territory of the Member States that is conferred directly on Union citizens by the Treaty, and it aims in particular to strengthen that right" (*Case C-371/08 Ziebell* 2011, ¶ 69).

Not only are EU citizens able to benefit from the rights under the Citizenship Directive but their families too. Originally, the concept of family was defined in Article 10 of Regulation 1612/68/EEC and therefore was solely linked to the *homo economicus*. However, this concept was redefined in the Citizenship Directive to include all citizens of the Union regardless of their economic activity, and the scope of the concept of family has also been broadened to reflect the evolution of family in EU member States (*Case C-673/16 Coman* 2018; *Case C-490/20 V.M.A.* 2021; *Case C-713/23 Cupriak-Trojan and Trojan* 2025; Citizenship Directive 2024, art. 2(2) and art. 3). The Court had anticipated this legislative change in the *Baumbast* case, which concerned a no longer economically active EU citizen who retained his right of lawful residence by virtue of his children's right to pursue their studies in the State of residence and his status of primary carer of his children (*Case C-413/99 Baumbast* 2002,

¶ 75; see *Case C-480/08 Teixeira* 2010, ¶ 70; *Case C-310/08 Ibrahim* 2010, ¶ 59).

> Reaffirming that "Union citizenship is destined to be the fundamental status of nationals of the Member States" (para 82), the Court stated that the Treaty on European Union does not require that EU citizens pursue a professional or trade activity in order to enjoy the rights deriving from European citizenship. Nor does it provide that EU nationals should be deprived of their rights as EU citizens after their professional activity has come to an end. (para 83) (see Dadomo and Quénivet 2020, 453; Reich and Harbacevica 2003, 632)

In simpler terms, the Court clarified that "a citizen of the European Union who no longer enjoys a right of residence as a migrant worker in the host Member State can, as a citizen of the Union, enjoy there a right of residence by direct application of Article [21(1) TFEU]" (*Case C-413/99 Baumbast* 2002, ¶ 94).

The next landmark case was *Zambrano* (*Case C-34/09 Zambrano* 2011), where the Court demonstrated that not only EU citizenship was a fundamental status as declared in *Grzelczyk* and *Baumbast* but also EU citizens were entitled to enjoy its rights. Mr and Mrs Zambrano were primary carers of dependants who were minor EU citizens and whose non-EU parents' deportation or refusal to enter the territory would have, owing to a relationship of dependency, irremediably led to them being denied "the genuine enjoyment of the substance of the rights conferred by virtue of their status as citizens of the Union" (*Case C-34/09 Zambrano* 2011, ¶ 42) although the minor Union citizens had never exercised their right to free movement (see *Case C-256/11 Dereci* 2011; *Case C-165/14 Rendón Marín* 2016; *Case C-133/15 Chavez-Vilchez* 2017; *Case C-82/16 K.A.* 2018). The case dispelled the claim that EU citizenship was merely a mercantile form of citizenship aimed at facilitating economic integration and for the benefit of a select few able to move to another country (see Kostakopoulou 2007, 625). It is precisely the autonomous nature of EU citizenship, disentangled from economic activity, that enabled the Court of Justice to prevent EU citizens from losing the enjoyment of their rights.

For the Court, not only is free movement an indicator of the effectiveness of EU citizenship (Neuvonen 2019, 8) but so is the right to residence. In a series of cases, the Court affirmed that the effectiveness of EU citizenship would be undermined if, as a consequence of refusing a third-country national who is a family member the right to join the EU citizen (even if the latter has not exercised their right to free movement), that "citizen would be obliged in practice to leave the territory of the European Union" and so be denied the "genuine enjoyment of the substance of the rights conferred by virtue of the status of citizen of the European Union" (*Case C-86/12 Alopka* 2013, ¶ 32; *Case C-40/11 Iida* 2011, ¶ 71; *Case C-256/11 Dereci* 2011, ¶¶ 64, 66 and 67; *C-87/12 Ymeraga* 2013, ¶ 36; *Case C-165/14 Rendón Marín* 2016, ¶ 74; *Case C-304/14 C.S.* 2016, ¶ 29; *Case C-82/16 K.A.* 2018, ¶ 41; *Case C-133/15 Chavez-Vilchez* 2017, ¶ 63; *Case C-836-18 Subdelegación del Gobierno en Ciudad Real v. R.H.* 2020, ¶ 39; *Joined Cases C-420/22 and C-528/22 N.W. and P.Q.* 2024, ¶ 60).

Yet, it can be argued that in protecting the "possibility of exercising the freedom of movement", the Court was, in effect, reinforcing the migrant identity (Hoogenboom 2015, 316; see Coutts 2019, 335–36) whilst moving away from the narrow focus on the *homo economicus*.

For the sake of comprehensiveness, it is important to note that the right of economically and non-economically active Union citizens to reside is nonetheless subject to limitations and restrictions laid down in the treaty (TFEU (Lisbon) 2025, art. 20(2) and 21(1); *Case C-393/13 Dano and Dano* 2014, ¶ 60) and the Citizenship Directive (Citizenship Directive 2024, arts 27, 28 and 29). The Court, in the *Baumbast* case, recalled that "the competent authorities and, where necessary, the national courts must ensure that those limitations and conditions are applied in compliance with the general principles of [Union] law and, in particular, the principle of proportionality" (*Case C-413/99 Baumbast* 2002, ¶ 94; See Spaventa 2019, 594).

2.4 Conclusion

Overall, even though it is possible to view the access and the exercise of rights derived from the status of EU citizens as working "*à géométrie variable*"—in the sense that such rights depend on the context in which EU citizenship is exercised (Shaw 2019, 440; see Garner 2018, 132)—the integrity of the concept of EU citizenship itself remains intact. The original starting point for EU citizens' rights is and remains the status of being an EU citizen. Accordingly, EU citizenship can be viewed as "only a means to access a certain number of rights guaranteed by the treaties and all linked to the plurality of connections [with the European Union] of an individual" (Pataut 2010; see Fernández 2012, 154).

References

Amended Proposal for a Council Directive on a Right of Residence for Nationals of Member States in the Territory of Another Member State COM/80/358 FINAL, OJ C188/7. 1980.

Arestis, G. 2010. *European Citizenship and the Elimination of Discriminatory Measures among European Citizens with Special Reference to Social Benefits.* Paper presented at Annual Conference of the Centre for Legal Research at the University of the West of England. October 4.

Barber, N. W. 2002. Citizenship, Nationalism and the European Union. *European Law Review* 27 (3): 241–259.

Barnard, Catherine, and Sarah Fraser Butlin. 2022. Ceding Control and Taking It Back: The Origins of Free Movement in EU Law. *Industrial Law Journal* 51 (3): 643–671. https://doi.org/10.1093/indlaw/dwab032.

Blumann, Claude. 1991. L'Europe des citoyens. *Revue Du Marché Commun de l'Union Européenne* 346:283–292.

Bux, Udo, and Mariusz Maciejewski. 2025. *The Citizens of the Union and Their Rights.* Fact Sheets on the European Union. European Parliament. https://www.europarl.europa.eu/factsheets/en/sheet/145/the-citizens-of-the-union-and-their-rights.

Case 143/87. 1988. Stanton and S.A. Belge d'Assurances 'L'Étoile 1905' v. Institut National d'Assurances Sociales Pour Travailleurs Indépendants (Inasti), ECLI:EU:C:1988:378 (ECJ).

Case 196/87. 1988. Udo Steymann v. Staatssecretaris van Justitie, ECLI:EU:C:1988:475 (ECJ).

Case 293/83. 1985. Françoise Gravier v. City of Liège, ECLI:EU:C:1985:69 (ECJ).

Case 53/81. 1982. D. M. Levin v. Staatssecretaris van Justitie, ECLI:EU:C:1982:105 (ECJ).

Case 75/63. 1964. M.K.H. Unger, the Wife of R. Hoekstra v. Bestuur Der Bedrijfsvereniging Voor Detailhandel En Ambachten, ECLI:EU:C:1964:19 (ECJ).

Case C-118/20. 2022. J.Y. v. Wiener Landesregierung, ECLI:EU:C:2022:34 (CJEU).

Case C-133/15. 2017. H.C. Chavez-Vilchez and Others v. Raad van Bestuur van de Sociale Verzekeringsbank and Others, ECLI:EU:C:2017:354 (CJEU).

Case C-135/08. 2010. Janko Rottman v. Freistaat Bayern, ECLI:EU:C:2010:104 (CJEU).

Case C-139/85. 1986. R. H. Kempf and Staatssecretaris van Justitie, ECLI:EU:C:1986:223 (ECJ).

Case C-165/14. 2016. Alfredo Rendón Marín v. Administractión Del Estado, ECLI:EU:C:2016:675 (CJEU).
Case C-181/23. 2025. European Commission v. Republic of Malta (Citizenship by Investment), ECLI:EU:C:2025:283 (CJEU).
Case C-184/99. 2001. Rudy Grzelczyk v. Centre Public d'Aide Sociale d'Ottignies-Louvain-La-Neuve, ECLI:EU:C:2001:458 (ECJ).
Case C-200/02. 2004. Kunqian Catherine Zhu and Man Lavette Chen v Secretary of State for the Home Department, ECLI:EU:C:2004:639 (ECJ).
Case C-221/17. 2019. M.G. Tjebbes and Others v. Minister van Buitenlandse Zaken, ECLI:EU:C:2019:189 (CJEU).
Case C-256/11 Murat Dereci and Others v. Bundesministerium Für Inneres, ECLI:EU:C:2011:734 (2011). (CJEU)
Case C-292/89. 1991. The Queen and The Immigration Appeal Tribunal, Ex Parte Gustaff Desiderius Antonissen, ECLI:EU:C:1991:80 (ECJ).
Case C-304/14. 2016. Secretary of State for the Home Department v. C.S., ECLI:EU:C:2016:674 (CJEU).
Case C-310/08. 2010. London Borough of Harrow v. Nimco Hassan Ibrahim and Secretary of State for the Home Department, ECLI:EU:C:2010:80 (CJEU).
Case C-316/13. 2015. Gérard Fenoll v Centre d'aide par le travail La Jouvene and Association de parents et d'amis de personnes handicapées mentales (APEI) d'Avignon, ECLI:EU:C:2015:200 (CJEU).
Case C-34/09. 2011. Gerardo Ruiz Zambrano v. Office National de l'Emploi (ONEm), ECLI:EU:C:2011:124 (CJEU).
Case C-371/08. 2011. Nural Ziebell v. Land Baden-Württemberg, ECLI:EU:C:2011:809 (CJEU).
Case C-378/97. 1999. Criminal Proceedings against Florus Ariël Wijsenbeek, ECLI:EU:C:1999:144 (Advocate General Cosmas).
Case C-393/13. 2014. Elisabeta Dano and Florin Dano v. Jobcenter Leipzig, ECLI:EU:C:2014:2358 (CJEU).
Case C-4/23. 2024. M.-A. A. v. Direcţia de Evidenţă a Persoanelor Cluj, Serviciul Stare Civilă, Direcţia Pentru Evidenţa Persoanelor Şi Administrarea Bazelor de Date Din Ministerul Afacerilor Interne, Municipiul Cluj-Napoca, ECLI:EU:C:2024:845 (CJEU).
Case C-40/11. 2011. Yoshikazu Iida v. Stadt Ulm, ECLI:EU:C:2012:691 (ECJ).
Case C-413/99. 2002. Baumbast and R. v. Secretary of State for the Home Department, ECLI:EU:C:2002:493 (ECJ).
Case C-438/14. 2016. Nabiel Peter Bogendorff von Wolffersdorff v. Standesamt Der Stadt Karlsruhe and Zentraler Juristischer Dienst Der Stadt Karlsruhe, ECLI:EU:C:2016:401 (CJEU).
Case C-480/08. 2010. Maria Teixeira v. London Borough of Lambeth and Secretary of State for the Home Department, ECLI:EU:C:2010:83 (CJEU).

Case C-490/20. 2021. V.M.A. v. Stolichna Obshtina, Rayon "Pancharevo", ECLI:EU:C:2021:1008 (CJEU).

Case C-524/06. 2008. Heinz Huber v. Germany, ECLI:EU:C:2008:194 (Advocate General Maduro).

Case C-673/16. 2018. Relu Adrian Coman and Others v. Inspectoratul General Pentru Imigrări and Ministerul Afacerilor Interne, ECLI:EU:C:2018:385 (CJEU).

Case C-689/21. 2023. X v. Udlændinge-Og Integrationsministeriet, ECLI:EU:C:2023:626 (CJEU).

Case C-713/23. 2025. Jakub Cupriak-Trojan and Mateusz Trojan v. Wojewoda Mazowiecki, ECLI:EU:C:2025:917 (CJEU).

Case C-82/16. 2018. K.A. e.a. v. Belgische Staat, ECLI:EU:C:2018:308 (CJEU).

Case C-836/18. 2020. Subdelegación Del Gobierno En Ciudad Real v. R.H., ECLI:EU:C:2020:119 (CJEU).

Case C-85/96. 1998. María Martínez Sala v. Freistaat Bayern, ECLI:EU:C:1998:217 (ECJ).

Case C-86/12. 2013. Adzo Domenyo Alokpa et al v. Ministre Du Travail, de l'Emploi et de l'Immigration, ECLI:EU:C:2013:645 (CJEU).

Case C-87/12. 2013. Kreshnik Ymeraga and Others v. Ministre Du Travail, de l'Emploi et de l'Immigration, ECLI:EU:C:2013:291 (CJEU).

Charter of Fundamental Rights of the European Union, OJEU C326/391. 2012. http://data.europa.eu/eli/treaty/char_2012/oj/eng.

Closa, Carlos. 1992. The Concept of Citizenship in the Treaty on European Union. *Common Market Law Review* 29 (6): 1137–1169.

Consolidated Version of Treaty on European Union (Lisbon). 2025. http://data.europa.eu/eli/treaty/teu_2016/2025-03-15.

Consolidated Version of Treaty on the Functioning of the European Union (Lisbon). 2025. http://data.europa.eu/eli/treaty/tfeu_2016/2025-03-15.

Council Directive 68/360/EEC of 15 October 1968 on the Abolition of Restrictions on Movement and Residence within the Community for Workers of Member States and Their Families, OJ L257/13. 1968.

Council Directive 93/109/EC of 6 December 1993 Laying down Detailed Arrangements for the Exercise of the Right to Vote and Stand as a Candidate in Elections to the European Parliament for Citizens of the Union Residing in a Member State of Which They Are Not Nationals, OJ L329/34. 1993.

Council Directive 94/80/EC of 19 December 1994 Laying Down Detailed Arrangements for the Exercise of the Right to Vote and to Stand as a Candidate in Municipal Elections by Citizens of the Union Residing in a Member State of Which They Are Not Nationals, OJ L368/38. 1994.

Council Directive 364/90/EEC on the Right of Residence, OJ L180/26. 1990.

Council Directive 90/365/EEC on the Right of Residence for Employees and Self-Employed Persons Who Have Ceased Their Occupational Activity, OJ L180/28. 1990.

Council Directive 90/366/EEC Replaced by Council Directive 93/96/EEC on the Right of Residence for Students, OJ L317/59. 1993.

Coutts, Stephen. 2019. The Shifting Geometry of Union Citizenship: A Supranational Status from Transnational Rights. *Cambridge Yearbook of European Legal Studies* 21 (December): 318–341. https://doi.org/10.1017/cel.2019.19.

Dadomo, Christian, and Noëlle Quénivet. 2020. *European Union Law*. 3rd ed. Hall & Stott Publishing.

Davis, Roy W. 2002. Citizenship of the Union ... Rights for All? *European Law Review* 27 (2): 121–137.

Delanty, Gerard. 2007. European Citizenship: A Critical Assessment. *Citizenship Studies* 11 (1): 63–72. https://doi.org/10.1080/13621020601099872.

Directive 2004/38/EC of the European Parliament and the of the Council of 29 April 2004 on the Rights of Citizens of the Union and Their Family Members to Move and Reside Freely within the Territory of the Member States Amending Regulation (EEC) No 1612/68 and Repealing Directives 64/221/EEC, 68/360/EEC, 72/194/EEC, 73/148/EEC, 75/34/EEC, 75/35/EEC, 90/364/EEC, 90/365/EEC, and 93/96/EEC, OJ L158/77. 2024.

Dubucs, Hadrien, and Stéphane Mourlane. 2017. Les migrations intra-européennes d'hier à aujourd'hui. *Hommes & Migrations* 1317–1318 (April): 1317–1318. https://doi.org/10.4000/hommesmigrations.3863.

Edens, D. F., and S. Patijn. 1972. The Scope of the EEC System of Free Movement of Workers. *Common Market Law Review* 9 (3): 322–328. https://doi-org.uwe.idm.oclc.org/10.54648/cola1972026.

Elsmore, M. J., and P. Starup. 2007. Union Citizenship-Background, Jurisprudence, and Perspective: The Past, Present, and Future of Law and Policy. *Yearbook of European Law* 26 (1): 57–113. https://doi.org/10.1093/yel/26.1.57.

European Commission. 1975. *Report on European Union (29 December 1975)*. Bulletin of the European Communities, Supplement 1/76. European Communities. http://www.cvce.eu/obj/report_on_european_union_29_december_1975-en284c9784-9bd2-472b-b704-ba4bb1f3122d.html.

European Commission. 1985. *A People's Europe*. Bulletin of the European Communities Supplement 7/85. https://repositori.uji.es/server/api/core/bitstreams/0b38d568-7a56-41c3-a026-6a38f0f1455a/content.

Evans, A. C. 1982. European Citizenship. *The Modern Law Review* 45 (5): 497–515.

Evans, A. C. 1984. European Citizenship: A Novel Concept in EEC Law. *American Journal of Comparative Law* 32 (4): 679–716.

Evans, Andrew. 1991. Nationality Law and European Integration. *European Law Review* 16 (3): 190–215.

Fernández, Christian. 2012. Patriots in the Making? Migrants, Citizens, and Demos Building in the European Union. *Journal of International Migration and Integration* 13 (2): 147–163. https://doi.org/10.1007/s12134-011-0210-8.

Final Communiqué of the Meeting of Heads of Government of the Community (Paris, 9 and 10 December 1974). 1974. Paris. https://www.cvce.eu/content/publication/1999/1/1/2acd8532-b271-49ed-bf63-bd8131180d6b/publishable_en.pdf.

Garner, Oliver. 2018. The Existential Crisis of Citizenship of the European Union: *The Argument for an Autonomous Status. Cambridge Yearbook of European Legal Studies* 20:116–146. https://doi.org/10.1017/cel.2018.6.

Hoogenboom, A. 2015. In Search of a Rationale for the EU Citizenship Jurisprudence. *Oxford Journal of Legal Studies* 35 (2): 301–324. https://doi.org/10.1093/ojls/gqu023.

Ipsen, H. P., and G. Nicolaysen. 1964. Haager Kongress für Europarecht und Bericht über die aktuelle Entwicklung des Gemeinschaftsrecht. *Neue Juristische Wochenschrift* 17:339–344.

Jacobs, Francis G. 2007. Citizenship of the European Union—A Legal Analysis. *European Law Journal* 13 (5): 591–610. https://doi.org/10.1111/j.1468-0386.2007.00385.x.

Jessurun d'Oliveira, H. U. 1995. 'Union Citizenship: Pie in the Sky? In *A Citizen's Europe. In Search for a New Order*, ed. Allan Rosas and Esko Antola. Sage.

Joined Cases 286/82 and 26/83. 1984. Graziana Luisi and Guiseppe Carbone v. Ministero Del Tesero, ECLI:EU:C:1984:35 (ECJ).

Joined Cases C-420/22 and C-528/22. 2024. N.W. and P.Q. v Országos Idegenrendészeti Főigazgatóság and Miniszterelnöki Kabinetirodát Vezető Miniszter, ECLI:EU:C:2024:344 (CJEU).

Joined Cases C-65/95 and C-111/95. 1996. The Queen v. Secretary of State for the Home Department, Ex Parte Mann Singh Shingara and Ex Parte Abbas Radiom, ECLI:EU:C:1996:451 (Advocate General Colomer).

Kochenov, Dimitry. 2013. The Right to Have *What* Rights? EU Citizenship in Need of Clarification. *European Law Journal* 19 (4): 502–516. https://doi.org/10.1111/eulj.12043.

Kostakopoulou, Theodora. 1998. European Citizenship and Immigration after Amsterdam: Openings, Silences, Paradoxes. *Journal of Ethnic and Migration Studies* 24 (4): 639–656. https://doi.org/10.1080/1369183X.1998.9976658.

Kostakopoulou, Dora. 2005. Ideas, Norms and European Citizenship: Explaining Institutional Change. *The Modern Law Review* 68 (2): 233–267. https://doi.org/10.1111/j.1468-2230.2005.00536.x.

Kostakopoulou, Dora. 2007. European Union Citizenship: Writing the Future. *European Law Journal* 13 (5): 623–646. https://doi.org/10.1111/j.1468-0386.2007.00387.x.

Kostakopoulou, Dora. 2008. The Evolution of European Union Citizenship. *European Political Science* 7 (3): 285–295. https://doi.org/10.1057/eps.2008.24.

Kostakopoulou, Dora. 2018. Scala Civium: Citizenship Templates Post-Brexit and the European Union's Duty to Protect EU Citizens. *Journal of Common Market Studies* 56 (4): 854–869. https://doi.org/10.1111/jcms.12683.

Laursen, Finn, and Sophie Vanhoonacker, eds. 1992. *The Intergovernmental Conference on Political Union: Institutional Reforms, New Policies, and International Identity of the European Community.* Professional Research Paper. Intergovernmental Conference on Political Union, Dordrecht. Martinus Nijhoff.

Maas, Willem. 2021. European Citizenship in the Ongoing Brexit Process. *International Studies* 58 (2): 168–183. https://doi.org/10.1177/00208817211002008.

Mancini, G. Federico. 1989. The Making of a Constitution for Europe. *Common Market Law Review* 26 (4): 595–614. https://doi-org.uwe.idm.oclc.org/10.54648/cola1989031.

Meehan, Elizabeth M. 1996. European Integration and Citizens' Rights: A Comparative Perspective. *Publius: The Journal of Federalism* 26 (4): 99–121. https://doi.org/10.1093/oxfordjournals.pubjof.a029886.

More, Gillian. 2020. From Union Citizen to Third-Country National: Brexit, the UK Withdrawal Agreement, No-Deal Preparations and Britons Living in the European Union. In *European Citizenship under Stress—Social Justice, Brexit and Other Challenges*, ed. Nathan Cambien, Dimitry Kochenov, and Elise Muir. Brill.

Neuvonen, Päivi Johanna. 2019. Retrieving the "Subject" of European Integration. *European Law Journal* 25 (1): 6–20. https://doi.org/10.1111/eulj.12301.

Olsen, Espen D. H. 2008. The Origins of European Citizenship in the First Two Decades of European Integration. *Journal of European Public Policy* 15 (1): 40–57. https://doi.org/10.1080/13501760701702157.

Pataut, Etienne. 2010. Citoyenneté de l'Union et nationalité étatique. *Revue Trimestrielle de Droit Européen* 3:617–632.

Pataut, Étienne. 2018. Les conflits de nationalités face au droit de l'Union. *Revue Critique de Droit International Privé* 2 (2): 241–256. https://doi.org/10.3917/rcdip.182.0241.

Plender, Richard. 1976. An Incipient Form of European Citizenship. In *EU Law and the Individual*, ed. Francis Geoffrey Jacobs. North Holland.

Preuß, Ulrich K. 1998. Citizenship in the European Union: A Paradigm for Transnational Democracy. In *Re-Imagining Political Community*, ed. Daniele Archibugi, David Held, and Martin Köhler. Stanford University Press.

Proposal for a Council Directive on a Right of Residence for Nationals of Member States in the Territory of Another Member State COM/79/215 FINAL, OJ C207/14. 1979.

Ramos, Rui Manuel, and Moura. 1992. Les nouveaux aspects de la libre circulation des personnes. Vers une citoyenneté européenne. *Boletim da Faculdade de Direito: Universidade de Coimbra* 68:17–57.

Regulation (EEC) No 1612/68 of the Council of 15 October 1968 on Freedom of Movement for Workers within the Community, OJ L257/2. 1968.

Regulation (EU) No 492/2011 of the European Parliament and of the Council of 5 April 2011 on Freedom of Movement for Workers within the Union. 2011. *OJ* L141/1.

Reich, Norbert, and Solvita Harbacevica. 2003. Citizenship and Family on Trial: A Fairly Optimistic Overview of Recent Court Practice with Regard to Free Movement of Persons. *Common Market Law Review* 40 (3): 615–638. https://doi.org/10.54648/COLA2003032.

Schönberger, C. 2007. European Citizenship as Federal Citizenship - Some Citizenship Lessons of Comparative Federalism. *European Review of Public Law* 19 (1): 61–81.

Shaw, Jo. 2007. E.U. Citizenship and Political Rights in an Evolving European Union. *Fordham Law Review* 75 (5): 2549–2578.

Shaw, Jo. 2019. "Shunning" and "Seeking" Membership: Rethinking Citizenship Regimes in the European Constitutional Space. *Global Constitutionalism* 8 (3): 425–469. https://doi.org/10.1017/S2045381719000133.

Shuibhne, Niamh Nic. 2010. The Resilience of EU Market Citizenship. *Common Market Law Review* 47 (6): 1597–1628. https://doi.org/10.54648/COLA2010068.

Simon, Denys, and Robert Kovar. 1993. La citoyenneté européenne. *Cahiers de Droit Européen* 3–4:285–316. https://doi.org/10.54648/COLA2004023.

Spaventa, Eleanor. 2004. From Gebhard to Carpenter: Towards a (Non-) Economic European Constitution. *Common Market Law Review* 41 (3): 743–773.

Spaventa, Eleanor. 2008. Seeing the Wood Despite the Trees? On the Scope of Union Citizenship and Its Constitutional Effects. *Common Market Law Review* 45 (1): 13–45. https://doi.org/10.54648/COLA2008002.

Spaventa, Eleanor. 2019. Mice or Horses?: British Citizens in the EU 27 after Brexit as "Former EU Citizens". *European Law Review* 44 (5): 589–604.

Stephanou, Constantin A. 1991. Identité et citoyenneté européennes. *Revue du Marché Commun de l'Union Européenne* 343:30–39.

The Granting of Special Rights. Implementation of Point 11 of the Final Communiqué Issued at the European Summit Held in Paris on 9 and 10 December 1974. 1975. COM (75) 321 final. Bulletin of the European Communities, Supplement 5/75. Commission.

Top v. Dulles, 356 US 86 (US Supreme Court). 1958.

Treaty Establishing the European Community (Consolidated Version 1997—Amsterdam), 340 OJ C. 1997. http://data.europa.eu/eli/treaty/tec_1997/oj.

Treaty Establishing the European Economic Community (Rome). 1957. http://data.europa.eu/eli/treaty/teec/sign.

Treaty on European Union, Together with the Complete Text of the Treaty Establishing the European Community, OJ 92/C 224/01. 1992. https://eur-lex.europa.eu/legal-content/EN/TXT/PDF/?uri=OJ:C:1992:224:FULL.

van den Berghe, Guido, and Christian H. Huber. 1981. European Citizenship. In *Das Europa der Zweiten Generation. Gedächtnisschrift für Christophe Sasse*, ed. Roland Bieber and Dietmar Nickel II. N.P. Engel Verlag.

van den Brink, Martijn. 2019. The Problem with Market Citizenship and the Beauty of Free Movement. In *The Internal Market and the Future of European Integration: Essays in Honour of Laurence W. Gormley*, ed. Dimitry Kochenov, Fabian Amtenbrink, Gareth Davies, and Justin Lindeboom. Cambridge University Press. https://doi.org/10.1017/9781108565417.018.

Vignes, Daniel-Henri. 1961. La libération de l'établissement et des services dans la Communauté Economique Européenne. *Annuaire Français de Droit International* 7:668–725. https://doi.org/10.3406/afdi.1961.1114.

Weiler, J. H. H. 1996. Citizenship and Human Rights. In *Reforming the Treaty on European Union*, ed. J. A. Winter, D. M. Curtin, A. E. Kellermann, and B. de Witte. Kluwer Law International.

White, Robin C. A. 2005. Free Movement, Equal Treatment, and Citizenship of the Union. *International and Comparative Law Quarterly* 54 (4): 885–905. https://doi.org/10.1093/iclq/lei041.

Wouters, Jan, Sanderijn Duquet, and Katrien Meuwissen. 2014. Caring for Citizens Abroad: The European Union and Consular Tasks. *European Foreign Affairs Review* 19:563–580.

CHAPTER 3

The Transformative Value of EU Citizenship

Abstract This chapter explores the transformative value of European Union citizenship, introduced by the Treaty of Maastricht as a complement to the internal market and subsequently elevated to a fundamental status. EU citizenship functions as an additional layer to national citizenship, conferring rights that enable individuals to embed themselves socially, economically, and politically within their host Member State. Using the metaphor of vinaigrette, the chapter illustrates the interplay between nationality and EU citizenship, arguing that the right to free movement acts as the "emulsifier" that activates its full potential. Three rights, the right to residence, the principle of non-discrimination, and the right to vote and stand in local elections, are identified as key to this transformative process. These rights foster integration, transforming EU citizens from "foreigners" into quasi-nationals. Further, EU citizenship is presented as experiential, shaping everyday practices and relationships. By examining both rights and lived realities, the chapter contends that EU citizenship transcends its mercantile origins, creating a socio-political identity rooted in participation and belonging.

Keywords EU citizenship • Nationality • Right to residence • Principle of non-discrimination • Principle of equality • Right to vote • Brexit • Integration

C. Dadomo, N. Quénivet, *The Transformative Value of EU Citizenship after Brexit*,
https://doi.org/10.1007/978-3-032-20595-7_3

3.1 Introduction

Introduced by the Treaty of Maastricht, EU citizenship was initially perceived as a symbolic addition to the internal market, designed to strengthen the Union's democratic legitimacy and foster a sense of belonging among its peoples. Over time, however, this status has evolved beyond its original mercantile rationale, acquiring a distinct constitutional dimension that is additional to nationality. Yet, its "predication upon nationality of a Member State means that no direct connection was created between the individual and the European constitutional order" (Garner 2018, 120; see *Case C-673/20 EP v. Préfet du Gers (A.G.)* 2022a, ¶ 22) and polity.

It confers a set of rights, including free movement, residence, equal treatment, and political participation, the last three of which take particular relevance when the first one, free movement, is realised. These rights are not merely formal entitlements; they constitute the foundation of an experiential citizenship that enables individuals to embed themselves socially, economically, and politically within their host Member State. As Aristotle stressed in a broader context, "a citizen is not a citizen because he lives in a certain place, for resident aliens and slaves share in the place; nor is he a citizen who has legal rights to the extent of suing and being sued; for this right might be enjoyed under the provisions of a treaty" (Aristotle 1996, 62). Therefore, more is required than just residence and rights.

This chapter presents the conceptual framework of the book, examining the transformative value of EU citizenship through a legal-participatory lens, focusing on three core rights: the right of residence, the principle of non-discrimination, and the right to vote and stand in local elections. It argues that these rights have redefined the status of EU citizens, transforming them from "foreigners" into quasi-nationals and fostering integration at multiple levels. By exploring the interplay between law and practice, this chapter contends that EU citizenship is not a static legal category but a dynamic status that shapes everyday experiences. As Coutts observes, EU citizenship is "a status of transnational social integration" (Coutts 2020, 133).

Using the culinary metaphor of the vinaigrette, the first section of this chapter introduces the relationship between EU citizenship and nationality. It suggests that these elements, viewed as layers, can morph into a new type of citizenship. The next section then engages in an analytical presentation of the rights that underpin the transformative nature of EU citizenship. It argues in a last section that EU citizenship is ultimately an experiential citizenship, one rooted in *practice*, and that is where its transformative value lies fundamentally.

3.2 The Relationship Between European Union Citizenship and Nationality: An Intricate Affair

Brexit has undeniably exacerbated the duality of EU citizenship which exists both as an independent status and a complementary (pre-Lisbon) or additional (post-Lisbon) over-layer to national citizenship. For EU citizens in the UK, the loss of recognition of their EU citizenship underscores that this status of EU citizen exists as such. Whilst they retain their EU citizenship in the European Union, they have lost its associated benefits in the UK. Without EU citizenship, rights are not automatic; they can be renegotiated, redefined (as seen with the EU settled status, see Sect. 4.3), or even completely revoked (e.g., the right to vote and stand at elections). For UK nationals in the EU27, the consequence of the loss of EU citizenship is even more drastic as such a loss transforms them into third-country nationals under EU law.

This situation is the product of the fact that EU citizenship is a "derived and superposed citizenship" ("citoyenneté dérivée et superposée") (Pertek 2013, 432). The best way to understand the value of EU citizenship is, using the metaphor of the vinaigrette, to consider it an additional, yet separate layer of citizenship derived from nationality.

3.2.1 A Layer Additional to National Citizenship

Already in 1991, it was clear that the rights and obligations attached to EU citizenship "apply in addition to the rights and obligations existing at national level" (Resolution on Union Citizenship 1991, preamble ¶ E). As Advocate General Szpunar explained in 2021, "Union citizenship confers on the nationals of the Member States a citizenship 'beyond the State'" (*Case C-118/20 J.Y. (A.G.)* 2021, ¶ 33; see *Case C-135/08 Rottman (A.G.)* 2009, ¶ 16). This citizenship is derived from nationality. Yet, it is also additional to it: "[c]itizenship of the Union is thus not only derived but also additional, in so far as it affords supplementary rights to citizens of the Union, such as the right to move and reside freely within the territory of the Member States or the right to vote and to stand as candidates in elections to the European Parliament and municipal elections" (*Case C-118/20 J.Y. (A.G.)* 2021, ¶ 33). The Court reiterated in clear terms that it follows from Articles 9 TEU and 20(1) TFEU that "Union citizenship is ***additional*** to national citizenship but does not replace it" (*Case C-673/20 E.P. v. Préfet du Gers* 2022b, ¶ 47 (emphasis added); *Case C-181/23 Citizenship by Investment* 2025, ¶ 79; *Case C-181/23 Citizenship by Investment (A.G.)* 2024, ¶ 42).

Shuibhne posits that whilst "'additional to' could be said to convey its value ***added*** character", it can also be negatively interpreted "as a more calculated affirmation of Member State control over national citizenship" (Shuibhne 2012, 139). The authors however assert that to understand the use of the word "additional", it is necessary to go back in time and contrast "additional to" and "complement". Indeed, the Amsterdam treaty specified that "Union citizenship shall *complement* national citizenship", whereas the current version under the Lisbon Treaty (Articles 9 TEU and 20 TFEU) explains that "[c]itizenship of the Union shall be ***additional*** to [...] national citizenship" (emphasis added). As the authors have argued elsewhere, "[t]he word 'complement' was unfortunate as it suggested that European citizenship was a subsidiary element of national citizenship. By contrast, the word 'additional' rather suggests that EU nationals have the benefit of dual citizenship" (Dadomo and Quénivet 2020, 451) as was suggested in Article 5 of the Preliminary Draft Treaty Establishing a Constitution for Europe (Preliminary Draft Treaty Establishing a Constitution for Europe 2002). De Waele rightly elucidates that to complement can be defined

> as "to make complete or perfect, to supply what is wanting", whereas an "addition" is "the putting or joining of one thing to another so as to increase it, or the joining together of several things into one amount". Clearly then, a complement is something that works to the benefit of the object it complements; an addition can however hold its own, with or without the thing it adds to. Thus, an additional good appears to command a greater significance than a complementary one. (de Waele 2010, 323)

Rieder also argues that the word "additional" can mean that "both 'entities' at one point can exist independently from each other" (Rieder 2013, 171).

Although Kostakopoulou argues that "European citizenship constitutes a unique experiment for stretching social and political bonds beyond national boundaries and for creating a political community in which diverse peoples become associates in a collective experience and institutional designers" (Kostakopoulou 2007, 624), history is replete of examples of individuals belonging to a variety of communities (e.g., pan-hellenism (Rhodes 2015) and pan-Africanism (Kuryla 2025)) transcending national allegiance (Stephanou 1991, 33) and based on a variety of identification factors such as language, political opinion, faith, history, destiny, etc. As Maduro explained, "this new form of citizenship does not put in question our first allegiance to our national bodies politic" but "forms the basis of a new political area from which rights and duties emerge, which are laid down by [EU] law and do not depend on the State" (*Case C-135/08 Rottman (A.G.)* 2009, ¶ 23; see Bux and Maciejewski 2025). Likewise, citizens of multinational States have plural national identities. A British national can also identify as English, Scottish, or Welsh, for example. In fact, in a 2001 report, the Commission explained that "[c]itizenship of the Union [...] is thus 'superimposed' on national and in some cases regional or local citizenship to give the effect of multiple levels" (European Commission 2001, 7). As a matter of fact, a uniform sense of belonging is neither required nor generated by the nationality of these individuals (Jenson 2007, 64). This reinforces the idea that EU citizenship is additional rather than complementary to nationality.

3.2.2 A Layer Derived from Nationality

EU citizenship is derived because it is linked to the nationality of a Member State (Frau 2019, 511). This follows from Articles 9 TEU and 20(1) TFEU which provide respectively that "[e]very national of a Member State shall be a citizen of the Union" and "[e]very person holding the nationality of a Member State shall be a citizen of the Union".

As the Commission stressed, "[h]olding the nationality of a Member State is a prerequisite for being a citizen of the Union" (European Commission 2017, preamble ¶ 2). The Court confirmed that "[b]y Article 9 TEU and Article 20 TFEU, the authors of the Treaties thus established an inseparable and exclusive link between possession of the nationality of a Member State" (*Case C-673/20 E.P. v. Préfet du Gers* 2022b, ¶ 48). As Pataut explains, nationality is the entrance key to EU citizenship, a status that creates rights (Pataut 2021, 517). And in his opinion in the more recent *Citizenship by Investment* case, Advocate General Collins also explains

> [t]he status of EU citizenship is inseparably linked to, and entirely dependent upon, the possession of the nationality of a Member State. The acquisition of Member State nationality results in the automatic and unconditional acquisition of EU citizenship. The loss of Member State nationality has the consequence that the person concerned automatically loses his or her status as an EU citizen. (*Case C-181/23 Citizenship by Investment (A.G.)* 2024, ¶ 42)

It is therefore a legal identity by transitivity (Chaltiel 2008), a *jus tractum* (Kochenov 2008). Whilst some might bemoan that EU citizenship is derived from the nationality of the Member States of the European Union (see Sect. 6.3), this approach is similar to how the US and German nationalities were formerly conceived (see Faist 2001, 48; Maas 2008, 587). Until the Fourteenth Amendment in 1868, US citizenship was derived from sub-federal citizenship (see Schönberger 2007, 70). German citizenship operated under a similar principle until 1934: Article 1 of the Imperial and State Nationality Law which read "A German is someone who possesses citizenship in a federal State (paras 3 to 32) or direct imperial citizenship (paras 33 to 35)" (Reichs-Und Staatsangehörigkeitsgesetz 1913) was repealed by the 1934 Ordinance on German citizenship that created one single citizenship granted by the State (Verordnung Über Die Deutsche Staatsangehörigkeit 1934, ¶ 1(1) and 2). The difference with the US approach, however, was that from 1913, a direct imperial nationality had been introduced alongside nationality from federated states (see Lepoutre 2019). Certain contemporary federations allow a form of dual citizenship, whereby individuals belong to two political communities within the same State (van den Brink 2019, 251; Schönberger 2007, 66). In Switzerland, Swiss citizenship is a consequence of citizenship of a canton (Schönberger 2007, 62 and 70). Albeit in reverse, the Fourteenth Amendment, Section 1 of the US Constitution holds that "all persons born or naturalized in the United States, and subject to the jurisdiction thereof, are citizens of the United States and of the State wherein they reside" (Fourteenth Amendment to the Constitution of the United States, n.d.).

3.2.3 The "Vinaigrette" Metaphor

In this light, EU citizenship is not that iconoclastic: it is derived from and additional to another nationality/citizenship.

Let's use the culinary metaphor of the vinaigrette. It is the result of the emulsification process of oil and vinegar. As non-polar and polar substances, respectively, oil and vinegar are immiscible and, as a result, the oil floats on top of the vinegar. Shaken together, they will turn into vinaigrette; when the vinaigrette rests, the two liquids separate again. Without vinegar, there is no vinaigrette.

Equally, nationality and EU citizenship are "inextricably linked and independent" (*Case C-135/08 Rottman (A.G.)* 2009, ¶ 23), the latter resting on top of the former without replacing it. Thus, while "Union citizenship assumes nationality of a Member State", once free movement is exercised (the emulsification process), EU citizenship takes its full significance as "a legal and political concept independent of that of nationality" (*Case C-135/08 Rottman (A.G.)* 2009, ¶ 23). Until free movement is exercised, nationality and EU citizenship coexist independently.

Its legal, abstract construct is irrelevant to individuals on a daily basis. Although this approach treats EU citizenship as an additional layer to nationality, it is argued that it has acquired intrinsic value for EU citizens living in another EU Member State. The two layers are intertwined, much like oil and vinegar mixed together to create a vinaigrette, which has a different flavour from its separate ingredients. As a result, EU citizenship is transformative; it is not just a "top up" but has fundamentally altered how individuals are treated and how they perceive themselves in another EU Member State. It has become an integral part of a Union citizen's legal heritage.

3.3 Rights that Create the Transformative Value

Though EU citizenship appears to be unique in its status, the treatment of EU citizens is multifaceted ("*à géométrie variable*") depending on whether these citizens are exercising their right to free movement, have exercised it and have returned to their country of origin (as *Surinder Singh* (*Case C-370/90 Singh* 1992, ¶ 25) demonstrates), or are prevented, actually or potentially, from exercising it (as the *Zambrano* line of jurisprudence reveals). As such, as Becker suggests, "European citizenship takes on practical meaning once the opportunities it conveys are seized upon by those to whom it is available" (Becker 2004, 141; see Fernández 2012, 149). Mobility plays a key role in determining the constellation of rights available to EU citizens (Pertek 2013, 432). This stands in stark contrast to national citizenship, which could be described as a "sedentary status"

(Kostakopoulou 2018, 856). Yet, the recent jurisprudence stressing the potential mobility and the possibility of denying the "genuine enjoyment" of EU rights suggests that whilst mobility remains crucial, its significance might be gradually diminishing.

Nonetheless, "if one right defines EU citizenship, it is the right to move and reside freely throughout the EU" (van den Brink 2019, 249). As shown in the vinaigrette metaphor, the right to move is not only traditionally considered the most important right (Cambien et al. 2020, 4) but also the most well-known and appreciated by EU citizens (*EU Citizenship 2020 Final Report—Results of the Public Consultation on EU Citizenship Rights 2020* 2020, 10) and, as of 1 January 2024, it was enjoyed by 14 million individuals (European Council 2025). It is the emulsifying element that makes EU citizenship what it really and truly is. As Recchi states, EU citizenship "glorifies free movement as a first-rank, generalized individual right" (Recchi 2008, 205; see Thym 2016, 299). EU citizenship offers numerous benefits to those living abroad, as it facilitates integration (Fernández 2012, 149; Coutts 2018, 236). This is mainly due to its nature as a "citizenship of movement"; it essentially materialises itself outside the territory of an individual's State and throughout the Union territory (Pertek 2013, 432). As noted by Fernández, the initial EEC/EC policies were aimed at nationals who were exercising their right to freedom of movement (Fernández 2012, 154). As mentioned above, many of the Union citizens' rights are linked to mobility; in fact, "free movement can be viewed as the bedrock upon which the entire construction of European rights has been built" (Maas 2008, 583; see van den Brink 2019, 258; Hoogenboom 2015, 309–10). Or, as Shuibhne states "movement is still, for good or ill, the guts of EU citizenship" (Shuibhne 2010, 1611).

The crucial importance of EU citizenship to "movers" can be explained by the fact that "[c]itizenship is defined and negotiated through *de jure* rules and regulations as well as the *de facto* everyday practices that constitute belonging to a particular state or community" (Ferbrache and Yarwood 2015, 73). These *de jure* and *de facto* practices are linked to their very status as EU citizens living outside their country of nationality. Unlike nationals, these citizens are dependent on the rights conferred upon them by EU law (Fernández 2012, 160), though many of these rights simply stipulate that national law is to be extended to EU citizens. Moreover, as Advocate General Jacobs explained, they are "entitled to assume that [...] [they] will be treated in accordance with a common code of fundamental values" (*Case C-168/91 Konstantinidis (A.G.)* 1992, ¶ 46). EU citizens effectively become quasi-insiders within their host countries (Coutts 2018, 238).

This has been enabled by a variety of rights, three of which, the authors believe, show that EU citizenship is transformative in nature: the right to residence, the principles of non-discrimination and equality, and the right to vote. Other authors also consider such rights to be fundamentally important. For example, Sredanovic argues that "[t]he main rights linked to EU citizenship include the right to move and reside in all the EU member states (with some limitations), to be treated as equals of national citizens in most cases when accessing social rights, and to vote both in EU elections and in the local elections of the member state of residence" (Sredanovic 2021, 96). In the context of Brexit specifically, Brändle et al. contend that "the right to move and reside freely in the EU, the right to non-discrimination on the basis of nationality [...] and the right to vote in European Parliament (EP) and local elections" have highlighted the status of EU citizenship as one providing exclusive rights for EU citizens (Brändle et al. 2018, 812). Whilst other rights, such as access to health care, access to welfare, and the recognition of professional qualifications, also play a role, they are likely less fundamental in shaping the transformative nature of EU citizenship (see Ferbrache 2019a, 82).

3.3.1 *The Right to Residence*

First, the right to residence in another EU Member State is deemed to have a transformative value. Whilst EU citizenship is often referred to as a "citizenship of movement", it is equally a "citizenship of residence". Whereas it was initially viewed as a corollary of the freedom to exercise an economic activity, it is now a fundamental right of all EU citizens. By providing the legal framework for EU citizens to live abroad, provided they fulfil the required conditions (see Sect. 2.2), EU citizenship has not only enabled EU citizens to embed themselves into the local fabric but also provides them with stability. Moving to another EU Member State can thus be of any duration, as long as the relevant legal requirements are met.

Free movement rights are regulated by the Citizenship Directive. Accordingly, EU citizens can move to another EU Member State for up to three months without any conditions, provided they have a valid identity card or passport (Citizenship Directive 2024, art. 6). EU citizens can stay longer if they can demonstrate that they are job-seekers and have a genuine chance of being engaged (Citizenship Directive 2024, art. 14(4)(b)). Additionally, workers and self-employed persons (economically active persons) are allowed to stay for more than three months. So are persons of independent means and students (non-economically active persons), provided they have sufficient resources for themselves and their family members not to become a burden on the social assistance system of the host Member State during their period of residence, and have comprehensive sickness insurance cover in the host Member State (Citizenship Directive 2024, art. 7(1)(a), 7(1)(b) and 7(1)(c) respectively).

Furthermore, the family members of EU citizens, irrespective of their nationality, have a derived right of residence under the Citizenship Directive (Citizenship Directive 2024, art. 8(5) for EU nationals and art. 9 for non-EU nationals). The rationale for extending this right of residence is straightforward as explained in recital 6 of the Preamble to the Citizenship Directive (to maintain family unity) and in recital 6 of the Preamble to Regulation 492/2011 (Regulation (EU) No 492/2011 2011) on workers' and their families' rights (workers' right to be joined by their families and the conditions for the integration of these families into the host country). As Davies notes: "[w]ithout family people will not move" (Davies 2024, 275). The CJEU has further clarified in the *Lounes* case that this right also exists under Article 21 TFEU though

> only when it is necessary in order to ensure that the Union citizen can exercise his freedom of movement effectively. The purpose and justification of a derived right of residence are therefore based on the fact that a refusal to allow such a right would be such as to interfere, in particular, with that freedom and with the exercise and the effectiveness of the rights which Article 21(1) TFEU affords the Union citizen concerned. (*Case C-165/16 Lounes* 2017, ¶ 48)

Undoubtedly, the right of residence for family members of EU citizens not only facilitates the mobility of EU citizens but also helps their integration into the local society.

The crux is that, whilst EU citizens and their families reside on the basis of a system of rights spelt out in EU law, non-EU citizens are allowed to enter and stay in a country on the basis of a system of privileges that can be revoked at any time. Unlike other "foreigners", EU citizens are not subject to national requirements such as visas to seek the right to enter and reside, and they do not need to renew their right to stay. Indeed, after a continuous stay of five years, EU citizens become permanent residents without the need to formally apply for such status (Citizenship Directive 2024, art. 16). As permanent residents, EU citizens and their families no longer have to meet prior residence conditions and have access to the full panoply of rights and benefits, including social assistance, that are available to nationals (Citizenship Directive 2024, art. 16(1) and (2)). As recital 17 of the Preamble to the Citizenship Directive notes, that status was designed to "strengthen the feeling of Union citizenship" and is viewed as "a key element in promoting social cohesion" (Citizenship Directive 2024, recital 17 of preamble).

What is more, EU citizens benefit from enhanced protection against expulsion (Citizenship Directive 2024, art. 28(2) and (3), and preamble ¶¶ 17 and 24; see Dadomo and Quénivet 2020, sect. 20.5.3). As explained in recital 24 of the Preamble to the Citizenship Directive, "the greater the degree of integration of Union citizens and their family members in the host Member State, the greater the degree of protection against expulsion should be" (see Carrera and Colombi 2025, 55). However, the Court has been cautious, excluding such protection for migrant EU citizens who do not share the values of the host State and are not deemed integrated enough (Coutts 2019, 328–29). In several cases (*Case C-378/12 Onuekwere* 2014, ¶ 31; *Case C-400/12 M.G.* 2014, ¶¶ 33–38; *Joined Cases C-316/16 and C-424/16 B. and Vomero* 2018, ¶ 70), the Court stated that years spent in prison did not count towards the acquisition of permanent residence (Citizenship Directive 2024, art. 28(2)) and thus the enhanced protection under Article 28(3) of the Citizenship Directive. The Court has indeed ruled in *M.G.* that with regard to the calculation of the 10-year period of residence, "a period of imprisonment is, in principle, capable both of interrupting the continuity of the period of residence and of affecting the decision regarding the grant of the enhanced protection provided for thereunder, even where the person concerned resided in the host Member State" (*Case C-400/12 M.G.* 2014, ¶ 38). But the Court also added in the same paragraph that "the 10 years prior to imprisonment may be taken into consideration as part of the overall assessment required in order to determine whether the integrating links previously forged with the host Member State have been broken".

In reference to individuals serving a custodial sentence, in the Joined Cases of *B.* and *Vomero*, the Court discusses at greater length the issues of "integrative links" forged within the host Member State (*Joined Cases C-316/16 and C-424/16 B. and Vomero* 2018, ¶¶ 44–60) and of "disconnect[ion] from the society of the host Member State" (*Joined Cases C-316/16 and C-424/16 B. and Vomero* 2018, ¶ 77). In particular, the Court refers to an individual's prior level of social integration, the nature and the circumstances of the commission of their crime and their attitude during detention, and notably, whether it either reinforces that disconnection or, in contrast, "help[s] to maintain or restore links previously forged with the host Member State with a view to his future social reintegration in that State" (*Joined Cases C-316/16 and C-424/16 B. and Vomero* 2018, ¶¶ 70–75). This in fact reinforces the idea that integration and residence are clearly interlinked, thus supporting the proposal that the right to residence has a transformative value.

3.3.2 The Principles of Non-discrimination and Equality

Second, the fundamental principle of non-discrimination on the basis of nationality, originally enshrined in Article 7 of the Treaty of Rome (TEEC (Rome) 1957) (now 18 TFEU (TFEU (Lisbon) 2025)), has cemented this "embedment" and transformed those so-called foreigners into EU citizens who are entitled to the same treatment as national citizens. Equality, as a general principle of EU law, is defined as "comparable situations should not be treated differently and that different situations should not be treated in the same way, unless such different treatment is objectively justified" (*Case C-930/19 X* 2021, ¶ 57). The rationale for the application of such a principle to apply to EU citizens was very clear: since "nationality was the original proxy for prohibited discrimination" (Neuvonen 2019, 14), without this protective right "the free movement rights could not be exercised to their full effect since possible discriminatory treatments would deter EU citizens from exercising or continuing to exercise their free movement rights" (D'Alfonso et al. 2017, 16). Whilst some consider the principle of non-discrimination as one linked to the original common market and the intention to avoid social dumping (Giubboni 2007, 365), others explain that it is associated with inclusion and equality (Mourão Permoser 2017, 2538; Shaw 1998, sect. II.A) and thus more aligned with the idea of enabling EU citizens to embed themselves into the society of the host State.

As Thym explains, "[n]on-discrimination on grounds of nationality is the historic backbone of EU citizenship" (Thym 2016, 314). Although it is not specifically listed as an EU citizenship right, it "is a fundamental, constitutional aspect of EU citizenship" (More 2020, 459). The principle requires that, whenever the situation falls within the scope *ratione materiae* of EU law (*Case C-393/13 Dano and Dano* 2014, ¶ 59), EU citizens be given "the same treatment in law irrespective of their nationality, subject to such exceptions as are expressly provided for in that regard" (*Case C-393/13 Dano and Dano* 2014, ¶ 58 see also ¶ 60). Originally, this right was further delineated in Article 48(2) of the Treaty of Rome (TEEC (Rome) 1957) (now 45(2) TFEU (TFEU (Lisbon) 2025)) and developed in early regulations (Regulation (EEC) No 1408/71 of the Council of 14 June 1971 on the Application of Social Security Schemes to Employed Persons and Their Families Moving within the Community 1971, art. 3; repealed and replaced by Regulation (EC) No 883/2004 2004; Regulation (EEC) No 1612/68 1968, art. 7; repealed and replaced by Regulation (EU) 492/2011 2011) with regard to workers, and in Article 52 second paragraph (TEEC (Rome) 1957) (now 49(2) TFEU (TFEU (Lisbon) 2025)) and Article 59 first paragraph of the Treaty of Rome (TEEC (Rome) 1957) (now 56 first paragraph TFEU (TFEU (Lisbon) 2025)) with regard to self-employed persons exercising their right to free establishment and to provide services respectively. It is important to note that the principle was not exclusively granted to market citizens (Olsen 2008, 47). The Court interpreted this principle broadly to protect individual rights effectively (Jacobs 2007, 593) and extend its application to further social and economic aspects (Giubboni 2007, 369). The principle gained an even wider scope of application following the introduction of EU citizenship and the adoption of the Citizenship Directive (Muir 2020, 181–82), which in Article 24 refers to the principle of equal treatment and sets out exceptions to the principle (*Case C-709/20 C.G.* 2021). Article 24(1) conditions the principle of equal treatment in the following manner: "[s]ubject to such specific provisions as are expressly provided for in the Treaty and secondary law," whilst Article 24(2) allows States not to confer entitlement to social assistance. This means that Member States are not obliged to provide social assistance (as defined in *Brey* (*Case C-140/12 Brey* 2013, ¶¶ 60–61)) to non-national EU citizens during the first three months of residence or a longer period whilst they are jobseekers (see Spaventa 2008, 30; Giubboni 2007, 371–72) and that students are not entitled to receive maintenance grants and loans (see Davies 2024). Such exceptions have, in some cases, been mitigated by a broad interpretation of the texts (see Davies 2024, 289–90). Whilst the CJEU has at times stressed the need to show the bonds between the individual and the host State, that is, some form of integration or sense of belonging (*Case*

C-209/03 Bidar 2005, ¶¶ 49–63), in the vast majority of cases it has linked such right to lawful residency (*Case C-413/99 Baumbast* 2002, ¶ 92; *Case C-456/02 Trojani* 2004, ¶ 43; *Case C-85/96 Sala* 1998, ¶ 63; see Arestis 2010). As Elsmore and Starup explain, "[t]he interpretation has been that the right to equal treatment follows from (legal) residence" (Elsmore and Starup 2007, 101). Demonstrating such a connection is irrelevant after a period of five years; the principle of non-discrimination then applies to all EU citizens as they are viewed as "fully integrated and almost akin to a native" (Davies 2024, 287).

There is no doubt that this principle has gained a transformative value over the years. It has encouraged individuals to integrate into various sectors of society, including employment, education, and healthcare, as well as different groups, such as social, cultural, and ethnic communities (Azoulai et al. 2016, 7). It has entitled EU citizens to "home treatment" (Cîrlig 2020, 2). As a result, equality has enabled those who were once considered "outsiders" to become "insiders" in their country of residence (Kostakopoulou 2018, 857). As Advocate General Jacobs explained in his opinion in the case of *Collins*,

> [EU citizens] must not simply be tolerated as aliens, but welcomed by the authorities of the host State as Community nationals who are entitled, "within the scope of application of the Treaty", to all the privileges and advantages enjoyed by the nationals of the host State. No other aspect of Community law touches the individual more directly or does more to foster that sense of common identity and shared destiny without which the "ever closer union among the peoples of Europe", proclaimed by the preamble to the Treaty, would be an empty slogan. (*Case C-138/02 Collins (A.G.)* 2003, ¶ 11)

As such, the principle of equal treatment, as enshrined in the original Treaty of Rome, has been significantly enhanced by the concept of EU citizenship, which grants individuals equal rights and duties (TFEU (Lisbon) 2025, art. 20(2); Shaw 1998, sect. II.A). Moreover, the principle of non-discrimination on the basis of nationality is a fundamental aspect of citizenship more generally; it is revealing that "[i]n its Grzelczyk judgment, the Court regarded non-discrimination as the nucleus of citizenship" (Reich and Harbacevica 2003, 617). This is precisely what highlights the transformative value of EU citizenship: a national of an EU Member State is regarded as equal to a national of the host Member State.

The combined application of the concept of EU citizenship and the principle of non-discrimination or equal treatment has fundamentally transformed the EU citizens' life and influenced national law. As a result, EU citizens are treated differently from third-country nationals at both the national and local levels. In contradistinction to other "foreigners", EU citizenship, alongside the principle of non-discrimination, has prevented EU citizens from becoming "second class citizens" (Oosterom-Staples 2018, 435). Back in 1992, Closa emphasised that "[c]itizens of a Member State are still regarded as 'aliens' for [sic] 'foreigners' by other Member States and they may suffer discrimination in those fields of activity not protected by Community law (for instance, political rights)" (Closa 1992, 1139). Interestingly, seven years later, Kostakopoulou reported that "[n]otions such as 'immigrant', 'resident alien' or 'temporary guest' have been replaced by that of 'Union citizen'" (Kostakopoulou 1998a, 393; see Kostakopoulou 2007, 628 and 634) in national legislation. She explains that the presence of such individuals "is no longer a matter of state toleration and consent. It is, instead, an issue of exercising fundamental right" (Kostakopoulou 2007, 634). In contrast, third-country nationals are still viewed as "immigrants", and the legislation regarding them reflects this perspective. Consequently, the principle of non-discrimination has transformed EU nationals living in an EU Member State other than their own into individuals who can be considered "nationals-like".

This principle extends to the family members of EU citizens through the Citizenship Directive (Citizenship Directive 2024, art. 24), though not through Article 18 TFEU as it only applies to those with EU nationalities (*Joined Cases C-22/08 and C-23/08 Vatsouras and Koupatantze* 2009, ¶ 52; see Davies 2024, 274; *Case C-673/20 E.P. v. Préfet du Gers* 2022b, ¶ 78). The principle, as applied to family members, becomes a corollary to the primary rights of the EU citizen (Davies 2024, 275). The rationale for this is quite simple: an EU citizen "will be significantly discouraged from remaining in a host Member State if their TCN family members are unable to participate in society on fair and equal terms—to work, study, and engage in other activities" (Davies 2024, 275). Even in situations that fall outside of the scope of the Citizenship Directive, as Davies bluntly notes, "[n]o family, no meaningful free movement for Citizens" (Davies 2024, 276). Extending the principle of non-discrimination to family members further embeds EU citizens in the local fabric as not only they but also their family can meaningfully take part in the life of the host State.

In conclusion, the principle of non-discrimination on grounds of nationality has evolved from an economic safeguard into a constitutional cornerstone of EU citizenship. Initially designed to prevent obstacles to free movement, it now reflects a broader normative commitment to equality and integration within the Union. It embeds EU citizens into the social, economic, and cultural life of their host Member State. Its extension to family members further consolidates this effect, ensuring that free movement is meaningful and, in that regard, underscores the transformative value of EU citizenship.

3.3.3 The Right to Vote and Stand as a Candidate in Local Elections

The third right that has given EU citizenship a transformative value is the right to vote and stand as a candidate in local elections or in European elections in their country of residence rather than in their country of nationality under Article 22 TFEU.

Generally, "migrants place a high value on the right to vote" as it gives them a voice both as individuals and as a community (Leitner and Ehrkamp 2006, 1625). The establishment of the right to vote in and be elected at local elections was the product of decade-long discussions (see Blumann 1991, 288). Indeed, already at the Paris Summit held from 19 to 21 October 1972, Giulio Andreotti, Prime Minister of the Republic of Italy, argued that the then EC Member States

> could [then] decide to establish a European citizenship, which would be in addition to the citizenship which the inhabitants of [those] countries [then possessed]. It should permit the citizens of the Community countries, after a stay of a certain length in one of [those] countries, to exercise some political rights, such as that of participating in communal elections. (Andreotti 1972, 46; see Strudel 2003, 20)

The proposal was based on the understanding that whilst local decisions impact EU migrants, their participation in local political life does not affect a State sovereignty (Evans 1991, 201; Closa 1992, 1148) as participation in general or presidential elections would. It is indeed assumed that, as foreigners are guests in a State, they should observe political neutrality and thus should not have the right to vote in any national elections (van den Berghe and Huber 1981, 43).

Still in 1975 "The Granting of Special Rights" report highlighted that whilst the idea of *equal treatment* for foreigners concerning economic and social rights was accepted by public opinion at the time, political rights faced greater resistance (*Granting of Special Rights* 1975, 30). Yet over time, this hurdle was overcome, and now the right to vote and stand in local elections is an expression of the principle of non-discrimination as Article 22(1) specifies that it must be granted "under the same conditions as nationals of that State". Whilst the right to vote and stand as a candidate is "a corollary to the right of freedom of movement" (Anglmayer 2021, 2), allowing EU citizens to be quasi-nationals within their State of residence, the application of the principle of non-discrimination in this context aligns with the modern notion of democratic citizenship as profoundly egalitarian (Tamara Lenard 2016, 73).

The aim of conferring such political rights was undoubtedly to enable individuals to participate in the political life of their local communities and engage with local affairs in their State of residence, if they chose to do so. For example, in France, British nationals participated in local politics (Ferbrache and Yarwood 2015, 80), with some being elected as local councillors (Drake and Collard 2008, 227; Ferbrache 2019b, 509). The political participation was valued and seen as meaningful as they took an active role in their place of residence, were part of the local community, and built and strengthened social relationships (Ferbrache 2019b, 513). As Ferbrache observes, these local elections were considered "as forms of civic inclusion that foster a sense of belonging" (Ferbrache 2019b, 514). In fact, there was little "connection between interest in national politics and active local participation" (Drake and Collard 2008, 227). In some countries, because of the way local election registers are used, EU citizens have been able to vote in regional and national elections (see Kochenov 2009, 209). For example, in the UK, EU citizens were able to vote in the elections for the devolved Parliaments in Wales, Scotland, and Northern Ireland, which have legislative competences (see Shaw 2007, 2570). This ability to participate in local and regional politics has led to stronger connections with the local and regional social and political environments (see Ferbrache 2019b, 515), as citizenship is ultimately associated with bounded territory. It turns out that the right to vote, especially at local elections, has played a significant role in helping EU citizens integrate into the local life and become part of the social and political fabric of their communities (see Pataut 2010). Yet, whilst such a right exists, it does not mean that it is exercised by all EU citizens. Evidence indicates that turnout rates and candidacies are lower than those of (sedentary) nationals, likely due to a combination of factors, including difficulties with registration, a lack of electoral information, a poor understanding of the country's political system (Anglmayer 2021, 4), and, more fundamentally, a lack of knowledge of their right to vote and stand as candidate in municipal elections (Anglmayer 2021, 10). In fact, the overwhelming majority of mobile EU citizens voted in the EU Member State of which they were nationals (European Commission 2020, 29).

Further, EU citizens cannot take part in national elections. Already in 1975, the Commission had acknowledged that "complete assimilation with nationals as regards political rights [was] desirable in the long term from the point of view of a European Union" (*Granting of Special Rights* 1975, 28); yet, it understood that Member States would be reluctant to allow EU citizens to vote at all three levels of political representation: local, national, and European. Despite calls for the extension of this voting right to EU citizens (see e.g., Resolution of 16 February 2017 on Possible Evolutions of and Adjustments to the Current Institutional Set-up of the European Union 2017, ¶ 50) and European Citizens' Initiatives (see *Let Me Vote* 2013; *Voters without Borders, Full Political Rights for EU Citizens* 2020), EU Member States have not yet taken this step. Electoral participation is deemed an exclusive "right of democratic citizenship within a political community" (Ferbrache 2019b, 504). The denial of EU citizens' voice in the national elections has been criticised by scholars (see, e.g., Kochenov 2009, 207), notably for creating factually two groups of EU citizens: those who are nationals of the host State and those who are not (Lardy 1996, 625). Those without such a political right may be perceived as "outsiders", impeding their integration into the wider society since they do not enjoy full community membership. However, the reality on the ground is more mixed. For example, some UK nationals living in France felt excluded from full citizenship because they could not vote in national elections, whereas others placed greater importance on their local community and did not mind the exclusion (Ferbrache and Yarwood 2015, 80; Ferbrache 2019b, 502; Drake and Collard 2008, 227).

Overall, the right to vote and stand in local elections is considered to enable EU citizens to embed themselves in the local fabric. Ferbrache correctly observes that "[t]he significance of local voting rights might be something that becomes valued through practice" (Ferbrache 2019b, 516).

This section has demonstrated that the right to residence, the principle of non-discrimination and the right to vote and stand in local elections have all enabled EU citizens to embed themselves into the society of the EU Member State. Using a legal-participatory vision of EU citizenship (based on rights) enables the authors to conclude that these three rights have transformative value. It shows that EU citizenship, particularly concerning the three aforementioned elements, "*de facto* amounts to the possession of a quasinationality of the Member State of residence of which the citizen is not a national" (Kochenov 2013, 117).

3.4 An Experiential Citizenship

Although the argument that EU citizenship has enabled EU nationals to integrate within the local fabric can be supported by using a legal-participatory vision of EU citizenship (Becker 2004, 140 and 143–45) focusing on the *status* and *rights* of EU citizens, as described in Chap. 2 and Sect. 3.2, the authors maintain that this approach relates to the *practice* of EU citizenship, too. Whilst it is true that the legal-participatory approach towards EU citizenship emphasises "legal status and a clearly defined but narrow set of rights [which] might be called a 'minimalist conception' of European citizenship" (Becker 2004, 142), EU citizenship has, as will be demonstrated, enabled the development of a socio-legal environment that transcends this formalistic approach.

As much as scholars in the wake of the adoption of the Treaty of Maastricht believed that the new provisions did not significantly change the mercantile approach towards citizenship, they viewed the additional rights, such as the right to vote, as part of an "empty rhetoric" (see Kostakopoulou 1998b, 639). After all, EU citizenship "was not *in itself* much of a policy innovation" (Shaw 1997, 556). Writing in 1996, Herzog lamented the lack of a civic link ("*lien civique*") in the European Union, affirming that the only connections between the European peoples were the market and a couple of transnational programmes. Yet, there was no transnational public relation ("*relation publique transnationale*") (Herzog 1996, 39) and, as Delors famously said, "it is difficult to fall in love with a large market" (*Discours of Delors* 1989). Despite being marked by mobility and an internal market, the concept of EU citizenship was meant to evolve into a "political status [...], in an attempt to strengthen the democratic basis of the Community" (Kostakopoulou 1998b, 641; see Fernández 2012, 153; Shuibhne 2010, 1611) and to be the beginning of a new phase in both the enlargement and deepening of European integration (Simon and Kovar 1993, 286).

The concept of European citizenship was originally designed by politicians as a means to bring the European integration process closer to European nationals (*Tindemans Report—Report on European Union* 1975, 18) with the view to fostering greater awareness among them regarding their citizenship status and rights. As Barber underlines, "[i]ts authors hoped that its effects would extend beyond the legal realm, that it would create a psychological sense of attachment between the people of Europe and the structures of the Union and, in political terms, provide them with reasons to obey and support its institution" (Barber 2002, 247; see Resolution on EU Citizenship for Sale 2014, ¶ 7).

The idea of EU citizenship was designed to go beyond mere formal bonds (Resolution on EU Citizenship for Sale 2014, ¶ 7). EU citizenship means becoming and being recognised as a member of "a political community of citizens who (should) think of themselves as demos" (Fernández 2012, 159). Yet, as Barber points out, fostering such a psychological sense of attachment is challenging owing to the differences in languages, cultures, and traditions across the EU (Barber 2002, 247). People struggle to conceptualise themselves as a united group. Weiler also emphasises that, for a genuine sense of attachment to exist, there needs to be a "resonant fiction of relatedness" (Weiler 1997). Much hope was put in mobile citizens, who were seen as individuals likely to embrace European Union values and support European unification more readily. They were regarded as "a 'carrier group' of a firmer legitimacy for the EU and the champions of a borderless, ever closer Union" (Recchi 2008, 213).

The authors argue that although EU citizenship might not have reached its aim of creating this EU citizens togetherness (see, e.g., Drake and Collard 2008, 227 and 229; Coutts 2018, 244; Damay and Mercenier 2016, 1144–45), it has stirred a socio-psychological process in which EU citizens have integrated into the host State. As Schoenberger explains, when the Frenchman integrates into Italian society, he is "italianised" rather than "Europeanised" (Schönberger 2007, 79) or in Azoulai's words, "[a]s a Frenchman, I am 'European' by being given the opportunity to reside in Italy and to become 'quasi-Italian' with regard to the main aspects of my social life" (Azoulai 2017, 179–80).

This embeddedness is influenced by both external factors and the internal dynamics of each individual's relationships with others. Undoubtedly, free movement and its associated rights already facilitated some embedment. As Kostakopoulou stresses, the market citizen engaged in economic transactions, but these were "embedded within a social and political context" (Kostakopoulou 2005, 238–39). Yet, it was the very concept of EU citizenship that encapsulated this process in a single term. Through mobility, EU citizens have formed formal, informal, and emotional bonds with another EU Member State and its population.

Fundamentally, citizenship involves a direct and immediate relationship between the individual and their entity, polity or community (Vasiljević 2006, 117). Citizenship is as much a status as it is a set of relationships (Staeheli 2011, 394), built on the connection between an individual and a set of institutions guided by the "shared principles of justice, social and cultural norms and rules that establish the procedures of political participation, and day-to-day practices of citizen participation in the polity/community" (Vasiljević 2006, 117). Furthermore, citizenship is described as "of action and not of mode of being" (Tassin 1994, 109) in the sense that it is defined and enacted through ordinary (Staeheli et al. 2012, 630) and everyday social practices and political action (Bauder 2014, 91; see the work on the notion of *jus nexi* Shachar 2009, 2011). The process of embeddedness, or settlement, is developed by "experiencing, performing, and constructing a multitude of emotions, social relations, materialities, and imaginations" (Miller 2019).

Being an EU citizen is thus constructed through practice, involving not only interactions with the national structures and institutions (see Aradau et al. 2010, 956), but also encounters with the local population that foster and nurture sociability between EU citizens and nationals of the country of residence (Aradau et al. 2010, 945; Godin and Sigona 2022, 1136). Individuals "are bound by various kinds of connecting factors based on residence, employment, family ties, education and so on" (Azoulai 2016, 212), establishing a "genuine link with the society" of the host State (*Case C-209/03 Bidar* 2005, ¶ 62).

EU citizenship enables integration by default (Mügge and van der Haar 2016, 82); there is no explicit expectation that EU citizens integrate. Unlike other foreign nationals, EU citizens "are freed from the imperatives of migrant integration" (see Nancheva and Ranta 2022, 1983; Ranta and Nancheva 2019; Barbulescu and Favell 2020, 153). Nevertheless, they achieve social acceptance and have access to an array of rights and services. EU citizens in the UK had incorporated in their communities "in successful and sustainable patterns" and this without the need for integration governance (Nancheva and Ranta 2022, 1998). In the case of long-term residents, one can almost speak of full integration as there is "parity of life chances with members of the majority group" and "legitimacy of membership" (see Nancheva and Ranta 2022, 1986).

Four points must yet be stressed to provide a more accurate and less monolithic picture of the experience of mobile EU citizens. First, the quality of their experience is not solely determined by their status and rights; it also depends on how they are perceived within the society, localities, and neighbourhoods (Guma and Dafydd Jones 2019). For example, whilst white, professional British migrants were positively received in Berlin, this was less the case for non-white British migrants (Kulz 2023, 224–26). In the UK, Central and Eastern European nationals were "labelled, made to feel like and, to a considerable extent, accepted a lower-class EU citizen categorisation" (Siklodi 2023, 3).

Second, the embeddedness is essentially practised and experienced at the local rather than at the national level. It could be argued that it is a citizenship based on domicile (see Ferbrache and Yarwood 2015, 80–82) as the "person is a citizen of the polity in which she or he resides" (Bauder 2014, 92). However, in this context, the territory is less significant than the opportunity to come together and engage in activities within these local spaces and communities (Ferbrache and Yarwood 2015, 81–82; see Miller 2019). As Azoulai notes, this type of embeddedness is linked to specific sites of social and civil integration rather than the national political community (Azoulai 2016, 212).

Third, the embeddedness can be temporary and short-lived (Miller 2019). After all, it is an open and ongoing process that is built and forged on a daily basis; it is a temporal phenomenon that can be disrupted at any time under any given circumstance (Guma and Dafydd Jones 2019). However, in many cases, short encounters can be significant. For instance, "time spent in the UK and the personal decision to settle" were important embeddedness factors (Nancheva and Ranta 2022, 1996). This book, however, does not address such situations as it focuses on long-term residents.

Fourth, since embeddedness is created through constant negotiation with political, legal, economic, and social structures (see Ferbrache and Yarwood 2015, 75), it is subjective, almost unique to individuals and certainly impossible to define using a limited set of criteria. Nationality, gender, education, class, disability, etc., all affect the way EU citizens "encounter different life chances and face profoundly different opportunities for prosperity" (Trenz and Triandafyllidou 2017, 553). Further, such aspects also influence the way individuals, communities, and structures interact. As this book cannot address all these aspects, it takes a broad(er) brush but highlights, whenever possible and relevant, disparities in treatment and experiences.

Fifth, "citizenship as practice emphasises an alternative perspective from the bottom-up" (Ferbrache 2019a, 84) and thus puts individuals at the heart of the process. It relies on how individuals perceive their local community and their willingness to engage with it. For example, UK nationals living in Spain had little to no contact with the local population, which hindered their ability to embed themselves into Spanish society (see Giner-Monfort and Huete 2021, 75; Giner-Monfort and Hall 2024, 2).

In conclusion, more than a formal construct, EU citizenship is experiential, shaping everyday practices and relationships, impacting (more or less) mundane moments in EU citizens' personal, family, and social lives. In doing so, it transforms a legal status that grants rights into a lived reality.

3.5 Conclusion

In this light, the authors contend that EU citizenship is an experiential citizenship because it is rooted in the experience of first enjoying free movement and then accessing the right to residence, the principle of non-discrimination and the right to vote and stand in local elections, which the authors believe hold transformative value. It is only by experiencing free movement from one State to another and residing in another State that EU citizens can fully understand and appreciate the full implications of their rights as EU citizens. Whilst these rights are directly or indirectly conferred by the European Union, their practical application occurs within national and local settings (Fernández 2012, 156).

Ultimately, this experience allows the concept of EU citizenship to converge with that of "ordinary (national) citizenship" which "fuses legal structures, normative orders, and the practices and experiences of individuals, social groups and communities" (Staeheli et al. 2012, 631), and therefore translates into rights that can be exercised and enjoyed in everyday life.

As a result, the host State's social structures and institutions become meaningful objects to the individual (see, e.g., Ferbrache and Yarwood 2015, 80), and the experience can lead to a transformative understanding of EU citizenship. What began as a purely functional experience of the freedom of movement and residence, along with associated rights, has evolved into a fully transcendental and transformative experience of citizenship.

References

Andreotti, Guilio. 1972. *Speech at the Paris Summit between 19 and 21 October 1972.* Vol. 5, No. 11. Bulletin of the European Communities.

Anglmayer, Irmgard. 2021. Voting and Candidacy Rights of Mobile EU Citizens in Municipal Elections under Directive 94/80/EC. European Parliamentary Research Service. https://www.europarl.europa.eu/RegData/etudes/BRIE/2021/694233/EPRS_BRI(2021)694233_EN.pdf.

Aradau, Claudia, Jef Huysmans, and Vicki Squire. 2010. Acts of European Citizenship: A Political Sociology of Mobility. *Journal of Common Market Studies* 48 (4): 945–965. https://doi.org/10.1111/j.1468-5965.2010.02081.x.

Arestis, G. 2010. *European Citizenship and the Elimination of Discriminatory Measures among European Citizens with Special Reference to Social Benefits.* Paper presented at Annual Conference of the Centre for Legal Research at the University of the West of England. October 4.

Aristotle. 1996. *The Politics and the Constitution of Athens.* Edited by S Everson. Cambridge University Press.

Azoulai, Loïc. 2016. The European Individual as Part of Collective Entities (Market, Family, Society). In *Constructing the Person in EU Law: Rights, Roles, Identities*, ed. Loïc Azoulai, Barbou des Places, and Étienne Pataut. Hart Publishing. https://doi.org/10.5040/9781782259367.

Azoulai, Loïc. 2017. Transfiguring European Citizenship: From Member State Territory to Union Territory. In *EU Citizenship and Federalism: The Role of Rights*, ed. Dimitry Kochenov. Cambridge University Press. https://doi.org/10.1017/9781139680714.008.

Azoulai, Loïc, Ségolène Barbou des Places, and Etienne Pataut. 2016. Being a Person in the European Union. In *Constructing the Person in EU Law: Rights, Roles, Identities*, ed. Loïc Azoulai, Ségolène Barbou des Places, and Etienne Pataut. Hart Publishing.

Barber, N. W. 2002. Citizenship, Nationalism and the European Union. *European Law Review* 27 (3): 241–259.

Barbulescu, Roxana, and Adrian Favell. 2020. Commentary: A Citizenship without Social Rights? EU Freedom of Movement and Changing Access to Welfare Rights. *International Migration* 58 (1): 151–165. https://doi.org/10.1111/imig.12607.

Bauder, Harald. 2014. Domicile Citizenship, Human Mobility and Territoriality. *Progress in Human Geography* 38 (1): 91–106. https://doi.org/10.1177/0309132513502281.

Becker, Michael A. 2004. Managing Diversity in the European Union: Inclusive European Citizenship and Third-Country Nationals. *Yale Human Rights & Development Law Journal* 7:132–183.

Blumann, Claude. 1991. L'Europe des citoyens. *Revue Du Marché Commun de l'Union Européenne* 346:283–292.

Brändle, Verena K., Charlotte Galpin, and Hans-Jörg Trenz. 2018. Marching for Europe? Enacting European Citizenship as Justice During Brexit. *Citizenship Studies* 22 (8): 810–828. https://doi.org/10.1080/13621025.2018.1531825.

Bux, Udo, and Mariusz Maciejewski. 2025. The Citizens of the Union and Their Rights. Fact Sheets on the European Union. European Parliament. https://www.europarl.europa.eu/factsheets/en/sheet/145/the-citizens-of-the-union-and-their-rights.

Cambien, Nathan, Dimitry Kochenov, and Elise Muir. 2020. European Citizenship under Stress: Introduction. In *European Citizenship under Stress - Social Justice, Brexit and Other Challenges*, ed. Nathan Cambien, Dimitry Kochenov, and Elise Muir. Brill.

Carrera, Sergio, and Davide Colombi. 2025. Irregularising Human Mobility. *EU Migration Policies and the European Commission's Role.* SpringerBriefs in Law. Springer. https://i-claim.eu/project/irregularising-human-mobility/.

Case C-118/20. 2021. J.Y. v. Wiener Landesregierung, ECLI:EU:C:2021:530 (Advocate General Szpunar).

Case C-135/08. 2009. Janko Rottman v. Freistaat Bayern, ECLI:EU:C:2009:588 (Advocate General Maduro).

Case C-138/02. 2003. Brian Francis Collins v. Secretary of State for Work and Pensions, ECLI:EU:C:2003:409 (Advocate General Colomer).

Case C-140/12. 2013. Pensionsversicherungsanstalt v. Peter Brey, ECLI:EU:C:2013:565 (CJEU).

Case C-165/16. 2017. Toufik Lounes v. Secretary of State for the Home Department, ECLI:EU:C:2017:862 (CJEU).

Case C-168/91. 1992. Christos Konstantinidis v. Stadt Altensteig—Standesamt and Landratsamt Calw—Ordnungsamt, ECLI:EU:C:1992:504 (Advocate General Jacobs).

Case C-181/23 2024. European Commission v. Republic of Malta (Citizenship by Investment), ECLI:EU:C:2024:849 (Advocate General Collins).

Case C-181/23. 2025. European Commission v. Republic of Malta (Citizenship by Investment), ECLI:EU:C:2025:283 (CJEU).

Case C-209/03. 2005. The Queen, on the Application of Dany Bidar v. London Borough of Ealing and Secretary of State for Education and Skills, ECLI:EU:C:2005:169 (ECJ).

Case C-370/90. 1992. The Queen v. Immigration Appeal Tribunal and Surinder Singh, Ex Parte Secretary of State for Home Department, ECLI:EU:C:1992:296 (ECJ).

Case C-378/12. 2014. Nnamdi Onuekwere v. Secretary of State for the Home Department, ECLI:EU:C:2014:13 (CJEU).
Case C-393/13 2014. Elisabeta Dano and Florin Dano v. Jobcenter Leipzig, ECLI:EU:C:2014:2358 (CJEU).
Case C-400/12. 2014. Secretary of State for the Home Department v. M.G., ECLI:EU:C:2014:9 (CJEU).
Case C-413/99. 2002. Baumbast and R. v. Secretary of State for the Home Department, ECLI:EU:C:2002:493 (ECJ).
Case C-456/02. 2004. Michel Trojani v. Centre Public d'aide Sociale de Bruxelles (CPAS), ECLI:EU:C:2004:488 (ECJ).
Case C-673/20. 2022a. E.P. v. Préfet Du Gers and Institut National de La Statistique et Des Études Économiques (INSEE), ECLI:EU:C:2022:129 (Advocate General Collins).
Case C-673/20. 2022b. E.P. v. Préfet Du Gers and Institut National de La Statistique et Des Études Économiques (INSEE), ECLI:EU:C:2022:449 (CJEU).
Case C-709/20. 2021. C.G. v. The Department for Communities in Northern Ireland, ECLI:EU:C:2021:602 (CJEU).
Case C-85/96 1998. María Martínez Sala v. Freistaat Bayern, ECLI:EU:C:1998:217 (ECJ).
Case C-930/19. 2021. X v Belgian State, ECLI:EU:C:2021:657 (CJEU).
Chaltiel, Florence. 2008. La citoyenneté européenne. Cahiers du Conseil Constitutionnel 23 (February). https://www.conseil-constitutionnel.fr/nouveaux-cahiers-du-conseil-constitutionnel/la-citoyennete-europeenne.
Cîrlig, Carmen-Cristina. 2020. EU and UK Citizens' Rights after Brexit: An Overview. PE 651.975. European Parliamentary Research Service. https://www.europarl.europa.eu/RegData/etudes/IDAN/2020/651975/EPRS_IDA(2020)651975_EN.pdf.
Closa, Carlos. 1992. The Concept of Citizenship in the Treaty on European Union. *Common Market Law Review* 29 (6): 1137–1169. https://doi.org/10.54648/cola1992065.
Consolidated Version of Treaty on the Functioning of the European Union (Lisbon). 2025. http://data.europa.eu/eli/treaty/tfeu_2016/2025-03-15.
Coutts, Stephen. 2018. Citizens of Elsewhere, Everywhere and ... Nowhere? Rethinking Union Citizenship in Light of Brexit. *Northern Ireland Legal Quarterly* 69 (3): 231–247. https://doi.org/10.53386/nilq.v69i3.161.
Coutts, Stephen. 2019. The Shifting Geometry of Union Citizenship: A Supranational Status from Transnational Rights. *Cambridge Yearbook of European Legal Studies* 21:318–341. https://doi.org/10.1017/cel.2019.19.
Coutts, Stephen. 2020. The Court, the Legislature and the Co-Construction of a Status of Social Integration. In *European Citizenship under Stress—Social Justice, Brexit and Other Challenges*, ed. Nathan Cambien, Dimitry Kochenov, and Elise Muir. Brill.

D'Alfonso, Alessandro, Eva-Maria Poptcheva, James McEldowney, and Laura Tilindyte. 2017. The Brexit Negotiations: Issues for the First Phase. PE 607.267. European Parliamentary Research Service. https://www.europarl.europa.eu/RegData/etudes/IDAN/2017/607267/EPRS_IDA(2017)607267_EN.pdf.

Dadomo, Christian, and Noëlle Quénivet. 2020. *European Union Law*. 3rd ed. Hall & Stott Publishing.

Damay, Ludivine, and Heidi Mercenier. 2016. Free Movement and EU Citizenship: A Virtuous Circle? *Journal of European Public Policy* 23 (8): 1139–1157. https://doi.org/10.1080/13501763.2016.1186212.

Davies, Gareth. 2024. When Do Union Citizens and Their Families Have the Right to Equal Treatment on Grounds of Nationality in EU Law? *European Journal of Migration and Law* 26 (3): 267–290. https://doi.org/10.1163/15718166-12340180.

de Waele, Henri. 2010. EU Citizenship: Revisiting Its Meaning, Place and Potential. *European Journal of Migration and Law* 12 (3): 319–336. https://doi.org/10.1163/157181610X520391.

Directive 2004/38/EC of the European Parliament and the of the Council of 29 April 2004 on the Rights of Citizens of the Union and Their Family Members to Move and Reside Freely within the Territory of the Member States Amending Regulation (EEC) No 1612/68 and Repealing Directives 64/221/EEC, 68/360/EEC, 72/194/EEC, 73/148/EEC, 75/34/EEC, 75/35/EEC, 90/364/EEC, 90/365/EEC, and 93/96/EEC, OJ L158/77. 2024.

Discours de Jacques Delors devant le Parlement Européen (17 Janvier 1989*)*. 1989. Bulletin des Communautés européennes. 1989, N° Supplément 1/89. https://www.cvce.eu/content/publication/2003/8/22/b9c06b95-db97-4774-a700-e8aea5172233/publishable_fr.pdf.

Drake, Helen, and Susan Collard. 2008. A Case Study of Intra-EU Migration: 20 Years of "Brits" in the Pays d'Auge, Normandy, France. *French Politics* 6 (3): 214–233. https://doi.org/10.1057/fp.2008.11.

Elsmore, Matthew J., and Peter Starup. 2007. Union Citizenship-Background, Jurisprudence, and Perspective: The Past, Present, and Future of Law and Policy. *Yearbook of European Law* 26 (1): 57–113. https://doi.org/10.1093/yel/26.1.57.

European Commission. 2020. *EU Citizenship*. 2020. *Final Report—Results of the Public Consultation on EU Citizenship Rights 2020*. https://commission.europa.eu/document/download/567dd687-43eb-4efc-b706-188df9906084_en?filename=report_on_the_public_consultation_on_eu_citizenship_rights_2020_en.pdf.

European Commission. 2001. *Third Report from the Commission on Citizenship of the Union*. COM(2001) 506 Final. https://eur-lex.europa.eu/LexUriServ/LexUriServ.do?uri=COM:2001:0506:FIN:EN:PDF.

European Commission. 2017. *Decision on the Proposed Citizens' Initiative Entitled 'EU Citizenship for Europeans: United in Diversity in Spite of Jus Soli and Jus Sanguinis' C(2017) 2001*. [2017] OJEU C81/18.

European Commission. 2020. *EU Citizenship 2020—Results of the Public Consultation on EU Citizenship Rights 2020*. https://commission.europa.eu/document/download/567dd687-43eb-4efc-b706-188df9906084_en?filename=report_on_the_public_consultation_on_eu_citizenship_rights_2020_en.pdf.

European Council. 2025. EU Mobile Citizens and Their Electoral Rights. August 5. https://www.consilium.europa.eu/en/policies/mobile-eu-citizens-and-their-electoral-rights/.

Evans, Andrew. 1991. Nationality Law and European Integration. *European Law Review* 16 (3): 190–215.

Faist, Thomas. 2001. Social Citizenship in the European Union: Nested Membership. *Journal of Common Market Studies* 39 (1): 37–58. https://doi.org/10.1111/1468-5965.00275.

Ferbrache, Fiona. 2019a. Acts of European Citizenship: How Britons Resident in France Have Been Negotiating Post-Brexit Futures. *Geography* 104 (2): 81–88. https://doi.org/10.1080/00167487.2019.12094067.

Ferbrache, Fiona. 2019b. Local Electoral Rights for Non-French Residents? A Case-Study Analysis of British Candidates and Councillors in French Municipal Elections. *Citizenship Studies* 23 (5): 502–520. https://doi.org/10.1080/13621025.2019.1623864.

Ferbrache, Fiona, and Richard Yarwood. 2015. Britons Abroad or European Citizens? The Negotiation of (Trans)National Space and Citizenship by British Migrants in France. *Geoforum* 62 (June): 73–83. https://doi.org/10.1016/j.geoforum.2015.03.021.

Fernández, Christian. 2012. Patriots in the Making? Migrants, Citizens, and Demos Building in the European Union. *Journal of International Migration and Integration* 13 (2): 147–163. https://doi.org/10.1007/s12134-011-0210-8.

Fourteenth Amendment to the Constitution of the United States. n.d. Accessed 1 January 2026. https://constitution.congress.gov/constitution/amendment-14/.

Frau, Robert. 2019. Ist das Brexit-Abkommen zu Recht gescheitert? *Europarecht* 5:502–521.

Garner, Oliver. 2018. The Existential Crisis of Citizenship of the European Union: *The Argument for an Autonomous Status. Cambridge Yearbook of European Legal Studies* 20:116–146. https://doi.org/10.1017/cel.2018.6.

Giner-Monfort, Jordi, and Kelly Hall. 2024. Older British Migrants in Spain: Return Patterns and Intentions Post-Brexit. *Population, Space and Place* 30 (1): e2730. https://doi.org/10.1002/psp.2730.

Giner-Monfort, Jordi, and Raquel Huete. 2021. Uncertain Sunset Lives: British Migrants Facing Brexit in Spain. *European Urban and Regional Studies* 28 (1): 74–79. https://doi.org/10.1177/0969776420972148.

Giubboni, Stefano. 2007. Free Movement of Persons and European Solidarity. *European Law Journal* 13 (3): 360–379. https://doi.org/10.1111/j.1468-0386.2007.00370.x.

Godin, Marie, and Nando Sigona. 2022. Intergenerational Narratives of Citizenship among EU Citizens in the UK after the Brexit Referendum. *Ethnic and Racial Studies* 45 (6): 1135–1154. https://doi.org/10.1080/01419870.2021.1981964.

Guma, Taulant, and Rhys Dafydd Jones. 2019. "Where Are We Going to Go Now?" European Union Migrants' Experiences of Hostility, Anxiety, and (Non-)Belonging During Brexit. *Population, Space and Place* 25 (1): e2198. https://doi.org/10.1002/psp.2198.

Herzog, Philippe. 1996. L'Europe peut-elle devenir l'affaire des citoyens? *Esprit* 224 (8/9): 32–53.

Hoogenboom, Alexander. 2015. In Search of a Rationale for the EU Citizenship Jurisprudence. *Oxford Journal of Legal Studies* 35 (2): 301–324. https://doi.org/10.1093/ojls/gqu023.

Jacobs, Francis G. 2007. Citizenship of the European Union—A Legal Analysis. *European Law Journal* 13 (5): 591–610. https://doi.org/10.1111/j.1468-0386.2007.00385.x.

Jenson, Jane. 2007. The European Union's Citizenship Regime. Creating Norms and Building Practices. *Comparative European Politics* 5 (1): 53–69. https://doi.org/10.1057/palgrave.cep.6110102.

Joined Cases C-22/08 and C-23/08. 2009. Athanasios Vatsouras and Josif Koupatantze v. Arbeitsgemeinschaft (ARGE) Nürnberg 900, ECLI:EU:C:2009:344 (ECJ).

Joined Cases C-316/16 and C-424/16 2018. B. v. Land Baden-Württemberg and Secretary of State for the Home Department v. Franco Vomero, ECLI:EU:C:2018:256 (CJEU).

Kochenov, Dimitry. 2008. Ius Tractum of Many Faces: European Citizenship and the Difficult Relationship between Status and Rights. *Columbia Journal of European Law* 15 (2): 169–238.

Kochenov, Dimitry. 2009. Free Movement and Participation in the Parliamentary Elections in the Member State of Nationality: An Ignored Link. *Maastricht Journal of European and Comparative Law* 16 (2): 197–224. https://doi.org/10.1177/1023263X0901600204.

Kochenov, Dimitry. 2013. The Essence of EU Citizenship Emerging from the Last Ten Years of Academic Debate: Beyond the Cherry Blossoms and the Moon? *International and Comparative Law Quarterly* 62 (1): 97–136. https://doi.org/10.1017/S0020589312000589.

Kostakopoulou, Dora. 1998a. Nested Old and New Citizenships in the European Union: Bringing Out the Complexity. *Columbia Journal of European Law* 5 (3): 389–413.

Kostakopoulou, Theodora. 1998b. European Citizenship and Immigration after Amsterdam: Openings, Silences, Paradoxes. *Journal of Ethnic and Migration Studies* 24 (4): 639–656. https://doi.org/10.1080/1369183X.1998.9976658.

Kostakopoulou, Dora. 2005. Ideas, Norms and European Citizenship: Explaining Institutional Change. *The Modern Law Review* 68 (2): 233–267. https://doi.org/10.1111/j.1468-2230.2005.00536.x.

Kostakopoulou, Dora. 2007. European Union Citizenship: Writing the Future. *European Law Journal* 13 (5): 623–646. https://doi.org/10.1111/j.1468-0386.2007.00387.x.

Kostakopoulou, Dora. 2018. Scala Civium: Citizenship Templates Post-Brexit and the European Union's Duty to Protect EU Citizens. *Journal of Common Market Studies* 56 (4): 854–869. https://doi.org/10.1111/jcms.12683.

Kulz, Christy. 2023. Spaces of the Local, Spaces of the Nation: Intersectional Bordering Practices in Post-Brexit Berlin. *European Urban and Regional Studies* 30 (3): 221–234. https://doi.org/10.1177/09697764221087644.

Kuryla, Peter. 2025. Pan-Africanism. In *Encyclopaedia Britannica*. December 12. https://www.britannica.com/topic/Pan-Africanism.

Lardy, Heather. 1996. The Political Rights of Union Citizenship. *European Public Law* 2 (4): 611–633. https://doi.org/10.54648/EURO1996055.

Leitner, Helga, and Patricia Ehrkamp. 2006. Transnationalism and Migrants' Imaginings of Citizenship. *Environment and Planning A: Economy and Space* 38 (9): 1615–1632. https://doi.org/10.1068/a37409.

Lepoutre, Jules. 2019. A Dysfunctional Eurozenship? The Question of Free Movement. *Verfassungsblog*, January 23. https://verfassungsblog.de/a-dysfunctional-eurozenship-the-question-of-free-movement/.

Let Me Vote. 2013. ECI(2013)000003. https://europa.eu/citizens-initiative/initiatives/details/2013/000003_en.

Maas, Willem. 2008. Migrants, States, and EU Citizenship's Unfulfilled Promise. *Citizenship Studies* 12 (6): 583–596. https://doi.org/10.1080/13621020802450668.

Miller, Rebekah Grace. 2019. (Un)Settling Home during the Brexit Process. *Population, Space and Place* 25 (1): e2203. https://doi.org/10.1002/psp.2203.

More, Gillian. 2020. From Union Citizen to Third-Country National: Brexit, the UK Withdrawal Agreement, No-Deal Preparations and Britons Living in the European Union. In *European Citizenship under Stress—Social Justice, Brexit and Other Challenges*, ed. Nathan Cambien, Dimitry Kochenov, and Elise Muir. Brill.

Mourão Permoser, Julia. 2017. Redefining Membership: Restrictive Rights and Categorisation in European Union Migration Policy. *Journal of Ethnic and*

Migration Studies 43 (15): 2536–2555. https://doi.org/10.1080/1369183X.2017.1301202.

Mügge, Liza, and Marleen van der Haar. 2016. Who Is an Immigrant and Who Requires Integration? Categorizing in European Policies. In *Integration Processes and Policies in Europe: Contexts, Levels and Actors*, ed. Blanca Garcés-Mascareñas and Rinus Penninx. Springer. https://doi.org/10.1007/978-3-319-21674-4_5.

Muir, Elise. 2020. EU Citizenship, Access to "Social Benefits" and Third-Country National Family Members: Reflecting on the Relationship between Primary and Secondary Rights in Times of Brexit. In *European Citizenship under Stress—Social Justice, Brexit and Other Challenges*, ed. Nathan Cambien, Dimitry Kochenov, and Elise Muir. Brill.

Nancheva, Nevena, and Ronald Ranta. 2022. Do They Need to Integrate? The Place of EU Citizens in the UK and the Problem of Integration. *Ethnic and Racial Studies* 45 (10): 1983–2003. https://doi.org/10.1080/01419870.2021.1977363.

Neuvonen, Päivi Johanna. 2019. Retrieving the "Subject" of European Integration. *European Law Journal* 25 (1): 6–20. https://doi.org/10.1111/eulj.12301.

Olsen, Espen D. H. 2008. The Origins of European Citizenship in the First Two Decades of European Integration. *Journal of European Public Policy* 15 (1): 40–57. https://doi.org/10.1080/13501760701702157.

Oosterom-Staples, Helen. 2018. The Triangular Relationship Between Nationality, EU Citizenship and Migration in EU Law: A Tale of Competing Competences. *Netherlands International Law Review* 65 (3): 431–461. https://doi.org/10.1007/s40802-018-0122-9.

Pataut, Etienne. 2010. Citoyenneté de l'Union et nationalité étatique. *Revue Trimestrielle de Droit Européen* 3:617–632.

Pataut, Étienne. 2021. Etre ou ne pas être (Européen). *Revue Trimestrielle de Droit Européen* 3:517–520.

Pertek, Jacques. 2013. *Droit des institutions de l'Union européenne*. 4th ed. Presses Universitaires de France.

Preliminary Draft Treaty Establishing a Constitution for Europe, EU Doc CONV 369/02. 2002. https://www.cvce.eu/content/publication/2013/8/1/a8e3c3ee-ecbd-40aa-acd4-11c8bfd2f69f/publishable_fr.pdf.

Ranta, Ronald, and Nevena Nancheva. 2019. Unsettled: Brexit and European Union Nationals' Sense of Belonging. *Population, Space and Place* 25 (1): e2199. https://doi.org/10.1002/psp.2199.

Recchi, Ettore. 2008. Cross-State Mobility in the EU: Trends, Puzzles and Consequences. *European Societies* 10 (2): 197–224. https://doi.org/10.1080/14616690701835287.

Regulation (EC) No 883/2004 of the European Parliament and of the Council of 29 April 2004 on the Coordination of Social Security Systems (Text with Relevance for the EEA and for Switzerland), OJ L166/1. 2004.

Regulation (EEC) No 1408/71 of the Council of 14 June 1971 on the Application of Social Security Schemes to Employed Persons and Their Families Moving within the Community, OJ L149/2. 1971.

Regulation (EEC) No 1612/68 of the Council of 15 October 1968 on Freedom of Movement for Workers within the Community, OJ L257/2. 1968.

Regulation (EU) No 492/2011 of the European Parliament and of the Council of 5 April 2011 on Freedom of Movement for Workers within the Union Text with EEA Relevance, OJ L141/1. 2011.

Reich, Norbert, and Solvita Harbacevica. 2003. Citizenship and Family on Trial: A Fairly Optimistic Overview of Recent Court Practice with Regard to Free Movement of Persons. *Common Market Law Review* 40 (3): 615–638. https://doi.org/10.54648/COLA2003032.

Reichs- und Staatsangehörigkeitsgesetz. 1913. http://www.verfassungen.de/de67-18/rustag13.htm.

Resolution of 16 February 2017 on Possible Evolutions of and Adjustments to the Current Institutional Set-up of the European Union, OJEU 2018 C252/201. 2017. https://www.europarl.europa.eu/doceo/document/TA-8-2017-0048_EN.html.

Resolution on EU Citizenship for Sale, 2013/2995(RSP). 2014. https://www.europarl.europa.eu/doceo/document/RC-7-2014-0015_EN.html?redirect.

Resolution on Union Citizenship, [1991] OJ C183/473. 1991. https://www.europarl.europa.eu/charter/docs/pe/union-citizenship/r3-139-91-en_en.pdf.

Rhodes, P. J. 2015. 'Panhellenism'. In Oxford Research Encyclopedia of Classics, by P. J. Rhodes. Oxford University Press. https://doi.org/10.1093/acrefore/9780199381135.013.4700.

Rieder, Clemens. 2013. The Withdrawal Clause of the Lisbon Treaty in the Light of EU Citizenship (Between Disintegration and Integration). *Fordham International Law Journal* 37 (1): 147–174.

Schönberger, Christoph. 2007. European Citizenship as Federal Citizenship—Some Citizenship Lessons of Comparative Federalism. *European Review of Public Law* 19 (1): 61–81.

Shachar, Ayelet. 2009. *The Birthright Lottery: Citizenship and Global Inequality*. Harvard University Press.

Shachar, Ayelet. 2011. Earned Citizenship: Property Lessons for Immigration Reform. *Yale Journal of Law & the Humanities* 23:110–158.

Shaw, Jo. 1997. The Many Pasts and Futures of Citizenship in the European Union. *European Law Review* 22 (6): 554–572.

Shaw, Josephine. 1998. *Citizenship of the Union: Towards Post-National Membership?* Jean Monnet Working Papers. https://jeanmonnetprogram.org/archive/papers/97/97-06-.html.

Shaw, Jo. 2007. E.U. Citizenship and Political Rights in an Evolving European Union. *Fordham Law Review* 75 (5): 2549–2578.

Shuibhne, Niamh Nic. 2010. The Resilience of EU Market Citizenship. *Common Market Law Review* 47 (6): 1597–1628. https://doi.org/10.54648/COLA2010068.

Shuibhne, Niamh Nic. 2012. EU Citizenship after Lisbon. In *The European Union after the Treaty of Lisbon*, ed. Diamond Ashiagbor, Nicola Countouris, and Ioannis Lianos. Cambridge University Press.

Siklodi, Nora. 2023. (Br)Exit Citizenship: Belonging, Rights and Participation. *Journal of Contemporary European Studies*, December 26, 1–17. https://doi.org/10.1080/14782804.2023.2298330.

Simon, Denys, and Robert Kovar. 1993. La citoyenneté européenne. *Cahiers de Droit Européen* 3–4:285–316. https://doi.org/10.54648/COLA2004023.

Spaventa, Eleanor. 2008. Seeing the Wood Despite the Trees? On the Scope of Union Citizenship and Its Constitutional Effects. *Common Market Law Review* 45 (1): 13–45. https://doi.org/10.54648/COLA2008002.

Sredanovic, Djordje. 2021. Brexit as a Trigger and an Obstacle to Onwards and Return Migration. *International Migration* 59 (6): 93–108. https://doi.org/10.1111/imig.12712.

Staeheli, Lynn A. 2011. Political Geography: Where's Citizenship? *Progress in Human Geography* 35 (3): 393–400. https://doi.org/10.1177/0309132510370671.

Staeheli, Lynn A., Patricia Ehrkamp, Helga Leitner, and Caroline R. Nagel. 2012. Dreaming the Ordinary: Daily Life and the Complex Geographies of Citizenship. *Progress in Human Geography* 36 (5): 628–644. https://doi.org/10.1177/0309132511435001.

Stephanou, Constantin A. 1991. Identité et citoyenneté européennes. *Revue du Marché Commun de l'Union Européenne* 343:30–39.

Strudel, Sylvie. 2003. Polyrythmie européenne : le droit de suffrage municipal des étrangers au sein de l'Union, une règle électorale entre détournements et retardements. *Revue Française de Science Politique* 53 (1): 3–34. https://doi.org/10.3917/rfsp.531.0003.

Tamara Lenard, Patti. 2016. Democracies and the Power to Revoke Citizenship. *Ethics & International Affairs* 30 (1): 73–91. https://doi.org/10.1017/S0892679415000635.

Tassin, Etienne. 1994. Identités nationales et citoyenneté politique. *Esprit* 198 (1): 97–111.

The Granting of Special Rights. 1975. *Implementation of Point 11 of the Final Communiqué Issued at the European Summit Held in Paris on 9 and 10*

December 1974. COM (75) 321 final. Bulletin of the European Communities, Supplement 5/75. Commission.

Thym, Daniel. 2016. "Citizens" and "Foreigners" in EU Law. Migration Law and Its Cosmopolitan Outlook. *European Law Journal* 22 (3): 296–316. https://doi.org/10.1111/eulj.12164.

Tindemans Report—Report on European Union. 1975. Bulletin of the European Communities, Supplement 1/76. European Communities. https://www.cvce.eu/en/education/unit-content/-/unit/02bb76df-d066-4c08-a58a-d4686a3e68ff/63f5fca7-54ec-4792-8723-1e626324f9e3/Resources#284c9784-9bd2-472b-b704-ba4bb1f3122d_en&overlay http://aei.pitt.edu/942/1/political_tindemans_report.pdf.

Treaty Establishing the European Economic Community (Rome). 1957. http://data.europa.eu/eli/treaty/teec/sign.

Trenz, Hans-Jörg, and Anna Triandafyllidou. 2017. Complex and Dynamic Integration Processes in Europe: Intra EU Mobility and International Migration in Times of Recession. *Journal of Ethnic and Migration Studies* 43 (4): 546–459. https://doi.org/10.1080/1369183X.2016.1251013.

van den Berghe, Guido, and Christian H. Huber. 1981. 'European Citizenship'. In *Das Europa der Zweiten Generation. Gedächtnisschrift für Christophe Sasse*, ed. Roland Bieber and Dietmar Nickel, II. N.P. Engel Verlag.

van den Brink, Martijn. 2019. The Problem with Market Citizenship and the Beauty of Free Movement. In *The Internal Market and the Future of European Integration: Essays in Honour of Laurence W. Gormley*, ed. Dimitry Kochenov, Fabian Amtenbrink, Gareth Davies, and Justin Lindeboom. Cambridge University Press. https://doi.org/10.1017/9781108565417.018.

Vasiljević, Snježana. 2006. The Concept of European Citizenship. In *Croatian Accession to the European Union (Volume 4)—Challenges of Participation*, ed. K. Ott. Institute of Public Finance and Friedrich Ebert Stiftung. https://d-nb.info/1191058271/34.

Verordnung über die deutsche Staatsangehörigkeit. 1934. http://www.verfassungen.de/de33-45/staatsangehoerigkeit34.htm.

Voters without Borders, Full Political Rights for EU Citizens. 2020. ECI(2020)000002. https://europa.eu/citizens-initiative/initiatives/details/2020/000002_en.

Weiler, J. H. H. 1997. To Be a European Citizen—Eros and Civilization. *Journal of European Public Policy* 4 (4): 495–519. https://doi.org/10.1080/135017697344037.

CHAPTER 4

Brexit: A Challenge to the EU Citizenship as a Fundamental Status

Abstract This chapter explores whether EU citizenship, described as the fundamental status of nationals of Member States, can be retained by UK nationals post-Brexit and concludes that it cannot, given its derivative nature from Member State nationality. The analysis rebuts arguments based on the *Rottman* jurisprudence, the fundamental status doctrine, the notion of a direct legal relationship with the EU, and the theory of acquired rights, demonstrating that EU citizenship remains contingent on nationality and is therefore revocable under Article 50 TEU. Brexit thus validates a minimalist conception of EU citizenship as a status conferring rights. The chapter then assesses how the EU and UK addressed citizens' rights during the negotiations leading to the adoption of the Withdrawal Agreement. The prioritisation of citizens' rights during the negotiations underscores their importance for both the EU and the UK. Moreover, the various mechanisms established to ensure the correct application and implementation of the Withdrawal Agreement highlight a shared commitment to upholding the rights of EU citizens in the UK and UK nationals in the EU27. Ultimately, Brexit reveals both the fragility and transformative value of EU citizenship.

Keywords EU citizenship • Withdrawal Agreement • Nationality • Fundamental status • Acquired rights • Negotiations • Brexit

C. Dadomo, N. Quénivet, *The Transformative Value of EU Citizenship after Brexit*,
https://doi.org/10.1007/978-3-032-20595-7_4

4.1 Introduction

The referendum in favour of the UK's withdrawal from the European Union undoubtedly created uncertainty and instability for EU citizens residing in the UK, and UK nationals living in the EU27. Many raised concerns about whether UK nationals in the EU27 could retain their EU citizenship status, and whether EU citizens in the UK would continue to be treated the same way as before the withdrawal. Brexit certainly posed a challenge to the concept of EU citizenship and, most importantly, to its fundamental status (see Cambien 2018, 1344).

Brexit allows the authors to explore the transformative value of EU citizenship. As discussed in earlier chapters, EU citizenship should be seen through the triad of status, rights, and practice. This chapter will focus on the impact of Brexit on the status of EU citizenship and how the negotiating parties, the EU and the UK, have addressed the status and rights of EU citizens in the UK and UK nationals as former EU citizens.

To understand the effect of Brexit on EU citizenship as a fundamental status (see Sect. 2.3), the authors have devised two tests. The first test (see Sect. 4.1 below) is whether the status of EU citizens enjoyed by UK nationals can be revoked. If it is indeed fundamental in nature, then assuredly it should not be revocable. Yet, it was revoked because, in accordance with Article 50(3) TEU(TEU (Lisbon) 2025), on 1 February 2020, the day of the entry into force of the Withdrawal Agreement, the Treaties ceased to apply to the UK so that "that State [was] no longer, as from that date, a Member State" (*Case C-685/20 P Sharpston* 2021, ¶ 53; repeated verbatim in *Case C-673/20 E.P. v. Préfet du Gers* 2022b, ¶ 55). This examination suggests that EU citizenship is nothing but an over-layer; it largely validates the minimalist approach of EU citizenship, thereby supporting the legal-participatory theory (see Becker 2004, 140 and 144–45). EU citizenship functions as a bundle of *rights* based on a legal *status* (as explained in Chap. 2.). The vinaigrette reverts to oil and vinegar as separate and independent elements, once again.

The second test (see 4.3. below) assesses how the EU and the UK have approached the issue of EU citizenship and its derived status. Rather than scrutinising the content of various documents produced during the negotiations and the legal provisions of the Withdrawal Agreement (see Chap. 5.), this test aims to understand how both parties have *perceived* the importance, that is, the value, of this fundamental status in the post-referendum context.

4.2 Loss of EU Citizenship

One method to assess the transformative value of EU citizenship is to consider whether it can be lost. After all, if it is truly transformative, it should remain with those who have experienced it. After explaining the link between EU citizenship and nationality of a Member State, this section scrutinises and rebuts the various arguments and theories suggesting that UK nationals in the EU could retain EU citizenship. It thus concludes that EU citizenship, although fundamental in nature, can only be available to nationals of a Member State of the EU.

4.2.1 EU Citizenship and Nationality of a Member State

When the concept of EU citizenship was established in the 1992 Maastricht Treaty (TEU and TEC (Maastricht) 1992), the possibility of losing it was not anticipated, as the treaty did not include a withdrawal clause, a provision introduced later by the Lisbon Treaty. Ultimately, this raises the question of whether, under EU law, the removal of EU citizenship is permissible, given its fundamental importance. As a result, this led to a reflection on the nature of EU citizenship, the connection between EU citizenship and nationality, and the role of EU law in regulating the acquisition and withdrawal of EU citizenship through nationality.

It is essential to remember that the original treaties referred to nationality and not citizenship. The nationality of a Member State allowed individuals to access a wide range of rights granted by the EEC Treaty (see Chap. 2.). Whilst the concept of "national of a Member State" appeared in the EEC Treaty and secondary sources and was thus fundamental, the Court did not provide an autonomous definition for it (Reich 2001, 6). Instead, it was assumed that nationality was to be regulated by national laws in accordance with international law (see in particular *Nottebohm Case* 1955, 20). However, the Court's position may seem puzzling when considering how it has treated other fundamental concepts of EU law. For example, in the *Hoekstra* case, the concept of a worker was given an autonomous, "supranational" meaning on the basis that, if the Member States could unilaterally fix or modify the meaning of this concept, they could effectively "eliminate at will the protection afforded by the Treaty to certain categories of person" (*Case 75/63 Unger* 1964, ¶ 184). Similarly, the concept of a spouse under the Citizenship Directive (Citizenship Directive 2024, art. 2(2)(a)) was also assigned an autonomous EU meaning in the

Coman case (*Case C-673/16 Coman* 2018). If EU citizenship is, as described in *Grzelczyk,* "the fundamental status of nationals of the Member States" (*Case C-184/99 Grzelczyk* 2001, ¶ 31 (emphasis added); *Case C-413/99 Baumbast* 2002, ¶ 82), then EU law should establish clear rules and limitations regarding its interpretation. As Jessurun d'Oliveira champions, EU citizenship should not depend on the application of national law "but rather the EU can determine that certain groups of people who lose their member state nationality will nonetheless remain Union citizens" (d'Oliveira et al. 2011, 149).

So, why does the Court take a cautious approach to the concept of "national of a Member State"? This can only be explained by its reluctance to interfere in a matter that falls within the remit of and is at the core of State sovereignty. As Hall explains, "[t]he rule that States are free to make dispositions of their nationalities for domestic purposes is concomitant with their sovereign independence in international law" (Hall 1996, 130). Pataut argues that for the Court to directly intervene in this field would be a "coup de force" that would be difficult to justify legally and difficult to accept politically (Pataut 2010). From a legal perspective, nationality issues are within the *domaine reservé* of States (*Nationality Decrees Issued in Tunis and Morocco (French Zone) (Advisory Opinion)* 1923, 24; Convention on Certain Questions Relating to the Conflict of Nationality, n.d., art. 1; *Nottebohm Case* 1955, 20) and "in the European setting, citizenship is a last bastion of sovereignty" (Brubaker 2002, 180). As Advocate General Maduro states, "[w]hat is at stake, through the nationality relationship, is the formation of a national body politic, and it goes without saying that a Member State is free to define the limits of that body politic by determining the persons whom it considers to be its nationals" (*Case C-135/08 Rottman (A.G.)* 2009, ¶¶ 17–18).

In 1991, the European Parliament had already recognised that "citizenship, and the bond inherent therein, must necessarily be subject to criteria for acquiring and forfeiting it and [...] those criteria may, for the time being, be made to tally with the conditions under which the nationality of the different Member States may be acquired or is forfeited" (Resolution on Union Citizenship 1991, preamble ¶ D). Consequently, since EU citizenship is derived from nationality (see Sect. 3.2), the determination of EU citizenship rests solely with the Member States, without any input from EU law. The German and UK declarations on the definition of a national (see Evans 1991, 191; Simmonds 1984), as well as declarations by the Member States in the framework of EU negotiations (see, e.g., Declaration on Nationality of a Member State (Treaty of Maastricht) 1992; Denmark and the Treaty on European Union 1992), support the view that States are allowed to determine nationality according to their own criteria. If the EU were to establish criteria for the acquisition of EU citizenship, it would conceptually and politically lead to an EU citizenship based on a unique *demos* rather than multiple *demoi* along with a centralised system of determination and conferral of EU citizenship (Kunoy 2006).

Although the acquisition of EU citizenship is expressly regulated by EU law, the loss of EU citizenship is not addressed in similar terms. It was initially assumed that retaining EU citizenship was contingent upon retaining nationality. This assumption was first confirmed by the Court in the *Rottman* case (*Case C-135/08 Rottman* 2010), which addressed the implications of losing nationality, and consequently, losing EU citizenship. Whilst the Court did not challenge the State's competence to grant or revoke nationality, it did scrutinise how such competence was exercised (Pataut 2021, 63). In this context, the Court established certain limits to the Member States' discretion, ascertaining that, when regulating nationality, States must ensure that revocation serves a legitimate purpose (*Case C-135/08 Rottman* 2010, ¶¶ 51–52; *Case C-221/17 Tjebbes* 2019, ¶ 33; *Case C-118/20 J.Y.* 2022, ¶ 52; *Case C-689/21 X* 2023, ¶ 31; *Joined Cases C-684/22 to C-686/22 S.Ö. and Others* 2024, ¶ 37), complies with the "general principle of international law that no one is arbitrarily to be deprived of his nationality" (*Case C-135/08 Rottman* 2010, ¶ 53), and is proportionate (*Case C-135/08 Rottman* 2010, ¶¶ 55–56; *Case C-221/17 Tjebbes* 2019, ¶¶ 41–42; *Case C-118/20 J.Y.* 2022, ¶¶ 59–61; *Case C-689/21 X* 2023, ¶¶ 39–40; *Joined Cases C-684/22 to C-686/22 S.Ö. and Others* 2024, ¶¶ 43–44). Member States must also consider EU law in this process (*Case C-369/90 Micheletti* 1992, ¶ 10; *Case C-129/99 Kaur* 2001, ¶ 19; *Case C-135/08 Rottman* 2010, ¶¶ 39 and 41; *Case C-221/17 Tjebbes* 2019, ¶ 30; *Case C-118/20 J.Y.* 2022, ¶ 37; *Case C-689/21 X* 2023, ¶ 28; *Joined Cases C-684/22 to C-686/22 S.Ö. and Others* 2024, ¶ 34; see Kostakopoulou 2007, 626; Oosterom-Staples 2018; for earlier discussion, see de Groot 1998), as the consequences of withdrawing nationality are drastic: individuals lose the rights associated with EU citizenship. As the Court noted in *J.Y.*, national authorities must ensure that the loss of nationality does not "disproportionately affect the normal development of his or her family and professional life from the point of view of EU law" (*Case C-118/20 J.Y.* 2022, ¶ 59) and "is consistent with the fundamental rights guaranteed by the Charter of Fundamental Rights of the European Union", notably the right to respect for family life and the principle of the best interests of the child (*Case C-118/20 J.Y.* 2022, ¶ 61). This clarification highlights why the loss of nationality is generally subject to more stringent scrutiny under EU Law compared to its acquisition.[1]

4.2.2 *The Case for the Post-Brexit Retention of their Status as EU Citizens by UK Nationals*

Scholars who argued that UK nationals could not lose their EU citizenship primarily relied on four types of arguments which are at times intertwined. First, they claimed that the *Rottman* line of jurisprudence does not allow for the loss of EU citizenship. Second, they emphasised the nature of EU citizenship as a fundamental status. Third, they stressed the direct legal relationship between EU citizens and the Union. Fourth, they referred to the theory of "acquired rights". However, all four approaches are legally flawed.

4.2.2.1 The Rottman *Line of Jurisprudence*

Under the first approach, referring to the *Rottman* case, legal commentators claimed that "it may be incompatible with EU law for an EU-27 state to remove 'permanent' rights of residence acquired by EU citizens and their family member" as the CJEU introduced a test of proportionality when States wished to withdraw nationality if such action resulted in the deprivation of EU citizenship (Ryan 2017, 207–8), and that "withdrawal from the EU is an unproportional (sic) infringement of [the rights of the UK EU citizens], without any justification on the nation states side. After all, it cannot not be argued that all UK EU citizens unanimously agreed to leave the European Union" (Wesemann 2018, 135). However, this interpretation misreads the CJEU's case law as the Court clarified in the *E.P.* case, a preliminary reference from a French court seized by a British national who, as a result of Brexit, had lost her right to vote in French

[1] However, this view has now to be more nuanced since the CJEU has, for the first time, assessed a national law granting nationality, and therefore EU citizenship, in exchange for predetermined investments or payments through a transactional procedure to be incompatible with the concept of EU citizenship on the ground that it breaches the principle of sincere cooperation and puts into question the mutual trust between Member States regarding the grant of nationality (*Case C-181/23 Citizenship by Investment* 2025).

municipal elections (*Case C-673/20 E.P. v. Préfet du Gers* 2022b, ¶¶ 46–59). As the Court made it clear,

> […] the loss of [the status of EU citizen], and consequently the loss of the right to vote and to stand as a candidate in the municipal elections in the Member State of residence of that national, is, as a general rule […] an automatic consequence of the sole sovereign decision taken by the United Kingdom to withdraw from the European Union, by virtue of Article 50(1) TEU. (*Case C-673/20 E.P. v. Préfet du Gers* 2022b, ¶ 59)

This was reiterated in the cases *Silver*, *Shindler* and *Price* (*Case C-499/21 P Silver* 2023, ¶ 45; *Case C-501/21 P Shindler* 2023, ¶ 68; *Case C-502/21 P Price* 2023, ¶ 74).

First, the *Rottman* line of jurisprudence does not delink EU citizenship from nationality (see Peers 2021, 153; Shuibhne 2023, 490): as EU citizenship derives from nationality, Mr. Rottman's loss of both Austrian and German citizenships resulted in the loss of his EU citizenship and the rights attached to it. At no stage did the Court of Justice envisage the possibility that EU citizenship could be retained without a national bond. It was clear that the Member States concerned would have to take the decision of reinstating the original nationality or confirming his naturalisation so as not to deprive Mr. Rottman of his Union citizen status and accompanying rights. A similar reading applies to the *J.Y.* case, especially as the Court stressed that both EU Member States involved (i.e., Estonia and Austria) were under a duty to ensure that the granting and withdrawal of nationality did not, even temporarily, lead to the loss of EU citizenship and its related rights (*Case C-118/20 J.Y.* 2022, ¶¶ 48–51). As Advocate General Szpunar had already stated in the *J.Y.* case, "this means that the nationality of a Member State is the prerequisite for enjoyment of EU citizenship, to which all the rights and duties provided for in the FEU Treaty are attached" (*Case C-118/20 J.Y. (A.G.)* 2021, ¶ 33). During the Brexit negotiations, the Commission reiterated that "[c]itizenship of the Union of a person is therefore conditional on the membership of the Union of at least one of the states of which that person is a national" (*Commission Decision on CI 'United in Diversity'* 2017, preamble ¶ 2). The Amsterdam Court, seized by a group of UK nationals, explained that a textual interpretation of Article 20 TFEU (which the Court did not adopt) meant that the "acquisition of EU citizenship, with the associated rights and freedoms, is reserved for nationals of EU Member States. In this light, it is arguable that, as a flip side of this, the loss of the status of citizen of an EU Member State also leads to the loss of EU" (*State of the Netherlands / X and others* 2018, ¶ 5.14). The court on appeal also noted "that it is reasonable to doubt the correctness of an interpretation of Article 20 TFEU, which means that the loss of the status of citizen of an EU Member State automatically means that the citizenship rights and freedoms derived/to be derived, with regard to the right to free movement and residence, are lost" (*State of the Netherlands / X and others* 2018, ¶ 3.10 (translation by Google)). As van der Mei states, "[l]oss of a Member State nationality implies automatic loss of this privileged status. When a Member State withdraws from the EU its nationals become third country nationals" (Van der Mei 2018; see Peers 2016). It is thus no surprise that in *E.P.* the Court, citing Article 9 TEU and Article 20 TFEU, highlighted the "inseparable and exclusive link between possession of the nationality of a Member State and not only the acquisition, but also the retention, of the status of citizens of the Union" (*Case C-673/20 E.P. v. Préfet du Gers* 2022b, ¶ 48) and drew the conclusion that "[t]he loss of nationality of a Member State therefore entails, for the person concerned, the automatic loss of his or her status as a citizen of the Union" (*Case C-673/20 E.P. v. Préfet du Gers* 2022b, ¶ 57; see *Case C-499/21 P Silver* 2023, ¶ 44; *Case C-501/21 P Shindler* 2023, ¶ 67; *Case C-502/21 P Price* 2023, ¶ 73). Thus, EU citizenship does not exist without a clear bond to the nationality of an EU Member State. Indeed, as Kovar and Simon already wrote in 1993, EU citizenship cannot be acquired or lost independently of the nationality of a Member State (Simon and Kovar 1993, 292).

Second, in the situation of the UK's withdrawal from the EU, the decision to withdraw nationality was not based on the application of national law, as was the case in *Rottman,* nor was it the result of the applicant's choice to renounce her nationality to acquire another one, as in *J.Y.* Frau actually observes that the UK nationals did not lose their nationality (Frau 2019, 512–13) and thus the *Rottmann/J.Y.* jurisprudence is ill-suited for interpretation purposes (see, a contrario, *X. v. State of the Netherlands* 2018, ¶ 5.21). Instead, the loss of EU citizenship was the "result of collective decision adopted in accordance with their own democratic rules to exit the EU" (Van der Mei 2018; van den Brink and Kochenov 2019, 1368). Moreover, the Court's case-law specifies that the removal of national citizenship must serve a legitimate purpose. A decision made collectively for the "common good" (Frau 2019, 512) can indeed be seen as a legitimate purpose. As Advocate General Collins reminded in the

E.P. case, the Court had declared in *Wightman* that withdrawal under Article 50 TEU was of a "voluntary and unilateral nature" (*Case C-673/20 EP v. Préfet du Gers (A.G.)* 2022a, ¶ 27; referring to *Case C-621/18 Wightman* 2018, ¶ 68). Indeed, in contrast to the situation in other cases concerning the loss of EU citizenship, the Court in *E.P.* stressed that there were no (French) national legislative measures excluding EU citizens from access to the benefits and rights conferred by EU Law (*Case C-673/20 E.P. v. Préfet du Gers* 2022b, ¶ 62). Rather, it was a sovereign decision taken by the UK in accordance with its constitutional requirements (*Case C-621/18 Wightman* 2018, ¶ 50; see *Case C-673/20 E.P. v. Préfet du Gers* 2022b, ¶ 53). The State, that is, the UK, did not withdraw nationality from individual persons (*Case C-673/20 E.P. v. Préfet du Gers* 2022b, ¶ 62). Accordingly, there was no need to undertake an individual examination of the consequences of the loss of EU citizenship in light of the principle of proportionality used in previous case-law (*Case C-673/20 E.P. v. Préfet du Gers* 2022b, ¶ 61; for a critique, see Lashyn 2022, 743).

4.2.2.2 The Fundamental Status of EU Citizenship

A second approach argues that the status of EU citizenship is so fundamental to an individual that it cannot be revoked. First, citizenship is generally considered the "highest and most secure legal status" (Lenard 2016, 73). It is the domestic reflection of nationality, the bond between a State and an individual (Weiss 1979, 4–5). Second, EU citizenship is viewed as a "state-like legal bond directly with individuals, substantively comparable to nationality" (Worster 2018, 352 and 357). Some argue this perspective stems from the EU possessing state-like features (Worster 2018, 351–52), while others point to the Charter of Fundamental Rights of the European Union (EU CFR 2012) which outlines rights akin to those granted to citizens of States. Southey suggests that "EU nationality should be regarded as equivalent to nationality of a nation State" (Southey 2015, 142). For others, although EU citizenship is not identical to nationality, its essence, that of a durable legal bond as described by the German Federal Constitutional Court (*Re Maastricht Treaty* 1993, ¶ 97), is noteworthy (Rieder 2013, 171–72; Lashyn 2022, 742). Logically, it follows that EU citizenship, much like nationality, cannot be revoked, except under certain restrictions imposed by international law. Among the restrictions are the prevention of statelessness (Convention on the Reduction of Statelessness 1961) and the prohibition of arbitrary or discriminatory removal of nationality (International Covenant on Civil and Political Rights 1966, art. 12(4)). Third, the Court has repeatedly stressed the fundamental status of EU citizenship (see Ryan 2017, 207; Worster 2018, 352–53).

In the *E.P.* judgment, the Court did not entertain the claim that (Spaventa 2019, 600), because EU citizenship was a fundamental status, it could not be removed. As Fichera points out, the argument relies "on the almost 'missionary' nature of EU citizenship as an independent and fundamental status" (Fichera 2018, 264). Whilst the Court reiterated (cynically, according to Lashyn (Lashyn 2022, 741)) this fundamental status (*Case C-673/20 E.P. v. Préfet du Gers* 2022b, ¶ 49), it emphasised that this status could only be conferred on EU citizens and only nationals of EU Member States could be such citizens. As Lashyn starkly notes, "[t]heir 'fundamental status' was taken from them as an 'automatic' consequence of the choice made by their compatriots" (Lashyn 2022, 736). Yet, had the Court characterised EU citizenship as autonomous, it would have overstepped its powers, fundamentally altering the EU constitutional order.

4.2.2.3 The Direct Legal Relationship Between EU Citizens and the Union

A third, interrelated, approach is based on the principles outlined in the *Van Gend en Loos* jurisprudence (*Case 26–62 van Gend & Loos* 1963). Academics have characterised EU citizenship as a special relationship between individuals and the European Union, asserting that EU citizens were in "a direct legal relationship with the Union, from which they derive[d] certain rights" (Worster 2018, 342; Lashyn 2022, 742). This legal order, distinct from the national legal orders of its Member States, has directly conferred rights upon individuals, thereby establishing this direct legal relationship (Worster 2018, 353–54) irrespective of Union citizenship as a status (see Shuibhne 2023, 508). Additionally, it was emphasised that this jurisprudence had indicated that EU citizens (then nationals of Member States) had acquired a "legal heritage" that could not be taken away from them. However, as previously explained, the Court in *E.P.* could not go any further since it would have exceeded its powers. By withdrawing from the EU, the UK has severed the connection to the EU legal heritage for UK nationals.

4.2.2.4 The Acquired Rights Theory

A fourth approach that was considered was the theory of "acquired rights", which had been advocated by various academics and activists who contended that UK nationals could retain their EU citizenship or, at least, some of the rights attached to it. Before and during the Brexit referendum, a widely discussed solution was that EU citizens would be able to keep enjoying all the rights linked to their status. As Ryan explained, "the legal status acquired by an individual, through meeting qualifying conditions over a period of years, should not be lost because the wider political context has changed" (Ryan 2017, 207). This argument relied on the legal doctrine of "acquired rights". Whilst "the notion of acquired rights is a very useful label to describe people's expectations, having relied on EU rights in the past and wanting them to persist" (*Oral Evidence given by V. Lowe to the House of Lords European Union Committee* 2016), it is a topic "beset by confusion and misinformation" (Douglas-Scott 2016).

First, it is important to note that Article 50 TEU makes no reference at all to acquired rights. Even, as Douglas-Scott points out, the general principles of EU law, such as legal certainty, non-retroactivity, and legitimate expectations,[2] are not particularly helpful in a context where EU law no longer applies (Douglas-Scott 2016). Piris, Former Director-General of the Legal Service of the Council of the European Union, expressed his personal view that applying such theory, especially in relation to UK nationals in the EU27, "would not have any legal support in the Treaties and would lead to absurd consequences" (Piris 2015, 10). Yet, it is interesting to note that some delegates to the Constitutional Convention that led to the conclusion of the Lisbon Treaty suggested safeguarding existing rights (Eeckhout and Frantziou 2017, 718). That such amendments were not adopted reinforces the argument that they were deemed unsuitable.

Second, some have referenced Article 70 of the Vienna Convention on the Law of Treaties, which spells out that "the termination of a treaty […] does not affect any right, obligation or legal situation of the parties created through the execution of the treaty prior to its termination" (Vienna Convention on the Law of Treaties 1969). Nevertheless, it must be pointed out that the article refers to the rights of the parties, that is, the States, rather than those of legal and natural persons (House of Lords, European Union Committee 2016, ¶¶ 57–60; Douglas-Scott 2016; Repasi 2017, 31; Cambien 2018, 1339–40). Some academics counterargued that, given the "new legal order" doctrine established in *van Gend en Loos*, this legal provision should be interpreted to include nationals of

[2] The principle of legitimate expectations has also been used as a separate approach to justify the retention of rights. It is however not dealt with in this book.

Member States as well (Lashyn 2022, 743). Such an interpretation would, however, be overly broad. In addition, Article 70 specifies that it only applies, "unless the treaty otherwise provides or the parties otherwise agree" (Vienna Convention on the Law of Treaties 1969). In this case, Article 50 TFEU would be the *lex specialis* and, as explained earlier, it does not refer to "acquired rights" (see Cambien 2018, 1339).

Third, the doctrine of acquired rights is also of customary nature (*Case Concerning Certain German Interests in Upper Silesia* 1926, ¶ 132; see Cambien 2018, 1339) and could potentially be used to ensure that EU citizens keep their rights. Yet, as Lowe observes, the scope of application would be limited, as the majority of such rights relate to ownership, business goodwill, certain contractual rights, and court judgments and arbitration decisions (House of Lords, European Union Committee 2016, ¶ 63; see Douglas-Scott 2016; Repasi 2017, 31). Free movement rights, political rights, the right to non-discrimination, and the right to residence are not included (Repasi 2017, 31–32).

Fourth, the enforcement of those rights would be highly problematic in national (Peers 2016) and international courts (House of Lords, European Union Committee 2016, ¶¶ 67–68). An additional challenge, irrespective of the source of acquired rights, is that the doctrine raises a vast number of issues relating to its application to both pending and future situations (e.g., the rights of children of those who have acquired rights) (Peers 2016; Piris 2015, 10).

Some authors have suggested that an alternative way to consider withdrawal is to liken it to secession and thus use the *Kurić* case (*Case of Kurić and Others v. Slovenia* 2012) to argue that the rights of those with residence in the host State but no opportunity to accede to that State's citizenship are frozen (Shaw 2019, 451–52). However, there is a significant difference between withdrawal and secession under international law.

Finally, in *E.P.*, although the Court did not expressly mention the theory of acquired rights, it rather quickly dismissed the idea that UK nationals, having previously exercised their freedom of movement (*Case C-673/20 E.P. v. Préfet du Gers* 2022b, ¶ 52) and their right to reside in an EU Member State (*Case C-673/20 E.P. v. Préfet du Gers* 2022b, ¶¶ 52 and 58), could retain their status as EU citizens.

Overall, this solution of "acquired rights", although initially appealing, has proven not to be legally viable and thus cannot support a transformative vision of EU citizenship.

The conclusion is that, because EU citizenship is a legal *status* with accompanying *rights*, it can be revoked by law. Brexit emphasises the additional and derived nature of EU citizenship, with the EU Member States acting as "the gatekeepers to EU citizenship" (Barnard 2016, 364). The automatic loss of EU citizenship underscores its status as a juridico-political institution, that is, a *status* that is a gateway to *rights*, and confirms the minimalist approach towards EU citizenship. It is akin to the oil in a vinaigrette disappearing, simply because the vinegar no longer meets the required specifications. Or, using Spaventa's metaphor, the horses of Cinderella's carriage have turned back to mice (Spaventa 2019, 591). This situation would suggest that the *practice* of EU citizenship is fundamentally undermined. However, is that truly the case? The next step, therefore, is to scrutinise the negotiations surrounding the Withdrawal Agreement to better understand how both parties *perceived* the rights of EU citizens in the UK and UK nationals in the EU27.

4.3 Negotiating the Rights of EU Citizens in the Withdrawal Agreement

The negotiations leading to the Withdrawal Agreement, along with the manner in which the rights of EU citizens in the UK and UK nationals in the EU27 are enshrined and procedurally protected, convey the impression that both parties recognised the transformative value of EU citizenship: "[f]rom the outset of the discussions concerning Brexit, the EU and the UK government stated their commitment to protecting the rights of citizens affected by Brexit—both EU citizens in the UK and UK nationals in the EU" (More 2020, 462).

4.3.1 First Phase of the Negotiations: Prompt Recognition of the Importance of the Issue of Citizens' Rights

The impact of Brexit on EU Citizens and UK nationals in the EU27 has been profound, affecting various aspects of their lives. As explained earlier (see Sect. 4.2), the withdrawal has led to the loss of EU citizenship for UK nationals. For EU citizens in the UK who had built their lives on these rights, Brexit created uncertainty and disruption. The European Council Guidelines Following the UK's Notification under Article 50 TEU adopted on 29 April 2017 recognised that "the United Kingdom's decision to leave the Union create[d] significant uncertainties that have the potential to cause disruption", notably for "[c]itizens who have built their lives on the basis of the rights flowing from the British membership of the EU [and] face the prospect of losing those rights" (European Council 2017, preamble). As the CJEU acknowledged in *Wightman*, "any withdrawal of a Member State from the European Union is liable to have a considerable impact on the rights of all Union citizens, including, *inter alia*, their right to free movement, as regards both nationals of the Member State concerned and nationals of other Member States" (*Case C-621/18 Wightman* 2018, ¶ 64). On a more practical level, EU citizens in the UK were worried that "without the protection of EU law they could be subjected to right-to-work or right-to-rent controls" (Sredanovic 2021, 98).

Although the Brexit negotiations were approached in purely intergovernmental terms, that is, between the EU and the UK, thus setting aside EU citizens, and originally with a view to obtaining the best outcome from a British perspective (Eeckhout and Frantziou 2017, 732), the importance of addressing this issue was recognised early in the Brexit negotiations. Despite Article 50 TEU not explicitly mentioning the rights of EU citizens, both the UK and the EU acknowledged the need to address these rights promptly (see Fichera 2018, 252–54; Bernard 2020, 302–4). In February 2017, the UK stressed that "[s]ecuring the status of, and providing certainty to, EU nationals already in the UK and to UK nationals in the EU is one of this Government's early priorities for the forthcoming negotiations" (UK Government 2017, 30), and in the March 2017 European Council Guidelines, the EU observed that "[a]greeing reciprocal guarantees to safeguard the status and rights derived from EU law at the date of withdrawal of EU and UK citizens, and their families, affected by the United Kingdom's withdrawal from the Union will be the *first* priority for the negotiations" (European Council 2017, ¶ 8 emphasis added; Shuibhne 2023, 510). Similar wording was used in the Directives for the Negotiation of an Agreement with the United Kingdom of Great Britain and Northern Ireland Setting out the Arrangements for its Withdrawal from the European Union adopted by the Council on 22 May 2017 (*Annex to Council Decision* 2017, ¶ 11).

The EU adopted a phased approach towards the negotiations (*Annex to Council Decision* 2017, ¶ 9) and insisted that settling the issue of EU citizens in the UK was one of the three top priorities alongside the Northern Ireland question and the financial settlement in Phase 1 (Fischer 2020), thus reflecting the significance of the EU citizenship issue but also the need for "damage control and mitigating the losses of the UK leaving the EU" (Frennhoff Larsén and Khorana 2020, 867). The UK's acceptance of this sequencing can be understood as proof of the "accepted logic and pragmatism of this approach" (Frennhoff Larsén and Khorana 2020, 869). The first round of negotiations, held on 19 June 2017, established that citizens' rights would be a priority. Round 2 (17–20 July 2017) concluded with a Joint Technical Note from the European Commission, summarising the UK and EU positions on citizens' rights, highlighting several areas of disagreement (European Commission Task Force for the Preparation and Conduct of the Negotiations with the United Kingdom under Article 50 TEU and the UK 2017). Subsequent rounds continued to focus on this issue, with significant progress made by the sixth round, culminating in a joint report published on 8 December 2017 (*Joint Report of EU and UK during Phase 1* 2017). Whilst the negotiations were admittedly not easy, in contrast to the two other topics of the first phase, citizens' rights were the subject of a relatively early agreement (Fabbrini 2019, 3). The report specified that

> [t]he overall objective of the Withdrawal Agreement with respect to citizens' rights is to provide reciprocal protection for *Union and UK citizens, to enable the effective exercise of rights derived from Union law and based on past life choices*, where those citizens have exercised free movement rights by the specified date. (*Joint Report of EU and UK during Phase 1* 2017, ¶ 6 (emphasis in original))

Accordingly, UK nationals (and their families) residing in an EU27 country and EU citizens (and their families) residing in the UK would be able to maintain their rights and reside in the relevant country after Brexit. After all, "both parties had a shared goal in ensuring that the rights [...] remained as close as possible to the status quo" (Frennhoff Larsén and Khorana 2020, 860; Juverdeanu 2025, 281). It is striking that "Citizens' Rights" is not only the first area listed in the report but also comprises 36 out of 90 substantive paragraphs. This emphasis from both parties on citizens' rights "epitomises the nature of the EU polity and the reasons behind it", revealing the transformative value of EU citizenship in that the loss of EU citizenship for UK nationals and the loss of the possibility to rely on EU law for EU citizens in the UK would fundamentally alter their lives.

4.3.2 *Second Phase of the Negotiations: Protection of Citizens' Rights in an International Agreement*

The second phase of the negotiations focused on drafting and agreeing on an international treaty, known as the Withdrawal Agreement. Whilst this approach can be criticised as EU citizens in the UK and UK nationals in the EU27 are not protected by the more generous and enforceable provisions of EU law anymore, Ryan correctly stresses that the provisions of the Withdrawal Agreement are "preferable to the alternative of relying upon domestic public opinion, in the states of residence, which is not fixed, and over which foreign nationals generally have limited influence" (Ryan 2017, 224). An international agreement would provide a stable and predictable legal framework for protecting these rights, mitigating the effects of Brexit.

As the Commission explained, the protection of the rights of EU citizens and their family members who had exercised their right of free movement under EU law can "be safeguarded in an agreement pursuant to Article 50 TFEU" (see European Commission 2018, preamble ¶ 5; 2017) and the EU can adopt legal acts conferring to third-country nationals (i.e., UK nationals in the EU27) "certain rights similar to rights of citizens of the Union to move and reside freely within the territory of the Member States" (European Commission 2018, preamble ¶ 5; 2017). For EU citizens in the UK and UK nationals in the EU27, it was the Withdrawal Agreement, an international treaty rather than EU law, that would safeguard their rights (though not their status). This was not the first time in history that the EU negotiated a treaty relating to the rights and treatment of its citizens. For example, the Agreement between the European Community and its Member States, on the one part, and the Swiss Confederation, on the other, on the free movement of persons entitles EU citizens to enter and reside in Switzerland (Agreement between the European Community and Its Member States, of the One Part, and the Swiss Confederation, of the Other, on the Free Movement of Persons 2002, art. 1). Now, EU citizens in the UK and UK nationals in the EU27 have their rights protected and enforced under an international treaty between the EU and a third State. However, this situation was unique in that the negotiations concerned the retention of rights by EU citizens in a former EU Member State and the provision of rights to UK nationals living in the EU27 as former EU citizens.

The first draft was published on 19 March 2018, translating the joint report into legal terms. Whilst most sections relating to the citizens' rights had been agreed upon, there was still some dissension regarding the role of the Court of Justice of the European Union (Fabbrini 2019, 5). During the second phase of the negotiations, the European Parliament was extremely active in advocating for citizens' rights, notably adopting a holistic approach by defending not only the rights and interests of EU citizens in the UK (as the Council and the Commission did) but also of UK nationals living in the EU27 (Bernard 2020, 322). Moreover, the Parliament pushed for maintaining the role of the CJEU. The second phase thus demonstrates that the UK and the EU acknowledged the transformative value of EU citizenship.

4.3.3 *The Withdrawal Agreement: Acknowledgement of the Transformative Nature of EU Citizenship*

Eventually, the Withdrawal Agreement was concluded on 14 November 2018.[3] The fact that citizens' rights are enshrined in an international treaty is, no doubt, inferior to EU Law. Nevertheless, conscious of the "downgrading" in the effectiveness of the protection offered to EU citizens in the UK and UK nationals in the EU27, both parties agreed that specific measures needed to be adopted. In other words, the specific and transformative nature of EU citizenship has been acknowledged.

First, it was imperative that the Withdrawal Agreement be implemented in UK Law and EU Law. Bearing in mind that the UK legal system is dualist, the statutory incorporation of treaties is a prerequisite for the application. In this mind, the 2017 Joint Report stated in paragraph 36 that the UK government would introduce the Withdrawal Agreement & Implementation Bill, which would not only expressly refer to the Agreement but also fully incorporate the citizens' rights part of the agreement into UK law (*Joint Report of EU and UK during Phase 1* 2017). The Act would have effect in primary legislation, prevailing over any inconsistent or incompatible legislation, unless this Act was repealed by Parliament. This was implemented by the adoption of the European Union (Withdrawal

[3] When the negotiations re-opened in Autumn 2019 after a change in government, Part Two of the Agreement (Citizens rights) did not change.

Agreement) Act 2020 of 23 January 2020 (EU (Withdrawal Agreement) Act 2020), and the citizens' rights provisions of the Agreement are found in Appendix EU of the UK's Immigration Rules (see Chap. 5.). On the EU side, the Agreement is binding on the EU pursuant to Article 216(2) TFEU. The Commission can also adopt acts to implement the Withdrawal Agreement and issue guidance for a harmonised application of the Agreement in the EU Member States (Neville 2023, 7). It has, for example, amended the Visa Code to include an explicit reference to Withdrawal Agreement beneficiaries (*Report from the Commission Pursuant to Article 159(2) of the Withdrawal Agreement* 2025, 3).

Second, Article 4(1) of the Agreement provides that legal and natural persons can rely directly on the provisions contained or referred to in this Agreement, provided they meet the conditions for direct effect under Union law of clarity, precision, and unconditionality as developed by the CJEU in the *van Gend en Loos* case (see Porchia 2019, 591).

Third, the Agreement specifies that when implementing and applying its concepts and provisions, the judicial and administrative authorities of the UK must interpret them in conformity with the case law of the CJEU established before the end of the transition period (Withdrawal Agreement 2020, art. 4(4)) and pay due regard to relevant CJEU case law handed down after the end of the transition period (Withdrawal Agreement 2020, art. 4(5)). To some extent, this mechanism ensures that British courts align with the judgements of the CJEU.

Fourth, the CJEU continues to play an albeit limited role. The Withdrawal Agreement also specifies that a UK court or tribunal can, under Article 158, much alike under the procedure of Article 267 TFEU (TFEU (Lisbon) 2025) (though there is no obligation for courts of last instance to refer the matter (see, e.g., *Simkova v. S.S.W.P.* 2025, ¶¶ 82–84)) ask for a preliminary ruling to the CJEU (temporal limitations are, however, attached to this mechanism). The authors are aware of four cases in which the parties to the proceedings have suggested a preliminary reference. In three of them, the courts decided the case without making a preliminary reference (*Ali v. S.S.H.D.* 2024; *Simkova v. S.S.W.P.* 2025; *Fertré* 2025), and in one, it sent the question to the CJEU (*B.Z. v. S.S.W.P.* 2025). Additionally, the European Commission was granted the right, for four years from the date of the decision concerned, to "bring the matter to the Court of Justice of the European Union in accordance with the requirements laid down in Article 258 TFEU or the second subparagraph of Article 108(2) TFEU" if the UK did not comply "with a decision referred to in Article 95(1) of this Agreement, or fails to give legal effect in the United Kingdom's legal order to a decision, as referred to in that provision, that was addressed to a natural or legal person residing or established in the United Kingdom" (Withdrawal Agreement 2020, art. 87(2)). The CJEU's involvement, albeit for a limited time, and the ongoing relevance of its case-law highlight the UK's understanding of the importance of safeguarding the rights of EU citizens on its territory, especially considering that one of its red lines was to curtail the CJEU's involvement.

Fifth, Article 159(1) of the Withdrawal Agreement specifies that the UK must create an authority to monitor the implementation and application of Part Two with "powers equivalent to those of the European Commission acting under the Treaties". The existence of such a body certainly attests to a profound willingness to ensure that the rights of EU citizens in the UK are safeguarded, thus stressing the importance of the rights acquired by EU citizens. The Independent Monitoring Authority for the Citizens' Rights (Independent Monitoring Authority for the Citizens' Rights Agreements, n.d.-a) was thus established under Section 15 of the European Union (Withdrawal Agreement) Act 2020 as a corporate body. It aims to monitor the implementation and application of Part 2 of the Withdrawal Agreement (EU (Withdrawal Agreement) Act 2020, § 22(1) of Schedule 2) and to promote adequate and effective implementation in the UK of Part 2 (EU (Withdrawal Agreement) Act 2020, § 23(1) of Schedule 2). In this light, the Independent Monitoring Authority focuses on, inter alia, provisions relating to "residency" and "non-discrimination on the grounds of nationality and equal treatment" (Ministry of Justice and Independent Monitoring Authority for the Citizens' Rights Agreements 2024, ¶ 5.2), two of the three factors the authors consider to reflect the transformative value of EU citizenship (see Sect. 3.3). The Independent Monitoring Authority is independent (EU (Withdrawal Agreement) Act 2020, § 13 of Schedule 2) and carries out inquiries to determine whether the UK has failed to comply with Part 2 of the Withdrawal Agreement and to identify recommendations for relevant public authorities (EU (Withdrawal Agreement) Act 2020, § 25 of Schedule 2). It can bring legal action through judicial review in UK courts (see Independent Monitoring Authority for the Citizens' Rights Agreements 2022) and intervene in relevant cases (Withdrawal Agreement 2020, art. 159(1); EU (Withdrawal Agreement) Act 2020, § 30 of Schedule 2; see examples in Independent Monitoring Authority for the Citizens' Rights Agreements 2024, 19–21; 2025, 21–28). It also prepares annual reports for the Specialised Committee on Citizens' Rights established by Article 165(1) of the Withdrawal Agreement (Withdrawal Agreement 2020, art. 159(2); EU (Withdrawal Agreement) Act 2020, §

31 of Schedule 2).[4] It is noteworthy that the Authority can hear complaints from individuals;· in 2023–2024, it received 151 (Independent Monitoring Authority for the Citizens' Rights Agreements 2024, 27) and in 2024–2025, 116 complaints (Independent Monitoring Authority for the Citizens' Rights Agreements 2025, 31). Remarkably, the Authority set up a Citizens' panel (comprising over 80 members) (Independent Monitoring Authority for the Citizens' Rights Agreements 2025, 36) to hear directly from EU citizens and their family members, who can thus share their experiences of life as EU citizens (Independent Monitoring Authority for the Citizens' Rights Agreements n.d.-b). Areas of concern were, inter alia, equal treatment and non-discrimination, and residence (Independent Monitoring Authority for the Citizens' Rights Agreements 2024, 16). In other words, this Authority is not only responsible for ensuring that the *rights* of EU citizens are safeguarded, but also for considering how EU citizens *experience* these rights. This is notably achieved by setting up inquiries that may highlight systemic failings, articulating their concerns to relevant public bodies, and publishing reports. Article 159(3) of the Withdrawal Agreement nevertheless sets a temporal limit on Authority's existence, specifying that the Joint Committee, that is, the Specialised Committee on Citizens' Rights, shall assess its functioning after 8 years after the end of the transition period and may decide to abolish the Authority (see Ministry of Justice and Independent Monitoring Authority for the Citizens' Rights Agreements 2024, para. 35.1).

Sixth, on the EU side, the Commission, under Article 17 TFEU (TFEU (Lisbon) 2025) ensures the correct application of the Agreement, monitors compliance by the Member States, and, if required, enforces the Agreement (Neville 2023, 7; *Report from the Commission Pursuant to Article 159(2) of the Withdrawal Agreement* 2025, 2). For example, on 16 December 2024, the Commission referred the UK to the Court of Justice of the European Union "for failure to comply with EU law on free movement of EU citizens and their family members at the end of 2020" (European Commission 2024; *Case C-892/24 Commission v. United Kingdom*, n.d.). Although these proceedings started before the Withdrawal Agreement, the Commission has specified that such breaches "are considered to be of continuing relevance to the exercise of rights applicable

[4] The latest report was published on 23 October 2025 and is available at https://ima-citizensrights.org.uk/wp-content/uploads/2025/10/IMA-Annual-Report-to-the-Specialised-Committee-and-Joint-Committee-2024.pdf

under the Withdrawal Agreement" (European Commission 2024). Much of the monitoring and enforcement, however, takes place informally through bilateral relations between the Commission and individual Member States (*Report from the Commission Pursuant to Article 159(2) of the Withdrawal Agreement* 2025, 7–11).

Seventh, under Article 165(1) of the Withdrawal Agreement, a specialised Committee on Citizens' Rights was established as part of the Joint Committee. Composed of representatives of the EU and the UK, its purpose is to "draw up decisions and recommendations and refer them for adoption by the Joint Committee" (Withdrawal Agreement 2020, art. 165(2)) and report back to that Committee on the results and conclusions of their meetings (Withdrawal Agreement 2020, art. 165(4)).[5] The first meeting was held on 20 May 2020, and as of 2 January 2026, 17 meetings had been held. Under Article 159(2) of the Withdrawal Agreement, the Commission (see, e.g., *Report from the Commission Pursuant to Article 159(2) of the Withdrawal Agreement* 2025) and the Independent Monitoring Authority (see, e.g., Independent Monitoring Authority 2025) are obliged to report to it on the implementation and application of Part Two of the Agreement. Recurring themes include the importance of clear communication and support for vulnerable citizens, as well as issues relating to residence documentation, etc. The Committee has frequently invited representatives from "British in Europe" and "the3million", representing UK nationals in the EU27 and EU citizens in the UK, respectively, thus underscoring the importance of listening to the voices of those affected by Brexit and acknowledging the shift in status from EU citizens to that of "special foreigners". The Committee has consistently raised concerns regarding the registration of both EU nationals in the UK and UK nationals in the EU27 (which affect access to benefits and services), differences in interpretation regarding whether EU citizens in the UK fall under the Withdrawal Agreement or UK immigration rules, the importance of communication, family reunification, etc. Although the joint statements are far from painting a perfect picture, the fact that the two parties meet regularly to discuss outstanding issues shows their commitment to engagement and dialogue for the benefit of (former) EU citizens.

[5] All their reports can be found at https://commission.europa.eu/strategy-and-policy/relations-united-kingdom/eu-uk-withdrawal-agreement/meetings-eu-uk-joint-and-specialised-committees-under-withdrawal-agreement_en#meetingsofthespecialisedcommittees

To summarise, the negotiations surrounding the Withdrawal Agreement underscore the transformative nature of EU citizenship. From the outset, both the EU and the UK recognised that safeguarding citizens' rights was not merely a technical task. The phased approach adopted during the negotiations, prioritising citizens' rights, reflects this shared understanding. Although the resulting protections fall short of the robust guarantees offered under EU law, the Agreement nonetheless provides a stable and enforceable framework, that mitigates the disruptive effects of Brexit on millions of individuals. Moreover, the incorporation of the Agreement into UK and EU law, the establishment of monitoring mechanisms, and the continued, albeit limited, role of the CJEU illustrate a commitment to preserving rights acquired under EU membership. These measures, coupled with ongoing dialogue through specialised committees and the work of the Independent Monitoring Authority, demonstrate that both parties sought to maintain continuity and legal certainty for affected citizens.

4.4 Conclusion

In conclusion, the impact of Brexit on EU citizens' rights and freedoms has been significant. At first glance, Brexit seems to confirm this interpretation of EU citizenship as a *status* that is a gateway to *rights*. The withdrawal of the UK from the EU led to the loss of recognition of the status of EU citizens for those living in the UK, so that the rights attached to Union citizenship are no longer recognised by the UK authorities. After Brexit, the source of the legal rights of EU citizens in the UK is no longer the Union law provisions on citizenship. Still, EU citizens in the UK remain EU citizens for all other purposes. This approach towards EU citizenship seemed to be based on a minimalist approach towards EU citizenship, confirming that EU citizenship is a *status* that acts as the basis of *rights*. A similar conclusion can be drawn from the fact that all UK nationals have lost their EU citizenship.

The importance of EU citizenship was recognised early in the negotiations, and it remained a priority issue throughout the process. The use of an international law framework and the establishment of a special set-up for (former) EU citizens in the Withdrawal Agreement provides a stable and predictable legal framework for protecting these rights, mitigating the effects of Brexit on individuals who had exercised their right to reside in the UK or the EU before the end of the transition period. In other words, both parties have recognised the special (perhaps transformative) nature of EU citizenship.

References

Agreement between the European Community and Its Member States, of the One Part, and the Swiss Confederation, of the Other, on the Free Movement of Persons, OJ L114/6. 2002. https://eur-lex.europa.eu/LexUriServ/LexUriServ.do?uri=CELEX:22002A0430(01):EN:HTML.

Agreement on the Withdrawal of the United Kingdom of Great Britain and Northern Ireland from the European Union and the European Atomic Energy Community, OJ L 29/7. 2020. https://eur-lex.europa.eu/legal-content/EN/TXT/?uri=CELEX%3A02020W%2FTXT-20250430.

Annex to Council Decision: Directives for the Negotiation of an Agreement with the United Kingdom of Great Britain and Northern Ireland Setting out the Arrangements for Its Withdrawal from the European Union. 2017. XT 21016/17 ADD 1 REV 2. General Secretariat of the Council.

Barnard, Catherine. 2016. *The Substantive Law of the EU – The Four Freedoms*. 5th ed. Oxford University Press.

Becker, Michael A. 2004. Managing Diversity in the European Union: Inclusive European Citizenship and Third-Country Nationals. *Yale Human Rights & Development Law Journal* 7:132–183.

Bernard, Nicolas. 2020. Union Citizens' Rights Against Their Own Member State after Brexit. *Maastricht Journal of European and Comparative Law* 27 (3): 302–324. https://doi.org/10.1177/1023263X20908761.

Brubaker, Rogers. 2002. *Citizenship and Nationhood in France and Germany. 6. print*. Harvard University Press.

Case C-892/24 Commission v. United Kingdom, C/2025/1221. n.d. (not yet decided).

Cambien, Nathan. 2018. Residence Rights for EU Citizens and their Family Members: Navigating the New Normal. *European Papers—A Journal on Law and Integration* 3 (3): 1333–1352.

Case 26/62. 1963. N.V. Algemene Transport-En Expeditie Onderneming van Gend & Loos v. Netherlands Inland Revenue Administration, ECLI:EU:C:1963:1 (ECJ).

Case 75/63. 1964. M.K.H. Unger, the Wife of R. Hoekstra v. Bestuur Der Bedrijfsvereniging Voor Detailhandel En Ambachten, ECLI:EU:C:1964:19 (ECJ).

Case C-118/20. 2021. J.Y. v. Wiener Landesregierung, ECLI:EU:C:2021:530 (Advocate General Szpunar).

Case C-118/20. 2022. J.Y. v. Wiener Landesregierung, ECLI:EU:C:2022:34 (CJEU).

Case C-129/99. 2001. The Queen v. Secretary of State for the Home Department, Ex Parte: Manjit Kaur, Intervener: Justice, ECLI:EU:C:2001:106 (CJEU).

Case C-135/08. 2009. Janko Rottman v. Freistaat Bayern, ECLI:EU:C:2009:588 (Advocate General Maduro).
Case C-135/08. 2010. Janko Rottman v. Freistaat Bayern, ECLI:EU:C:2010:104 (CJEU).
Case C-181/23. 2025. European Commission v. Republic of Malta (Citizenship by Investment), ECLI:EU:C:2025:283 (CJEU).
Case C-184/99. 2001. Rudy Grzelczyk v. Centre Public d'Aide Sociale d'Ottignies-Louvain-La-Neuve, ECLI:EU:C:2001:458 (ECJ).
Case C-221/17. 2019. M.G. Tjebbes and Others v. Minister van Buitenlandse Zaken, ECLI:EU:C:2019:189 (CJEU).
Case C-369/90. 1992. Mario Vicente Micheletti and Others v. Delegación Del Gobierno En Cantabria, ECLI:EU:C:1992:295 (ECJ).
Case C-413/99. 2002. Baumbast and R. v. Secretary of State for the Home Department, ECLI:EU:C:2002:493 (ECJ).
Case C-499/21 P. 2023. Joshua David Silver and Others vCouncil of the European Union, ECLI:EU:C:2023:479 (CJEU).
Case C-501/21 P. 2023. Harry Shindler and Others v. Council, ECLI:EU:C:2023:480 (CJEU).
Case C-502/21 P. 2023. David Price v. Council, ECLI:EU:C:2023:482 (CJEU).
Case C-621/18. 2018. Andy Wightman and Others v. Secretary of State for Exiting the European Union, ECLI:EU:C:2018:999 (CJEU).
Case C-673/16. 2018. Relu Adrian Coman and Others v. Inspectoratul General Pentru Imigrări and Ministerul Afacerilor Interne, ECLI:EU:C:2018:385 (CJEU).
Case C-673/20. 2022a. E.P. v. Préfet Du Gers and Institut National de La Statistique et Des Études Économiques (INSEE), ECLI:EU:C:2022:129 (Advocate General Collins).
Case C-673/20. 2022b. E.P. v. Préfet Du Gers and Institut National de La Statistique et Des Études Économiques (INSEE), ECLI:EU:C:2022:449 (CJEU).
Case C-685/20 P. 2021. Eleanor Sharpston v. Council of the European Union and Representatives of the Governments of the Member States, ECLI:EU:C:2021:485 (CJEU).
Case C-689/21. 2023. X v. Udlændinge- Og Integrationsministeriet, ECLI:EU:C:2023:626 (CJEU).
Case Concerning Certain German Interests in Upper Silesia (the Merits)—Germany v. Poland, P.C.I.J. Ser. A, No. 7. 1926. (Permanent Court of International Justice). https://www.worldcourts.com/pcij/eng/decisions/1926.05.25_silesia.htm
Case of Kurić and Others v. Slovenia, 26828/06 (ECtHR) 2012. https://hudoc.echr.coe.int/fre?i=001-111634
Charter of Fundamental Rights of the European Union, OJEU C326/391. 2012. http://data.europa.eu/eli/treaty/char_2012/oj/eng.

Commission Decision on the Proposed Citizens' Initiative Entitled 'EU Citizenship for Europeans: United in Diversity in Spite of Jus Soli and Jus Sanguinis'. 2017. OJ L81/18. European Commission. https://eur-lex.europa.eu/legal-content/EN/TXT/?uri=CELEX:32017D0599.

Consolidated Version of Treaty on European Union (Lisbon). 2025. http://data.europa.eu/eli/treaty/teu_2016/2025-03-15.

Consolidated Version of Treaty on the Functioning of the European Union (Lisbon). 2025. http://data.europa.eu/eli/treaty/tfeu_2016/2025-03-15.

Convention on Certain Questions Relating to the Conflict of Nationality, 179 L.N.T.S. 89. n.d.

Convention on the Reduction of Statelessness, 989 U.N.T.S. 175. 1961.

de Groot, Gerard-Rene. 1998. The Relationship between the Nationality Legislation of the Member States of the European Union and European Citizenship. In *European Citizenship: An Institutional Challenge*, ed. M. La Torre, vol. 3. Kluwer Law International.

Declaration on Nationality of a Member State (Treaty of Maastricht), OJ C191/98. 1992. https://eur-lex.europa.eu/legal-content/EN/TXT/PDF/?uri=OJ:C:1992:191:FULL.

Denmark and the Treaty on European Union, OJ C348/2. 1992. https://eur-lex.europa.eu/legal-content/EN/TXT/HTML/?uri=CELEX:41992X1231&rid=1.

Directive 2004/38/EC of the European Parliament and the of the Council of 29 April 2004 on the Rights of Citizens of the Union and Their Family Members to Move and Reside Freely within the Territory of the Member States Amending Regulation (EEC) No 1612/68 and Repealing Directives 64/221/EEC, 68/360/EEC, 72/194/EEC, 73/148/EEC, 75/34/EEC, 75/35/EEC, 90/364/EEC, 90/365/EEC, and 93/96/EEC, OJ L158/77. 2024.

Douglas-Scott, Sionaidh. 2016. What Happens to "Acquired Rights" in the Event of a Brexit? *UK Constitutional Law Association*, May 16. https://ukconstitutionallaw.org/2016/05/16/sionaidh-douglas-scott-what-happens-to-acquired-rights-in-the-event-of-a-brexit/.

Eeckhout, Piet, and Eleni Frantziou. 2017. Brexit and Article 50 TEU: A Constitutionalist Reading. *Common Market Law Review* 54 (3): 695–734.

European Commission. 2017. *Decision on the Proposed Citizens' Initiative Entitled 'Retaining European Citizenship*. C(2007) 2002 final.

European Commission. 2018. Decision on the Proposed Citizens' Initiative Entitled 'Permanent European Union Citizenship. OJEU C264/4. European Commission. https://eur-lex.europa.eu/legal-content/EN/TXT/?uri=CELEX:32018D0726(01).

European Commission. 2024. Commission Refers the United Kingdom to the Court of Justice. Text. December 16. https://ec.europa.eu/commission/presscorner/detail/en/ip_24_6144.

European Commission Task Force for the Preparation and Conduct of the Negotiations with the United Kingdom under Article 50 TEU and the UK. 2017. *The Joint Technical Note Attached Summarises the UK and EU Positions and Compares Them Following the 2nd Round of Art. 50 Negotiations.* TF50 (2017) 10—Commission to EU27.

European Council. 2017. Guidelines Following the UK's Notification under Article 50 TEU. https://www.consilium.europa.eu/en/press/press-releases/2017/04/29/euco-brexit-guidelines/.

European Union (Withdrawal Agreement) Act 2020. 2020. https://www.legislation.gov.uk/ukpga/2020/1.

Evans, Andrew. 1991. Nationality Law and European Integration. *European Law Review* 16 (3): 190–215.

Fabbrini, Federico. 2019. The Brexit Negotiations and the May Government. *European Journal of Legal Studies*, no. Special Issue (October): 1–22. https://doi.org/10.2924/EJLS.2019.001.

Fichera, Massimo. 2018. Brexit and the Security of the European Project: Citizenship and Free Movement as a Case Study. *Northern Ireland Legal Quarterly* 69 (3): 249–269. https://doi.org/10.53386/nilq.v69i3.163.

Fischer, Paul. 2020. Lessons From Brexit on How (Not) to Negotiate. *Harvard Business Review*, December 8. https://hbr.org/2020/12/lessons-from-brexit-on-how-not-to-negotiate.

Frau, Robert. 2019. Ist das Brexit-Abkommen zu Recht gescheitert? *Europarecht* 5:502–521.

Frennhoff Larsén, Magdalena, and Sangeeta Khorana. 2020. Negotiating Brexit: A Clash of Approaches? *Comparative European Politics* 18 (5): 858–877. https://doi.org/10.1057/s41295-020-00213-6.

Gwladys Fertré v. Vale of White Horse District Council, EWCA Civ 1057. 2025. (Court of Appeal (Civil Division)).

Hall, Stephen. 1996. Loss of Union Citizenship in Breach of Fundamental Rights. *European Law Review* 21 (2): 129–143.

House of Lords, European Union Committee. 2016. Brexit: Acquired Rights. 10th Report of Session 2016–17. House of Lords.

Independent Monitoring Authority. 2025. *IMA's Annual Report to the Specialised Committee on Citizens' Rights Established under the Withdrawal Agreement and the Joint Committee Established under the EEA EFTA Separation Agreement.* https://assets.publishing.service.gov.uk/media/68e4d137750fcf90fa6ffe6a/ima-aunnal-report-specialised-joint-committees-2025-large-print.pdf.

Independent Monitoring Authority for the Citizens' Rights Agreements. 2022. Independent Monitoring Authority Successful in Landmark High Court Challenge against Home Office. December 21. https://ima-citizensrights.org.uk/news_events/independent-monitoring-authority-successful-in-landmark-high-court-challenge-against-home-office/.

Independent Monitoring Authority for the Citizens' Rights Agreements. 2024. *Annual Report and Accounts 2023–2024.* https://assets.publishing.service.gov.uk/media/672b7eaf40f7da695c921c42/ima-annual-report-2024.pdf

Independent Monitoring Authority for the Citizens' Rights Agreements. 2025. *Annual Report and Accounts 2024–2025.* https://ima-citizensrights.org.uk/wp-content/uploads/2025/10/IMA-Annual-Report-to-the-Specialised-Committee-and-Joint-Committee-2024.pdf.

Independent Monitoring Authority for the Citizens' Rights Agreements. n.d.-a. Independent Monitoring Authority for the Citizens' Rights Agreements. Accessed 1 January 2026. https://ima-citizensrights.org.uk/.

Independent Monitoring Authority for the Citizens' Rights Agreements. n.d.-b. Who We Are. Accessed 1 January 2026. https://ima-citizensrights.org.uk/about-us/who-we-are/.

International Covenant on Civil and Political Rights, 999 U.N.T.S. 171. 1966.

Joined Cases C-684/22 to C-686/22. 2024. S.Ö. and Others v. Stadt Duisburg and Others, ECLI:EU:C:2024:345 (CJEU)

Joint Report from the Negotiators of the European Union and the United Kingdom Government on Progress during Phase 1 of Negotiations under Article 50 TEU on the United Kingdom's Orderly Withdrawal from the European Union. 2017. TF50 (2017) 19.

Juverdeanu, Cristina. 2025. Brexit and the EU Settlement Scheme: Continuity and Rupture with the European Union. *Journal of Contemporary European Studies* 33 (1): 278–293. https://doi.org/10.1080/14782804.2024.2372677.

Kostakopoulou, Dora. 2007. European Union Citizenship: Writing the Future. *European Law Journal* 13 (5): 623–646. https://doi.org/10.1111/j.1468-0386.2007.00387.x.

Kunoy, Bjørn. 2006. A Union of National Citizens. The Origins of the Court's Lack of Avant-Gardisme in the Chen Case. *Common Market Law Review* 43 (1): 179–190. https://doi.org/10.54648/cola2005090.

Lashyn, Serhii. 2022. Sacrificing EU Citizenship on the Altar of Brexit. *Maastricht Journal of European and Comparative Law* 29 (6): 736–744. https://doi.org/10.1177/1023263X221146465.

Lenard, Patti Tamara. 2016. Democracies and the Power to Revoke Citizenship. *Ethics and International Affairs* 30 (1): 73–91.

Ministry of Justice and Independent Monitoring Authority for the Citizens' Rights Agreements. 2024. *Framework Document between the Ministry of Justice and Independent Monitoring Authority for the Citizens' Rights Agreements.* https://ima-citizensrights.org.uk/wp-content/uploads/2024/04/IMA-Framework-Document-web.pdf.

More, Gillian. 2020. From Union Citizen to Third-Country National: Brexit, the UK Withdrawal Agreement, No-Deal Preparations and Britons Living in the European Union. In *European Citizenship under Stress—Social Justice, Brexit and Other Challenges*, ed. Nathan Cambien, Dimitry Kochenov, and Elise Muir. Brill.

Nationality Decrees Issued in Tunis and Morocco (French Zone) (Advisory Opinion), 1921. P.C.I.J. Rep. 1923, Ser. B, No. 4 (Permanent Court of International Justice. https://www.worldcourts.com/pcij/eng/decisions/1923.02.07_morocco.htm.

Neville, Ann. 2023. Update on the Implementation of the Citizens' Rights Provisions of the Withdrawal Agreement. PE 739.351. European Parliamentary Research Service. https://www.europarl.europa.eu/RegData/etudes/BRIE/2023/739351/EPRS_BRI(2023)739351_EN.pdf.

Nottebohm Case (Liechtenstein v. Guatemala) (Second Phase), [1955] IC.J. Rep. 4 (International Court of Justice. 1955. icj-cij.org/sites/default/files/case-related/18/018-19550406-JUD-01-00-EN.pdf.

Oliveira, H. U. Jessurun d', Gerard René de Groot, and Anja Seling. 2011. Court of Justice of the European Union: Decision of 2 March 2010, Case C-315/08. *European Constitutional Law Review* 7 (1): 138–160. https://doi.org/10.1017/S1574019611100073.

Oosterom-Staples, Helen. 2018. The Triangular Relationship Between Nationality, EU Citizenship and Migration in EU Law: A Tale of Competing Competences. *Netherlands International Law Review* 65 (3): 431–461. https://doi.org/10.1007/s40802-018-0122-9.

Oral Evidence given by V Lowe to the House of Lords European Union Committee. 2016. http://data.parliament.uk/writtenevidence/committeeevidence.svc/evidencedocument/eu-justice-subcommittee/brexit-acquired-rights/oral/38196.html.

Pataut, Etienne. 2010. Citoyenneté de l'Union et nationalité étatique. *Revue Trimestrielle de Droit Européen* 3:617–632.

Pataut, Étienne. 2021. La nationalité étatique au défi du droit de l'Union. *Droit Constitutionnel. RED* 3 (2): 62–67. https://doi.org/10.3917/red.003.0062.

Peers, Steve. 2016. What Next After the UK Vote to Leave the EU? *EU Law Analysis*, June 2. http://eulawanalysis.blogspot.com/2016/06/what-next-after-uk-vote-to-leave-eu.html.

Peers, Steve. 2021. The End—Or a New Beginning? The EU/UK Withdrawal Agreement. *Yearbook of European Law* 39 (March): 122–198. https://doi.org/10.1093/yel/yeaa010.

Piris, Jean-Claude. 2015. Should the UK Withdraw from the EU: Legal Aspects and Effects of Possible Options. No. 355. Fondation Robert Schuman Policy Paper. Fondation Robert Schuman. https://www.robert-schuman.eu/en/european-issues/0355-if-the-uk-left-the-european-union-legal-aspects-and-consequences-of-the-various-possible-options.

Porchia, Ornella. 2019. Citizens' Rights in the Post Brexit Scenario. *ERA Forum* 19 (4): 585–595. https://doi.org/10.1007/s12027-018-0545-0.

R. (on the Application of Ali) v. Secretary of State for the Home Department Respondent. 2024. EWCA Civ 1546 (Court of Appeal [Civil Division]).

R. (on the Application of B.Z.) v. Secretary of State for Work and Pensions. 2025. EWHC 1814 (Admin) (High Court of Justice).

Re Maastricht Treaty, 2 BvR 2134/92, 2 BvR 2159/92 (German Federal Constitutional Court). 1993. https://www.bundesverfassungsgericht.de/SharedDocs/Entscheidungen/EN/1993/10/rs19931012_2bvr213492en.html.

Reich, Norbert. 2001. Union Citizenship—Metaphor or Source of Rights? *European Law Journal* 7 (1): 4–23. https://doi.org/10.1111/1468-0386.00116.

Repasi, René. 2017. Die Rechte der Unionsbürger und ihr Fortbestehen nach dem Brexit. *Ifo Schnelldienst* 11:30–33.

Report from the Commission Pursuant to Article 159(2) of the Withdrawal Agreement. 2025. C(2025) 7843 final. European Commission. https://commission.europa.eu/document/download/2cd42c73-9972-422d-b48e-5f906636 41f2_en?filename=annual_report_on_citizens_rights_2024%20en.pdf.

Resolution on Union Citizenship, OJ C183/473. 1991. https://www.europarl.europa.eu/charter/docs/pe/union-citizenship/r3-139-91-en_en.pdf.

Rieder, Clemens. 2013. The Withdrawal Clause of the Lisbon Treaty in the Light of EU Citizenship (Between Disintegration and Integration). *Fordham International Law Journal* 37 (1): 147–174.

Ryan, B. 2017. Negotiating the Right to Remain after Brexit. *Immigration, Asylum and Nationality Law* 31 (3): 197–226.

Shaw, Jo. 2019. "Shunning" and "Seeking" Membership: Rethinking Citizenship Regimes in the European Constitutional Space. *Global Constitutionalism* 8 (3): 425–469. https://doi.org/10.1017/S2045381719000133.

Shuibhne, Niamh Nic. 2023. Protecting the Legal Heritage of Former Union Citizens: EP v Préfet Du Gers. *Common Market Law Review* 60 (2): 475–516. https://doi.org/10.54648/cola2023028.

Simkova (Appellant) v. Secretary of State for Work and Pensions (Respondent). 2025. UKSC 41 (UK Supreme Court).

Simmonds, Kenneth R. 1984. The British Nationality Act 1981 and the Definition of the Term "National" for Community Purposes. *Common Market Law Review* 21 (4): 675–686. https://doi.org/10.54648/COLA1984033.

Simon, Denys, and Robert Kovar. 1993. La citoyenneté européenne. *Cahiers de Droit Européen* 3–4:285–316. https://doi.org/10.54648/COLA2004023.

Southey, Hugh. 2015. Is EU Citizenship Purely a Matter for Individual Member States? *Judicial Review* 20 (3): 141–146. https://doi.org/10.1080/10854681.2015.1073045.

Spaventa, Eleanor. 2019. Mice or Horses?: British Citizens in the EU 27 after Brexit as “Former EU Citizens”. *European Law Review* 44 (5): 589–604.

Sredanovic, Djordje. 2021. Brexit as a Trigger and an Obstacle to Onwards and Return Migration. *International Migration* 59 (6): 93–108. https://doi.org/10.1111/imig.12712.

The State of the Netherlands (Ministry of Foreign Affairs and the City of Amsterdam / X and others). 2018. ECLI:NL:GHAMS:2018:2009 (Court of Appeal of Amsterdam). https://uitspraken.rechtspraak.nl/details?id=ECLI:NL:GHAMS:2018:2009.

Treaty on European Union, Together with the Complete Text of the Treaty Establishing the European Community, OJ 92/C 224/01. 1992. https://eur-lex.europa.eu/legal-content/EN/TXT/PDF/?uri=OJ:C:1992:224:FULL.

UK Government. 2017. The United Kingdom’s Exit from and New Partnership with the European Union. Cm 9417.

van den Brink, Martijn, and Dimitry Kochenov. 2019. Against Associate EU Citizenship. *Journal of Common Market Studies* 57 (6): 1366–1382. https://doi.org/10.1111/jcms.12898.

Van der Mei, A. 2018. Brexit and Citizenship I: Retention of EU Citizenship. *Maastricht University Blog*, October 22. https://www.maastrichtuniversity.nl/blog/2018/10/brexit-and-citizenship-i-retention-eu-citizenship.

Vienna Convention on the Law of Treaties, 1155 U.N.T.S. 331. 1969. https://treaties.un.org/pages/ViewDetailsIII.aspx?src=treaty&mtdsg_no=xxiii-1&chapter=23&Temp=mtdsg3&clang=_en.

Weiss, P. 1979. *Nationality and Statelessness in International Law*. 2nd ed. Brill.

Wesemann, Anne. 2018. European Union Citizens in Post EU UK. In *Legal Implications of Brexit*. Ed. Karl August Prinz von Sachsen Gesaphe, Juan J. Garcia Plesa, and Nils Szuka. Vol. 2. MV-WISSENSCHAFT. https://ub-deposit.fernuni-hagen.de/receive/mir_mods_00001460.

Worster, William Thomas. 2018. Brexit and the International Law Prohibitions on the Loss of EU Citizenship. *International Organizations Law Review* 15 (2): 341–363. https://doi.org/10.1163/15723747-01502005.

X. v. State of the Netherlands and Municipality of Amsterdam. 2018. ECLI:NL:RBAMS:2018:605 (Amsterdam District Court). https://uitspraken.rechtspraak.nl/details?id=ECLI:NL:RBAMS:2018:605.

CHAPTER 5

Brexit as a Means to Assess the Transformative Value of EU Citizenship

Abstract This chapter uses Brexit as a case study to evaluate the transformative value of EU citizenship through the triad of status, rights, and practice. It examines how the Withdrawal Agreement preserved the right to residence while simultaneously re-migrantising individuals who had previously enjoyed quasi-national status. The analysis highlights that, although the right to residence was largely retained, its implementation through constitutive registration systems introduced significant hurdles, particularly for vulnerable groups. The principle of non-discrimination remains legally intact, yet administrative complexities and the rise of xenophobia undermine its practical application. In contrast, the right to vote and stand as a candidate in local elections, integral to the transformative value of EU citizenship, was excluded from the Withdrawal Agreement. This left UK nationals in the EU27 largely disenfranchised, whilst the UK acknowledged its practice by giving such rights to EU citizens. A counterfactual scenario without the Agreement underscores its importance in mitigating harsher immigration policies. Ultimately, Brexit demonstrates that EU citizenship is not merely a legal status with rights but a lived experience that has, overall, been acknowledged by the UK, the EU, and its Member States.

C. Dadomo, N. Quénivet, *The Transformative Value of EU Citizenship after Brexit*,
https://doi.org/10.1007/978-3-032-20595-7_5

Keywords EU citizenship • Withdrawal Agreement • Right to residence • Principle of non-discrimination • Right to vote • Brexit • (Re)migranticisation • Integration

5.1 Introduction

Using Brexit as a case study, this book assesses the transformative value of EU citizenship, focusing on the triad of *status*, *rights*, and *practice*, and emphasising their interrelationship. The previous chapter examined how Brexit impacted the fundamental *status* of EU citizenship and shed light on two key aspects. First, EU citizenship is essentially an overlay; it largely supports the minimalist view of EU citizenship as a mere collection of *rights* tied to a legal *status* (see Chap. 2): UK nationals have lost this citizenship, and EU citizens in the UK can no longer use, and rely on, it in the same manner. Second, although the EU citizen status is lost for UK nationals and unopposable for EU citizens in the UK, an in-depth analysis of the negotiation process and the mechanisms established to protect both the rights of UK nationals in the EU27 and those of EU citizens in the UK reveals that both the UK and the EU have regarded these *rights*, and, to some extent, the *practice* related to EU citizenship, as deserving to be dealt with first in the Brexit negotiations and safeguarded by specific measures and mechanisms.

As the Commission explained in its EU Citizenship Report 2020, "[t]he Withdrawal Agreement guarantees [EU citizens living in the UK at the time of Brexit] and their family members broadly the same rights as they have now: they can continue to live, study, work and travel between their host country and the UK or the EU-27" (European Commission 2020, 25). With regard to the UK nationals, who since 1 February 2020 are no longer EU citizens but still live in EU countries, the Agreement "safeguard[s] their right to live, work or study in their host country. It provides for residence rights, rights of entry and exit, right to work, the recognition of professional qualifications, and social security coordination" (European Commission 2020, 25). The next step is to assess how the Agreement was implemented and applied in law and in practice, and determine whether its legal provisions adequately protect the elements of EU citizenship that are the essence of its transformative value, that is, the right to residence, freedom from discrimination, and the right to vote and be a candidate in local elections.

This chapter examines the provisions of the Withdrawal Agreement, particularly those related to permanent residents, that is, individuals who have been residing in the UK or in the EU27 for more than five years. Analysing this category of individuals is likely to reveal the transformative value of EU citizenship. It is important to clarify that this book focuses on the transformative value of EU citizenship and does not aim to provide a comprehensive analysis of all provisions pertaining to EU citizens in the UK or UK nationals in the EU27. Instead, it seeks to explore whether the rights enshrined in the Withdrawal Agreement reflect the transformative value of EU citizenship. Applying these elements, this chapter highlights the transformative value of European citizenship, albeit one founded mainly on *rights*, while also considering the *practice* of EU citizenship.

In line with the Withdrawal Agreement, which is based on the "reciprocal protection for Union citizens and for United Kingdom nationals, as well as their respective family members" (Withdrawal Agreement 2020, preamble ¶ 6; see *Case C-673/20 E.P. v. Préfet du Gers* 2022b, ¶ 72), the first section of this chapter does not separate the discussions into two parts, one for EU citizens in the UK and another for UK nationals in the EU27. By not adopting this binary structure, attention is drawn to their shared experience. For EU citizens in the UK, Brexit has not only jeopardised their rights but also threatened their "participation, settlement and belonging in British society" (Guma and Dafydd Jones 2019, 2). For UK nationals in the EU27, the precarity of their situation became evident. The chapter evaluates the Withdrawal Agreement against the transformative value of EU citizenship, as described in Chap. 3, by examining the right to residence, the principle of non-discrimination, and the right to vote and stand in elections.

5.2 The Right to Residence and the "(Re-) Migrantisation" of EU Citizens

Whereas previously EU citizens could not "be equated with foreigners (i.e., third country nationals) anywhere in the Union" (Kochenov 2013, 117), EU citizens in the UK and UK nationals in the EU27 have returned to a situation where they are treated as "foreigners". They can no longer be considered as quasi-nationals. Such a situation, however, has been tempered by the Withdrawal Agreement, which, to some extent, recognises the transformative value of EU citizenship in relation to residence even though it does "re-migrantise EU citizens". In these two aspects, we analyse how Brexit has impacted the triad of *status*, *rights*, and *practice* related to EU citizenship. Furthermore, we compare the situation of EU citizenship post-Brexit with and without the agreement to emphasise how the right to residence has been maintained or diminished compared to a scenario where no withdrawal agreement would have been reached.

5.2.1 Retention of the Right to Residence

It is telling that Part II on Citizens' Rights of the Withdrawal Agreement identifies its personal scope of application by reference to the right to residence (Withdrawal Agreement 2020, art. 10(1)). The territorial criterion is thus crucial, although different statuses under national law are granted on the basis of a temporal criterion. Those who "have resided legally in the host State in accordance with Union law for a continuous period of 5 years or for the period specified in Article 17 of Directive 2004/38/EC, shall have the right to reside permanently in the host State under the conditions" specified in the Citizenship Directive (Withdrawal Agreement 2020, art. 15(1)). Those who were not yet permanent residents by the end of the transition period but were residents for more than three months "have the right to acquire the right to reside permanently" (Withdrawal Agreement 2020, art. 16). As Peers notes, the expression "in accordance with Union law" seems to indicate that residence can also be granted on the basis of provisions unrelated to free movement law (Peers 2021, 156–57), thus, adopting a broad approach.

Article 13 specifies the residence rights which are roughly modelled on the relevant provisions of the TFEU (Articles 21, 45 and 49) and the Citizenship Directive (Withdrawal Agreement 2020, art. 13(1)), clearly supporting the view that "Union Law still plays a pivotal role" as "the persons as well as the content of their rights are identified on the basis of EU categories" (Porchia 2019, 588). As Juverdeanu states, the residence rights "are not designed from scratch but display the UK's commitment to offer EU+ Citizens in the UK a status that is as close to the one they had before Brexit as possible" (Juverdeanu 2025, 279). Further, neither the UK nor the EU (or its Member States) can impose further requirements (Withdrawal Agreement 2020, art. 13(4); see Peers 2021, 157–58). The Agreement also specifies that persons within its scope of application enjoy lifelong protection unless they cease to meet the relevant conditions (Withdrawal Agreement 2020, art. 39). In this regard, the Withdrawal

Agreement undoubtedly recognises the right to permanent residence, an element of the transformative value of EU citizenship.

Whilst tagging along with these EU legal provisions seems at first glance a welcome step, the reality is that, aside from Article 13 of the Withdrawal Agreement, there is no other legal basis for the right to residence. Consequently, failing to meet these conditions results in a loss of the right to residence, equal treatment, and related rights. "Legal" residence as defined in Article 13(1) is thus crucial for falling within the purview of the Withdrawal Agreement. As Dougan noted, "[t]he decision to rely on Union law as a general baseline for the protection of citizens' rights under the Withdrawal Agreement might sound uncontroversial—but it is still potentially problematic" (Dougan 2020, 669). Indeed, not all EU citizens in the UK and UK nationals in the EU27 were able to demonstrate that they met the conditions referred to in Articles 21 (citizenship), 45 (workers), and 49 (self-employed) of the TFEU (TFEU (Lisbon) 2025) and in the Citizenship Directive (Citizenship Directive 2024). O'Brien observes that the conditions listed in the EU Citizenship Directive have systematically disadvantaged certain categories of individuals, notably those on short-term or casual contracts, those who have periods of incapacity for work due to disability, or those who have taken on caring responsibilities (O'Brien 2021, 433 and 438; see Dougan 2020, 669). Already in 2017, the European Parliament had highlighted that workers in atypical employment relationships, those with a fragmented or non-continuous working history, self-employed individuals, and economically inactive citizens might find it challenging to prove their right to permanent residence (Spaventa 2017, 32–33). The Withdrawal Agreement thus reproduces this model of distinguishing between economically active and non-active persons (see Shuibhne 2023, 510), thereby excluding certain categories of EU citizens.

Moreover, as More notes, "[t]he EU legal acquis on having a 'right to residence' is a dense and complicated patchwork of legislation and Court of Justice case-law" (More 2020, 464) and States have erred on the side of caution, adopting a strict approach (More 2020, 465). Remarkably, the UK adopted a broad approach under the EU Settlement Scheme, including allowing applications based on a derivative right for those who did not qualify for a right of residence under the Citizenship Directive (UK Home Office 2024, sect. 4). It should be noted that Article 38 of the Withdrawal Agreement allows States to adopt or retain laws that are more favourable. First, the EU Settlement Scheme did not require EU citizens to prove that they had exercised their rights to qualify for residence in the UK, thus deviating from the Withdrawal Agreement (Neville 2023, 3). In fact, the application requirements for the scheme were proof of identity, evidence of continuous residence (for a period of five years for settled status), and suitability (Neville 2023, 3; Cîrlig 2020, 9; Gove 2020, 1). In this regard, the UK marked a strong departure from the Citizenship Directive (Neville 2023, 3). As the Court of Justice of the European Union acknowledged, the UK established "more favourable rules than those laid down by the provisions of that directive" (*Case C-709/20 C.G.* 2021, ¶¶ 82 and 87). Second, although the Withdrawal Agreement does not include individuals covered by the *Surinder Singh* (see Sect. 3.3) (see More 2020, 469) or *Zambrano* (see Sect. 2.3) jurisprudence (Peers 2021, 156–57; Cîrlig 2020, 6), remarkably, the UK has unilaterally included individuals in a *Surinder Singh/Lounes* (see Sect. 3.3.1) (Immigration Rules Appendix EU 2025, ¶ EU12) and *Zambrano* (Immigration Rules Appendix EU 2025, ¶ EU11) situation within the scope of beneficiaries in its Immigration Rules. Third, the UK has allowed applications based on derivative rights following the *Chen* (see Sect. 2.3) and *Ibrahim* and *Teixeira* (see Sect. 2.3) cases (Immigration Rules Appendix EU 2025, ¶ EU11). This demonstrates that the UK has gone beyond a strict interpretation of EU law and adopted the CJEU's jurisprudence on the genuine enjoyment of the rights associated with EU citizenship, thereby confirming the transformative value of EU citizenship. Official statistics (which also include EEA applicants) dated August 2024 show that applications under the *Chen*, *Surinder Singh/Lounes*, *Ibrahim/Teixeira*, and *Zambrano* routes were successful (for both settled and pre-settled status) at rates of 73%, 88%, 66%, and 15%, respectively. The much lower success rate for *Zambrano* applicants is nonetheless concerning and is likely due to the guidance's highly restrictive approach (EU Settlement Scheme: Person with a Zambrano Right to Reside, Version 8.0 2023 2023) or the fact that, according to the *Akinsanya* case, they could prove that by the end of the transition period and throughout the relevant period they had a derived right to reside and no other way to apply to remain in the UK (*Akinsanya and S.S.H.D.* 2022; *Akinsanya & Anin-Adjei v. S.S.H.D.* 2024). The decision to include such individuals under the Scheme was criticised for effectively blurring the different statuses (O'Brien 2021, 450), as individuals do not know whether their status is covered under the Withdrawal Agreement or under "pure" UK law. Indeed, if the Withdrawal Agreement governs their status, it is fully protected under that legal instrument; however, if it exists only under national law, it can be revoked or altered at the whim of the British Parliament. Most importantly, this issue affects not only those with derivative rights but also anyone who does not meet the strict criteria set out in the Withdrawal Agreement. As the CJEU explained in *C.G.*, the right of residence granted by a State establishing more favourable rules is an "action [that] cannot be regarded as an implementation of that directive" (*Case C-709/20 C.G.* 2021, ¶ 87). The Court then further stated that the individual in the proceedings "ha[d] a right of residence on the basis of national law" (*Case C-709/20 C.G.* 2021, ¶ 89). In light of this jurisprudence, it appears that individuals whose residence rights have been granted beyond the Withdrawal Agreement's wording, which relies on the Citizenship Directive, have national status rather than status derived from the Withdrawal Agreement. Yet, as the Court noted, this does not absolve the State from ensuring that such individuals are treated in accordance with Article 1 of the Charter (*Case C-709/20 C.G.* 2021, ¶ 89). In effect, the EU Settlement Scheme has, as noted by the EU (Specialised Committee on Citizens' Rights 2021c), created two cohorts of beneficiaries: those who fulfil the requirements of the Withdrawal Agreement (the "true cohort"), and thus benefit from lifelong protection under Article 39 of the Withdrawal Agreement, and those who do not and are covered by UK (immigration) law (the "extra cohort"). Whilst the UK can be praised for acknowledging the transformative value of EU citizenship in relation to the *right* and the *practice* of residence, its approach was a cause for concern (Specialised Committee on Citizens' Rights 2022a, 2021c, 2021a). The EU brought the issue to the fore several times (Specialised Committee on Citizens' Rights 2023b, 2024b) and, eventually, the UK took legislative steps. In December 2025 the co-chairs "welcomed the solution on the true and extra cohort issue enacted in the Border Security, Asylum and Immigration Act 2025 that provides legal clarity for EU citizens with status under the EU Settlement Scheme (EUSS)" (Specialised Committee on Citizens' Rights 2025a). Section 45 of the Border Security, Asylum and Immigration Act 2025 (Border Security, Asylum and Immigration Act 2025 n.d.) now specifies that both the "true" and the "extra" cohort are to be treated as having rights in the UK under the Withdrawal Agreement (see GOV.UK n.d.).

The European Commission issued a Guidance Note to assist Member States in correctly implementing the citizens' rights provisions of the Withdrawal Agreement (Guidance Note Relating to Withdrawal Agreement—Citizens' Rights 2020). Unlike the UK, EU Member States did not adopt a broad approach; they often relied on the issuance of previously issued documents (in conformity with EU law) or required UK nationals to apply for new documentation (see Table 1 Cîrlig 2020, 10–13). In doing so, EU Member States applied the terms of the Withdrawal Agreement that allowed them to require demonstration of compliance with the Citizenship Directive, that is, proof of sufficient resources and comprehensive sickness insurance for economically inactive individuals and students. Research shows that UK nationals realised they did not fulfil the eligibility requirements while applying for recognition of their legal status. Following Brexit, France had put in place a constitutive system obliging all UK nationals to hold a residence permit (Cîrlig 2020, 11). It was estimated that 148,300 UK nationals lived in France, yet nearly 20,000 more applied for residence (Specialised Committee on Citizens' Rights 2022c, 35). The relative lack of scrutiny of their residence status in another EU Member State by national authorities that UK nationals had benefited from before Brexit played against them as they became conscious that they did not meet the requirements. As Benson explains, some could not prove that they had the right to remain (see, e.g., Benson 2019). In Spain, where registration with the local authority is mandatory, many UK nationals had failed to do so out of fear of losing economic and social advantages in the UK (Giner-Monfort 2018, 361). And so, as they were required to apply for a new document attesting their rights under the Withdrawal Agreement (Cîrlig 2020, 11) under a declaratory system, they realised they did not meet the requirements. Out of the estimated 430,000 UK nationals, only 187,200 applied for a new residence document (Specialised Committee on Citizens' Rights 2022c, 36). Whilst the *right* to residence is recognised in the Withdrawal Agreement, the issue is that the *practice*—namely, the fact that these individuals have lived in the host country, formed families, and integrated into local society—is not adequately recognised, since they did not fulfil the residence requirements of the Citizenship Directive or relevant Treaty provisions.

What is more, whereas under EU law permanent residence can be lost through absence from the host State after two consecutive years (Citizenship Directive 2024, art. 16(4)), under the Withdrawal Agreement, such a right is lost after five consecutive years (Withdrawal Agreement 2020, art. 15(3)). Truly, this provision recognises the transformative value of EU citizenship as it means that the new permanent residence status can be retained for much longer than the one under EU law. In other words, the practice of temporarily leaving and returning to the host country is recognised and allowed by law.

In addition, Part Two of the Withdrawal Agreement recognises the derived right to residence and accompanying rights of family members of EU citizens in the UK and UK nationals in the EU27. The Withdrawal Agreement covers both direct family members, as defined in Article 2(2) of the Citizenship Directive, and extended family members who may or may not be EU citizens. This aligns with EU legal provisions, and therefore, the rights and practices of family members of EU citizens deriving their rights from such citizens are maintained.

Another important point concerns the expulsion of EU citizens in the UK or of UK nationals in the EU27. As indicated in Article 20(2) of the Withdrawal Agreement, the expulsion of individuals is now based on national law. Moreover, even those with permanent residence can be expelled for criminal conduct. Whilst this might be a cause for concern, Article 21 of the Withdrawal Agreement specifies that the procedural guarantees enshrined in Article 15 and Chapter VI of the Citizenship Directive concerning the notification of decisions, the right to appeal, etc. apply. Further, the potential harshness of national rules is tempered by the State's human rights commitments, notably the European Convention on Human Rights (European Convention on Human Rights 1950). Despite such strong protections, it was noted that a number of EU citizens in the UK received orders to leave the UK and UK nationals were ordered to leave the EU Member States (Carrera and Colombi 2025, 56–57; see Henley 2023). As it is unknown on what basis EU citizens in the UK were issued orders to leave, it is not possible to determine whether such orders were lawful under the Withdrawal Agreement. Slightly more information is available regarding the reasons for the deportations of UK nationals. It appears that a number of UK nationals were required to leave because they "had never fully complied with the requirements set out by the Citizen's Rights Directive" and "their situation had only come to the attention of the authorities after they were required to formally register as residents" (Carrera and Colombi 2025, 57). Others had missed registration deadlines or seemed to have been provided with insufficient information to register (Henley 2023). Relatedly, EU citizens in the UK have been and continue to be denied (re-)entry at the border, despite being lawful residents (O'Carroll and Goodier 2023; Specialised Committee on Citizens' Rights 2024b, 2025b).

Overall, the right to (permanent) residence has been retained in a similar, albeit not identical, fashion as under EU law. Although the *status* of EU citizenship has been lost for UK nationals and is inapplicable for EU citizens in the UK, the *right* to residence, which is an essential element of the transformative value of EU citizenship, remains largely intact, at least for those who could demonstrate residence or "legal" residence under the TFEU and the Citizenship Directive. There are, nevertheless, several points of concern, namely:

1. for EU citizens in the UK who *practised* EU citizenship but were unable to show five continuous years of residence and/or those who received orders to leave the UK although they were lawful residents,
2. for UK nationals who *practised* EU citizenship but did not follow the EU rules, as they did not have a right to residence according to the Withdrawal Agreement.

5.2.2 Migranticisation of Status

That being said, Brexit has (re-)migranticised the status of EU citizens and UK nationals respectively, as under Article 18 of the Withdrawal Agreement, the host State may require EU citizens in the UK and UK nationals in the EU27, and their families, to apply for national immigration status. Early in the Brexit negotiations, the UK had declared that it wished EU citizens to apply for a specific status, that of "settled status" (O'Brien 2021, 443–44), a term more familiar to British immigration law than "permanent residents" (Smismans 2018, 470). To find a compromise (see More 2020, 466–67; Shuibhne 2023, 512) between the principle of reciprocity that underpins the Withdrawal Agreement and the long-standing EU law's approach, which asserts that residence rights derive from EU law rather than proof of a right to residence via registration (for EU citizens, see *Case C-325/09 Dias* 2011, ¶¶ 48–49; for third-country nationals, see *Case C-246/17 Diallo* 2018, ¶¶ 48–49), Article 18(1) provides that "[t]he host State *may* require Union citizens or United Kingdom nationals, their respective family members and other persons [...] to apply for a new residence status which confers the rights under this Title and a document evidencing such status which may be in a digital form" (Withdrawal Agreement 2020 (emphasis added)). In other words, States were given the choice between instituting a constitutive registration system whereby individuals have to apply for a status and adopting a declaratory approach, which grants rights automatically once the relevant conditions are fulfilled (see Barnard et al. 2024, 56). In the latter case, according to Article 18(4), UK nationals would receive a residence document evidencing their status. In February 2020, the European Commission issued an implementing decision establishing a uniform format for EU residence documents issued under both the declaratory and constitutive approaches (Commission Implementing Decision on Documents 2020). The UK required EU citizens to apply for settled status under a constitutive scheme, introduced in March 2019, and their status was then documented online (Immigration Rules Appendix EU 2025; see Porchia 2019, 589–91; Barnard et al. 2022). Fourteen EU Member States, including Spain, Germany, Portugal, and Italy, opted for a declaratory system, conferring post-Brexit residence status on UK nationals who were automatically lawfully resident, while 13 EU Member States obliged UK nationals to formally apply for residence status within a certain period of time (Henley 2023; for full list and all processes, see Specialised Committee on Citizens' Rights 2022c).

First, the very fact that they were obliged to apply for the right to reside was alien to them. Even though Article 18 specifies that as long as they met the conditions, they had to be granted the status, the point is that they never had to undergo a formal process to prove their deservingness and fitness to the host State and community (Ranta and Nancheva 2019, 1). Whilst "permanent residence [was] acquired as a matter of course and documents attesting to it [had] only evidentiary value" (Spaventa 2017, 32), following Brexit, they had to demonstrate that they were lawful residents in accordance with EU law (Withdrawal Agreement 2020, art. 15) and not only that, they had been in the country for more than five years (see *Joined Cases C-424/10 and C-425/10 Ziolkowski and Others* 2011, ¶¶ 46–47 and 51). According to the Withdrawal Agreement, the procedure for applications ought to be "smooth, transparent and simple" and "unnecessary administrative burdens [...] avoided" (Withdrawal Agreement 2020, art. 18(1)(e)), and the form "short, simple, user-friendly and adapted to the context of this Agreement" (Withdrawal Agreement 2020, art. 18(1)(f)). In addition, the competent host State authorities "shall help the applicants to prove their eligibility" (Withdrawal Agreement 2020, art. 18(1)(o)) and shall not require documents that "go beyond what is strictly necessary and proportionate to provide evidence" (Withdrawal Agreement 2020, art. 18(1)(n)). Furthermore, a specific timeline was agreed upon in the Withdrawal Agreement; yet, aware that this could mean that EU citizens in the UK and UK nationals in the EU27 lose their right to residence (and accompanying rights under the Withdrawal Agreement), the parties introduced not only Article 18(1)(d) to oblige the relevant authorities to assess the personal circumstances of a person for not applying on time and allow for an application but also Article 37 to compel EU Member States and the UK to disseminate information relating to the Withdrawal Agreement and more specifically to conduct awareness-raising campaigns.

Looking at statistics, the procedure adopted in the UK worked fairly well: about half (3,123,000) of EU citizens who applied for the EU Settlement Scheme (from 6,385,000 applications) were granted permanent residence (Article 15 of the Withdrawal Agreement), and 40% were granted non-permanent residence (Article 13 of the Withdrawal Agreement) (Specialised Committee on Citizens' Rights 2022c, 35). Yet, this "move from a declaratory to a constitutive Scheme cannot be overstated" (Juverdeanu 2025, 280). Think tanks and academics had already warned that vulnerable individuals might struggle to register. The Migration Observatory in a 2018 report drew the attention to four categories of individuals: those who do not realise that they can and need to apply (Sumption and Kone 2018, 8–12); vulnerable groups mostly because they face social exclusion or their autonomy is reduced (e.g., victims of domestic abuse, children in care, victims of exploitation or trafficking, people with low levels of literacy, elderly people) (Sumption and Kone 2018, 12–15); people who cannot provide evidence (e.g., individuals without bank accounts, proof of address, without evidence of formal work in the UK) (Sumption and Kone 2018, 15–18); and those who do not meet the eligibility criteria (e.g., those with significant absences from the UK) (Sumption and Kone 2018, 20). Children, women, and homeless people are also mentioned as categories of people for whom the EU Settlement Scheme did not work well (Cîrlig 2020, 10). O'Brien also warned in 2021 that those most likely to fail to register were individuals who were unaware of the registration requirement, who struggled to collect the necessary evidence, or lacked sufficient IT literacy skills or access to IT (O'Brien 2021, 433). Despite the UK providing financial support to vulnerable EU citizens through grants to various organisations (Gove 2020, 2), a 2022 study showed that, although the EU Settlement Scheme process was relatively easy to apply—it was free and could be undertaken via a smartphone app—it presented a number of challenges (Barnard et al. 2022, 645). Whilst for some the decision process was quick (within weeks), for others it took months (Barnard et al. 2024, 61). Some of the issues identified included a lack of awareness of the scheme, hidden costs, a lack of understanding that the scheme applied to them or that they had an obligation to register their children, difficulties for some vulnerable groups in applying, a lack of access to or understanding of digital technology, etc. (Barnard et al. 2022, 658; see 2024, 52, 66 and 68). In 2025, Juverdeanu published the results of her survey. Age and educational attainment were significant factors in determining the ease of the application process (Juverdeanu 2025, 290). Furthermore, she discovered that relying on the National Insurance Number and databases such as those of the HMRC (His Majesty's Revenue & Customs) and the DWP (Department for Work and Pensions) to verify information discriminated against applicants who were, or had been, in precarious employment situations or who were disabled (Juverdeanu 2025, 281; 288 and 290). This, in the eyes of some scholars, demonstrates that the concept of market-citizen (see Chap. 2) remains relevant (see Juverdeanu 2025, 290). To sum up, she explains, "the EUSS both continues and breaks with the EU Legacy offering dismantlement for the vulnerable and continuity for the rest" (Juverdeanu 2025, 278).

UK nationals in EU Member States faced an even more difficult situation (Zambelli et al. 2022, 11) because each State had its own registration requirements, recording, reporting, and processes. To help them, in autumn 2019, the UK invited its nationals living abroad to "citizens outreach" meetings (More 2020, 468 fn 59), worked closely with some States which organised meetings with the British community (Specialised Committee on Citizens' Rights 2022c, 8; 10; 11; 13; 16; 18; 19), and funded organisations assisting UK nationals in the UK (Gove 2020, 2). Communication was difficult and, as they were fewer in number (it is estimated that about 1 million UK nationals lived in EU Member States in contrast to the 3.5–4.1 million EU citizens in the UK) (Specialised Committee on Citizens' Rights 2022c, 35–36), were scattered across many states, each of them with their own domestic procedures and were less vocal and organised, which made their (individual) struggles even greater. In 2020, the UK government sent a letter to the Vice-President of the European Commission to highlight, among others, the lack of "major media campaigns required under Article 37 in EU countries" and the fact that information varied greatly in "content, scale and accessibility" (Gove 2020, 2) and that EU Member States had not made available information to vulnerable groups, such as the elderly (Gove 2020, 2). Even though in 2021, the UK indicated that the EU had "not provided a sufficient level of communications and support to UK nationals in the EU" (Specialised Committee on Citizens' Rights 2021c), the situation did improve. The sixth and final report of the Committee on the Implementation of Residence Rights indicates that in many EU Member States, dedicated websites were created, campaigns targeting specific groups of individuals (such as student organisations) were launched, brochures and leaflets were distributed, and UK nationals were personally contacted, often because they were already registered with the authorities (Specialised Committee on Citizens' Rights 2022c).

Whether residing in a State that adopted the constitutive or the declaratory approach, UK nationals struggled with the registration. For those who had lived in countries where they did not need to register prior to Brexit but were obliged under the constitutive approach to do so, proving that they met the legal conditions for residence was a first-time experience (Benson 2019). Indeed, if they lived in Member States with quite lax residence requirements, they never had to provide evidence of their lawful presence under EU law (Benson 2020, 503). The complexity of some processes, which involved gathering paper-based evidence and sometimes face-to-face appointments (Gove 2020, 2), was rather daunting. France, Latvia, Luxembourg, Malta, and the Netherlands required UK nationals to apply for a new residence status (Specialised Committee on Citizens' Rights 2021b, 2021c, 2022c). In France, some UK nationals struggled to provide relevant evidence, and others failed to do so (Benson 2019). In Member States that had adopted a declaratory approach, new documents were required (Specialised Committee on Citizens' Rights 2022c). The UK repeatedly highlighted the existence of non-compliant administrative procedures adversely affecting UK nationals when seeking to obtain new residence status or documentation (Gove 2020, 2; Specialised Committee on Citizens' Rights 2021a, 2022b, 2023a). Moreover, some EU Member States were slow in issuing residence documents, which meant that UK nationals faced difficulties in evidencing their status (Specialised Committee on Citizens' Rights 2023a). Family members of UK nationals also seem to encounter difficulties in registration (Specialised Committee on Citizens' Rights 2023a, 2024a).

The registration procedure was the EU citizens' paperwork encounter with Brexit. EU citizens resented the introduction of this procedure, as they found it risky and stigmatising (Sredanovic 2021, 99; Siklodi 2023, 11). They felt "questioned about their entitlement to live and move in and out of their country of choice based on will and/or need" (Zambelli et al. 2022, 10). Whilst their right to residence was preserved, the process of officially registering this right failed to recognise the *practice* of EU citizenship, which did not require them to register or explain themselves to the authority (i.e., to prove that they had a lawful right under EU law to reside in the host country).

Second, their right to reside, though preserved and supported by the Withdrawal Agreement, is found in national law and, so it seems, (former) EU citizens need an immigration status to be embedded in the society. The process "triggered their reckoning with the precarity embedded in their newly migrantised status" (Zambelli et al. 2022, 10; see Brahic and Lallement 2020, 19). EU citizens in the UK identified the process of Brexit as one of reclassification as migrants (Barnard et al. 2022, 369). As the status was based on national registration, some EU citizens in the UK even "looked with suspicion at the durability of the rights that these permits/cards afforded them and/or their family members" (Zambelli et al. 2022, 11). Brexit brought to the surface the "us v. them" discourse, a new division forced upon the migrants (Lulle et al. 2019, 2; Brahic and Lallement 2020, 18). This goes much against the transformative value of EU citizenship as EU citizens in the UK had found their place in society through work, family, education, location, and hobbies, and their "immigration status" did not play any role in their everyday life (Ranta and Nancheva 2019, 15), and they viewed themselves as equal EU citizens (Barnard et al. 2022, 369). Little information is available regarding UK nationals in the EU27 though. In Romania, UK nationals enjoy a separate status under national law; they are distinct from other non-EU nationals who are referred to as "foreigners" on the one hand and from EU citizens, citizens of the EEA and Switzerland on the other (Valcu 2022, 19).

Third, with Brexit, EU citizens' *practice* of EU citizenship was called into question. Whilst this may have surprised those who felt the transformative value of EU citizenship that made them quasi-nationals, the reality was that "many British people did not accept their right to settle and partake of the welfare system on equal terms" (D'Angelo and Kofman 2018, 332; see Kostakopoulou 2018, 859). EU citizens in the UK experienced Brexit as a challenge to their embeddedness in the host State as they, until then, "felt fully integrated and welcomed into British society" (Godin and Sigona 2022, 1144; see Brändle et al. 2018, 823). Even though their reaction to Brexit was highly determined by "their social statuses and sense of entitlement and self-worth" (Godin and Sigona 2022, 1138), many felt that they had become "foreigners". As Godin and Sigona poignantly emphasise, "Brexit can be understood as a process of 'unmaking' citizens, turning European nationals from 'mobile citizens' into 'worthless migrants' in the eyes of the public and of rebordering membership in British society" (Godin and Sigona 2022, 1145; see Brahic and Lallement 2020, 16). During the negotiations of the Withdrawal Agreement, EU citizens in the UK felt unsettled (Guma and Dafydd Jones 2019, 7), their lives disrupted, Brexit having undermined their "connections, attachments, and relationships that made [EU citizens] feel at ease in places and communities in which they lived, and affecting their lives and way they engaged in Welsh and British society" (Guma and Dafydd Jones 2019, 8). Some made less effort to maintain friendships and develop new contacts (Brahic and Lallement 2020, 18). The entire process left EU citizens in the UK feeling unwelcome (Sredanovic 2021, 99), rejected and alienated (Botterill 2018, 546), different (Botterill 2018, 546), "othered" (Sredanovic 2022, 3099; Barnard et al. 2022, 369) and, as a result, identified less with British society (Sredanovic 2022, 3104). This was particularly the case for EU citizens from the "old EU Member States" who, for the first time, felt "othered" (Barnard et al. 2024, 62). Even individuals who were firmly anchored in British society (Barnard et al. 2022, 371) or had acquired British nationality felt they no longer belonged in the UK (Guma and Dafydd Jones 2019, 7). This feeling of otherness was even felt within mixed families living in the UK. A study revealed that "Brexit appeared to have created a fissure within their family sphere, engendering negative emotions such as a sense of being 'different' in front of one another and/or under the law, as well as risks of drifting apart from each other" (Zambelli et al. 2022, 9). In fact, as Siklodi notes, Brexit deepened already existing hidden tensions and unresolved issues (Siklodi 2023, 8; see Sredanovic 2022, 3099) as Barnard et al. refer to a certain hierarchical structure of EU citizens in the UK (Barnard et al. 2022, 370). In particular, Brexit had a disproportionate impact on EU citizens from Central and Eastern Europe; it "strain[ed] further their already precarious status and EU and UK senses of belonging" (Siklodi 2023, 1 and 3) and they "begun to reclassify themselves as (im)migrants, outsiders and foreigners" (Siklodi 2023, 9; see Blachnicka-Ciacek and Budginaite-Mackine 2022, 1088–89).

In contradistinction, there was no uniform sentiment felt by UK nationals in the EU27. For example, UK nationals in France viewed Brexit as a "point of rupture along existing routines and practices of daily life, and a catalyst for questioning their citizenship, rights and the possibility of continuing a future in France" (Ferbrache 2019a, 85) and, for the first time, felt "othered" (Sredanovic and Della Puppa 2023, 728). On the other hand, some UK nationals in Germany did not recognise themselves as migrants (Kulz 2023, 225) and those in Spain did not seem bothered by Brexit, as Brexit did not act as a push factor (Giner-Monfort and Huete 2021, 76), probably because these UK nationals "engaged in a settlement process that is closer to tourism than to migration" (Giner-Monfort and Huete 2021, 75). Overall, most of those affected by Brexit, especially EU citizens in the UK, felt that their practice of EU citizenship had been questioned. This sentiment was often more pronounced among them compared to UK nationals in the EU27 and sparked resentment towards the new post-Brexit policies.

Undoubtedly, despite retaining the *right* to residence (though with some caveats), the process of registering and the general atmosphere, especially in the UK, where Brexit was most felt, meant that EU citizens in the UK and UK nationals in the EU27 felt "othered" and their *practice* of EU citizenship set aside.

5.2.3 *The Absence of Withdrawal Agreement as Counterfactual Scenario*

The importance of the Withdrawal Agreement and its recognition of the transformative value of EU citizenship regarding the right of residence is best understood when compared to what would have been the fallback or default position in the absence of a Withdrawal Agreement.

First, the Withdrawal Agreement secured settled status for EU citizens in the UK. It derailed "the aim pursued by the British government [...] to treat EU nationals not as fellow European citizens, but, once again, as mobile workers, hence more or less returning the British model of immigration to the pre-2004 situation, if not before" (D'Angelo and Kofman 2018, 338). EU citizens, aware of the hostile environment policy, feared being subjected to right-to-work and right-to-rent controls similar to that imposed on other foreigners (Sredanovic 2021, 98–99). Whilst the settled status is very much like the well-known status under domestic immigration law of indefinite leave to remain under UK law (D'Angelo and Kofman 2018, 338; see Maas 2021, 172), it is also "a special post-EU status, set out in a separate set of UK rules separate from the current leave under the immigration rules" (Immigration Law Practitioners' Association 2016, ¶ 79).

Second, it was the legal status of EU citizenship that drew a distinction between EU citizens and third-country nationals in the EU (Dadomo and Quénivet 2020, 451) and created a "bright line legal distinction between European citizens and their TCN neighbours" (Becker 2004, 138) that initially prevented UK nationals in the EU27 from being third-country nationals. Now, having lost their EU citizenship and "all the well-known perks of [it]" (Kochenov 2016, 3), without the Withdrawal Agreement, they would have become third-country nationals whose status would be regulated by a mixture of national and EU law. Indeed, the EU "has developed a patchwork of TCN provisions that vary by agreement and provide different rights regarding residency, employment, free movement, family reunification, and social security" (Becker 2004, 151; see Garner 2016, 13). Even those who had exercised their right to free movement and had been long-term residents in the EU27 would have been left to suffer from the loss of citizenship as "the legal regime for non-EU citizens is (much) less favourable compared to the generous provisions applicable to Union citizens" (Tilindyte 2017, 3; see Cambien 2018, 1341).

UK nationals who had resided in an EU Member State for more than 5 years continuously could be automatically regarded as EU long-term residents under Directive 2003/109 (Council Directive on Long-Term Resident Third-Country Nationals 2003).[1] However, two problems need to be highlighted here. First, the conditions for the right to residence under this Directive differ from those under the Citizenship Directive, as this Directive permits States to define legal residence in accordance with their national law, albeit within the limits of EU law (see More 2020, 475). For example, the host Member State can request compliance with "integration measures, in accordance with national law" (Council Directive on Long-Term Resident Third-Country Nationals 2003, art. 5(2); see Mourão Permoser 2017, 2543–44; Acosta Arcarazo 2015, 213), proof of "stable and regular resources which are sufficient to maintain themselves and the members of their families, without recourse to the social assistance of the Member State concerned" (Council Directive on Long-Term Resident Third-Country Nationals 2003, art. 15(2)(a); see Spaventa 2019, 601) or reject an application on grounds of public policy or public

[1] This is the case provided that they do not fall within the excluded categories listed in Article 3(2). It should also be noted that this Directive does not apply to Denmark and that UK nationals in Ireland are covered by the Common Travel Area.

security (Council Directive on Long-Term Resident Third-Country Nationals 2003, art. 17(1)). Moreover, the right of third-country nationals to stay in an EU Member State depends on the laws of the State of residence, which define the conditions for their exclusion and/or expulsion, although they enjoy enhanced protection from expulsion (Council Directive on Long-Term Resident Third-Country Nationals 2003, preamble ¶ 16). Long-term resident status acquired under the 2003 Directive can be revoked under certain circumstances and may be lost if a person leaves their country of residence for 12 consecutive months (Council Directive on Long-Term Resident Third-Country Nationals 2003, art. 9(1)(c)). Second, this directive grants fewer rights than those of EU citizenship. Clearly, "[t]he rights afforded to recipients of this status are inferior to those attached to EU citizenship status" (Kostakopoulou 2018, 860). The Withdrawal Agreement acknowledges the special and distinct status of UK nationals who had exercised their right to free movement and made one of the EU Member States their home.

The special and distinct status offered post-Brexit to EU citizens in the UK and to UK nationals in the EU27, compared with that of other foreigners and third-country nationals, respectively, is certainly proof that the transformative value of EU citizenship has been recognised by both the EU and the UK. As More summarises, they are "resident aliens with a special status" (More 2020, 481). Their previous *rights* and how they have *practised* them have been to a great extent recognised.

The only notable right that UK nationals in the EU27 have lost putting them on a par with third-country nationals under EU law is free movement. The UK did not push the matter as it seemed contradictory to end free movement for EU citizens post-Brexit whilst claiming to keep such a right for UK nationals in the EU27. The Commission argued that it was beyond the scope of its mandate (see Neville 2023, 6). Interestingly, it is a right that some scholars view as one associated with market citizenship (More 2020, 481) as it enables individuals to move to another EU Member State, usually for work-related purposes. The lack of such onward mobility, nevertheless, does not affect the transformative value of EU citizenship as defined by the authors since such value is only revealed once EU citizens have exercised their right to free movement.

In summary, Brexit has reshaped the legal and social environment for EU citizens in the UK and for UK nationals in the EU27, revealing the fragility of rights once considered inherent to the status of EU citizenship. While the Withdrawal Agreement safeguards residence rights and acknowledges the transformative value of EU citizenship in relation to the right to residence, its implementation reveals significant limitations. The transition from a declaratory to a constitutive system, coupled with stringent evidentiary requirements, created barriers for vulnerable individuals and undermined the seamless practice of mobility that characterises EU citizenship. Moreover, the registration process and the emergence of "true" and "extra" cohorts blurred the boundaries between rights guaranteed under the Withdrawal Agreement and those contingent on national discretion, generating uncertainty and precarity. Socially, Brexit re-migrantised individuals who had previously enjoyed quasi-national status, challenging their sense of belonging and integration. The counterfactual scenario without the Withdrawal Agreement underscores its importance: without it, millions would have faced harsher immigration regimes and diminished rights. Ultimately, while legal protections remain, Brexit has demonstrated that citizenship is not merely a *status* with *rights*, but also a lived *experience,* one that can be disrupted by political change, forcing individuals to renegotiate their identity and security within new frameworks.

5.3 The Principles of Non-discrimination and Equality

The second core principle, which contributes to the transformative value of EU citizenship, is that of non-discrimination. The Withdrawal Agreement and measures put in place at the national level show that, although the principle is enshrined as a right in law and thus has been preserved, its practical operation is more doubtful.

The principle of non-discrimination has been completely retained in the Withdrawal Agreement. Article 12 of the Withdrawal Agreement clearly stipulates that "discrimination on grounds of nationality [...] shall be prohibited in the host State and the State of work" (Withdrawal Agreement 2020). Not only does it refer to Article 18 TFEU, but it also mirrors this article. As O'Brien notes, such wording in combination with Article 4(4) of the Withdrawal Agreement, which requires "provisions [...] referring to Union law or to concepts of provisions [to be interpreted] in conformity with the relevant case law of the Court of Justice of the European Union handed down before the end of the transition period," means that the effects of Article 18 TFEU, such as elaborated in

Trojani and *Grzelczyk* (see Sect. 2.3), are retained (O'Brien 2021, 465). Mirroring Article 24 of the Citizenship Directive, the principle of non-discrimination is reiterated in Article 23 in the form of "all Union citizens or United Kingdom nationals residing on the basis of this Agreement in the territory of the host State shall enjoy equal treatment with the nationals of that State within the scope of this Part."

The principle of non-discrimination is invoked again with respect to specific categories of individuals, namely workers (Article 24) and self-employed persons (Article 25). Article 24(1) of the Withdrawal Agreement specifies that, subject to limitations set out in Articles 45(3) and (4) TFEU, workers retain their rights under Article 45 TFEU and Regulation 492/2011 (Regulation (EU) No 492/2011 2011) and Article 25(1) provides that, subject to the limitations set out in Articles 51 and 52 TFEU, self-employed persons enjoy the rights guaranteed by Articles 49 and 55 TFEU.

This principle also applies to relatives of EU citizens in the UK and UK nationals in the EU27. First, Article 12 of the Withdrawal Agreement covers "the persons referred to in Article 10 of this Agreement", which includes family members under paragraph 1(e). Second, Article 23 second sentence specifies that "[t]he benefit of this right shall be extended to those family members of Union citizens or United Kingdom nationals who have the right of residence or permanent residence."

The limits of the principle of non-discrimination are those set out in the Citizenship Directive as Article 23 of the Withdrawal Agreement, which safeguards the principle of equal treatment, uses similar wording to that of Article 24(2) of the Citizenship Directive (Bernard 2020, 310–11). Indeed, its second paragraph reiterates that the host State shall neither be obliged to confer entitlement to social assistance during the first three months of residence (under Article 6 of the Citizenship Directive) or those who entered the territory to seek employment (under Article 14(4) of the Citizenship Directive) nor to "grant maintenance aid for studies, including vocational training, consisting in student grants or student loans to persons other than workers, self-employed persons, persons who retain such status or to members of their families" prior to a person's acquisition of the right to permanent residence as stipulated under Article 15 of the Withdrawal Agreement. Since, by definition, persons with permanent resident status under the Withdrawal Agreement do not fall within the scope of these exceptions, this Article allows them and their relatives to claim social assistance and student study grants on a par with nationals.

Undoubtedly, the principle of non-discrimination and the right to equal treatment have been preserved in the Withdrawal Agreement, both in the way they were stated in EU law and in the way they were enjoyed in practice by EU citizens before Brexit.

In contrast, the application of the principle of non-discrimination has changed, notably because EU citizens in the UK and UK nationals in the EU27 now hold different statuses and are thus required to prove their right to non-discrimination. Whereas previously, they did not need to obtain a national status to demonstrate equal access to jobs, social security, and education, they are now required to demonstrate that they were lawfully in the country to access work, education, and other services. In the UK, EU citizens must produce a share code, generated online, and UK nationals in the EU27 must exhibit a residence card. The introduction of an entirely electronic status in the UK caused several issues. In some instances, institutions such as local authorities and the Department for Work and Pensions as well as employers were unsure how to use it (Juverdeanu 2025, 289). Moreover, the process was rather complex from the standpoint of these institutions, employers, landlords, etc. A study conducted by the Public Law Project highlighted that the process undergone by a third party consisted of nine steps (Tomlinson and Welsh, n.d.). This added complexity and extra step may discourage third parties from engaging with EU citizens, thus leading to indirect discrimination. Already in 2020, the European Parliament expressed its concern that a digital proof might increase the risk of discrimination against prospective employees or tenants (European Parliament 2020, para. 10). Employers and landlords may choose not to hire EU citizens or rent their properties to them because they prefer to avoid the additional requirement of online verification (such as obtaining a share code) or fear they might inadvertently find themselves in an unlawful situation (see Barnard et al. 2024, 69). Such concern must be understood in the context of the UK's hostile environment policy that requires non-nationals to prove they are lawfully resident in the country for a variety of everyday activities (For an explanation of the concept of hostile environment, see Griffiths and Yeo 2021; Barnard et al. 2024, 63; Neville 2023, 5). This policy, intended to discourage illegal residence, is enforced by third parties such as public bodies, employers, landlords, and companies, who are required to verify a person's migration status (see Griffiths and Yeo 2021, 526–29; Neville 2023, 5). Failure to do so results in penalties.

EU citizens reported feeling the "rise of xenophobia linked to the Brexit process" (Sredanovic 2021, 99). In the UK, instances of everyday xenophobia increased following Brexit (Davies and Carter 2025, 164). In particular, EU citizens from Central and Eastern Europe, who had already experienced discrimination and been targeted by an "orientalist" discourse (Antonucci and Varriale 2020, 48), became targets of xenophobic attacks and nationalist rhetoric (Siklodi 2023, 1; Blachnicka-Ciacek and Budginaite-Mackine 2022, 1084). Brexit was compounded by a "hostile environment" policy that impacted all non-nationals, becoming "an amplification of longer-standing structural and institutional discrimination and everyday racism" (Benson and Lewis 2019, 2213; Blachnicka-Ciacek and Budginaite-Mackine 2022, 1083–84). Indeed, some studies indicate that Brexit deepened social divides related to race. For example, Davies and Carter report that non-white EU citizens experienced racist microaggressions linked to Brexit (Davies and Carter 2025, 164). Benson and Lewis show that for both British People of Colour in the EU27 and some EU citizens in the UK, there was a sense of continuation of racism and exclusion (Benson and Lewis 2019, 2224–25). Whilst these reports of xenophobia primarily involve incidents in public spaces, for example, individuals being asked about their accent, followed by a question on how long they plan to stay in the UK (Siklodi 2023, 11) or "Brexit-talk laced with implicit racism coming up at work" (Davies and Carter 2025, 164), there are fewer reports of incidents linked explicitly to discrimination. In 2019, some EU citizens with long-term residency in the UK struggled to access universal credit, mainly due to additional complexities introduced into the benefits system, which were spurred by concerns surrounding "benefit tourism" (Butler and Rankin 2019). EU citizens were incorrectly labelled as "no recourse to public funds" and so could not make claims to welfare benefits (Barnard et al. 2024, 64).

Information on whether UK nationals in the EU27 were or felt discriminated against is more sparse and often lacks specificity. In meetings of the Specialised Committee on Citizens' Rights, the UK expressed concern that UK nationals had difficulties accessing benefits and services, citing instances of discrimination on the grounds of nationality (Specialised Committee on Citizens' Rights 2021c; 2021a). This seemed to be particularly problematic in declaratory EU Member States, as UK nationals struggled to demonstrate that they were entitled to benefits and services (Specialised Committee on Citizens' Rights 2022a, 2022b, 2023c, 2023b). The UK questioned the application of the principle of equal treatment with respect to property rights and, more specifically, the purchase of property (Specialised Committee on Citizens' Rights 2022b, 2023c, 2023b). Information gathered in academic studies paints a mixed picture. For example, in a study carried out in Belgium, interviewees did not report any specific hostilities they had encountered (Sredanovic 2021, 102). On the other hand, Benson explains that white Britons in France encountered their first experience of "othering" (Benson 2020). Racism also played an important part in this process: non-white Britons in the EU (e.g., in Germany (Kulz 2023, 225)) reported experiencing racism, partially exacerbated by Brexit (Benson and Lewis 2019).

Overall, Brexit has not challenged the principle of non-discrimination and equal treatment that, in combination with other rights, gives EU citizenship its transformative value. The *rights* and the *practice* of non-discrimination have been recognised; nonetheless, the practice is threatened by the introduction of a status rooted in immigration law and everyday encounters of xenophobia, some of which are exacerbated by racial prejudice.

5.4 The Right to Vote in and Stand for Elections

A notable right that contributes to the transformative value of EU citizenship, namely voting rights and the right to stand in elections, is completely absent from the Withdrawal Agreement. Such rights have not been recognised. In fact, more fundamentally, Article 127(1)(b) (Withdrawal Agreement 2020) clarifies that such rights were not granted even during the transition period. At first sight, such a hard stance might seem perplexing.

First, it is a fundamental right enshrined in Articles 39 and 40 of the Charter of Fundamental Rights of the European Union (EU CFR 2012); yet, Article 127(1)(b) of the Withdrawal Agreement expressly specifies that these two articles are not applicable, including during the transition period. It was contended that a closer examination of Article 127(1) revealed that EU law applied "to and in the United Kingdom" which seemed to indicate that this article did not apply outside the territory of the UK (see Fouchet 2020, 3–4; see argument by appellant *438696* 2020), an argument refuted by the French Conseil d'Etat (*Case Nr 438696* 2020, ¶ 4) and the CJEU, pointing out that this provision must be read in conjunction with Article 127(6) of the Withdrawal Agreement, which provides: "Unless otherwise provided in this Agreement, during the transition period, any reference to Member States in the Union law applicable pursuant to paragraph 1, including as implemented and applied by Member States, shall be understood as including the United Kingdom" (*Case C-673/20 E.P. v. Préfet du Gers* 2022b, ¶¶ 69–70). Therefore, Member States are no longer obliged to give British nationals the right to vote and stand as candidates in municipal elections (*Case C-673/20 E.P. v. Préfet du Gers* 2022b, ¶ 71; see Shuibhne 2023, 487).

Second, pursuant to the preamble to Directive 94/80/CE, the right to vote and to stand as a candidate in local elections "is an instance of the application of the principle of equality and non-discrimination between nationals and non-nationals and a corollary of the right to move and reside freely […]" (Council Directive 94/80/EC 1994; see Anglmayer 2021, 2). Since both the principle of equality and non-discrimination between nationals and non-nationals and the right to residence have been preserved in the Withdrawal Agreement, it is, to some extent, surprising that it was not maintained as well. However, as the Court correctly points out, the principle of non-discrimination as encapsulated in the Withdrawal Agreement only covers the rights listed in Part II of that agreement (*Case C-673/20 E.P. v. Préfet du Gers* 2022b, ¶ 76), which does not include the right to vote and to stand as a candidate in municipal elections (*Case C-673/20 E.P. v. Préfet du Gers* 2022b, ¶ 77). Thus, it was clear to the negotiators that the right to vote and stand in elections was not a non-discrimination right.

Yet, such a stance is not particularly perplexing because the EU treaties reserve the right to vote and to stand as a candidate in municipal elections exclusively to EU citizens, and there is no legal basis in the Treaties that would grant EU institutions the power to confer the right to vote on third-country nationals (European Commission 2017, preamble ¶ 3). As the Court of Justice of the European Union stated, it is within the competences of the EU Member States to grant foreign nationals a right to vote and to stand as candidates (*Case C-673/20 E.P. v. Préfet du Gers* 2022b, ¶ 82). Moreover, the EU only enters into international agreements on the basis of reciprocity and mutual advantages and is thus "not required to grant, unilaterally, third-country nationals rights such as the right to vote and to stand as a candidate in municipal elections in the Member State of residence" (*Case C-673/20 E.P. v. Préfet du Gers* 2022b, ¶ 99). However, as the Advocate General Collins noted in his Opinion in the *Préfet du Gers* case, the decision was ultimately a political choice made by the UK that did not seek to grant voting rights to its nationals residing in the EU27 in exchange for granting reciprocal rights to EU citizens in the UK (*Case C-673/20 EP v. Préfet du Gers (A.G.)* 2022a, ¶ 73). As a result, voting rights are now prescribed solely at the national level.

In the UK, the eligibility rules regarding the right to vote in local and devolved elections hinge upon the place where a person lives. Roughly, the electoral system is divided into three: England and Northern Ireland, Scotland, and Wales. In the latter two, since any legally resident foreign national is allowed to vote, Brexit did not affect EU citizens, who can still vote in local elections and either the Scottish Parliament or the Senedd Cymru elections. In England and Wales, following the Elections Act 2022 amending the Representation of the People Act 1983 1983, two categories of EU citizens are eligible to vote:

1. "EU citizens with retained rights", i.e., those who were lawfully resident in the UK before 1 January 2020, had permission to enter or stay in the UK and have remained resident without a break (RPA 1983, § 203B) and
2. citizens of countries with which the UK has a bilateral agreement (i.e., Denmark (Agreement between UK and Denmark 2024), Luxembourg (Agreement between UK and Luxembourg 2019), Poland (Agreement between UK and Poland 2020), Portugal (Agreement between UK and Portugal 2019), and Spain (Agreement between UK and Spain 2019)) who are resident in the UK and have permission to enter or stay in the UK (RPA 1983, § 203A).

The fact that England and Northern Ireland distinguish between EU citizens who were in the UK before the end of the transition period of the Withdrawal Agreement shows that the UK made true its declaration in a policy paper dated June 2021 to respect "the rights of EU citizens who chose to make their home in the UK before this change" (UK Government 2021, pt. 1.2). As the explanatory notes to the Elections Act 2022 explain, "[t]he policy intention is to provide continuity in relation to the voting and candidacy rights of EU citizens who have been living in the UK since before Implementation Period Completion Day [...] and who hold lawful immigration status" (*Elections Act 2022, Explanatory Note* 2022, ¶ 456). Furthermore, it is worth noting that EU citizens in both categories are also eligible to be candidates in local elections. In taking this decision, the UK noted that this "mirrors the stance taken on the EU Settlement Scheme" and, rightfully, that it "goes beyond our obligations in the Withdrawal Agreement" ('Statement by Chloe Smith, Minister of State for the Constitution and Devolution; Statement UIN HCWS99' 2021). That being said, to vote, one must register with the local authority. The latest data (dated 2022) from the Electoral Commission shows that whilst 87% of UK/Irish nationals eligible to vote were registered to vote, this fell to only 68% for EU citizens (Electoral Commission, n.d.). The Migration Observatory surmises that this might be because of a lack of information about the electoral process, difficulties with registration owing to linguistic or bureaucratic barriers, the belief that registration is automatic (as it is often the case in EU Member States), or simply that EU citizens planning to return to their country of origin do not see the benefit of registering (Cuibus 2025). There is, however, no data on whether EU citizens go and vote (Cuibus 2025). Undoubtedly, the UK has acknowledged the *practice* of EU citizenship of long-term residents and therefore (at least one of the elements of) the transformative value of EU citizenship.

This stands in contrast to UK nationals in the EU27 who have lost the right to vote and stand in local elections unless either an agreement has been concluded between the UK and EU Member States (e.g., Spain, Portugal, Luxembourg, and Poland (Johnston 2022, 34)) or national legislation of EU Member States allows non-EU citizens to vote in local elections. With regard to the former, the UK has continued to invite EU Member States to enter into such agreements, hoping that these "measures [...] ensure that British nationals living overseas in the EU benefit from the Government's approach" ('Statement by Chloe Smith, Minister of State for the Constitution and Devolution; Statement UIN HCWS99' 2021). Whilst an agreement could be struck, no agreement could be made with France and Germany (Anglmayer 2021, 5). With regard to the second option, as the CJEU acknowledges, Member States are free "to grant, under conditions which they lay down in their national law, a right to vote and to stand as a candidate to nationals of a third State residing in their territory" (*Case C-673/20 E.P. v. Préfet du Gers* 2022b, ¶ 82). In that case, the State often requires individuals to fulfil certain requirements, usually related to residency (e.g., Belgium, Denmark, Estonia, Finland, Ireland, Lithuania, Netherlands, Slovakia, Slovenia, and Sweden (Johnston 2022, 34)) to show some form of integration. Belgium, Estonia, Finland, Hungary, the Netherlands, Lithuania, Slovenia, Slovakia, and Sweden allow legally resident foreigners to register for local elections, though not all allow them to stand as candidates (Anglmayer 2021, 6; see Cîrlig 2020, 16–17). Unfortunately, by the end of 2021, the overwhelming majority of UK nationals in the EU27 resided either in Spain (estimated 430,000 with 187,000 residence applications), France (estimated 148,000 with 165,000 residence applications), or Germany (estimated 85,000 though no data available for the number of residence applications) (data available at Specialised Committee on Citizens' Rights 2022c, 35–36))[2] and only Spain allows, on the basis of an agreement with the UK, UK nationals to exercise their right to vote and stand in local elections. This means that a large portion of UK nationals have lost their right to vote. A survey conducted in 2021–2022 revealed that 46% of UK nationals had no voting rights in their host country (Benson et al. 2022, 12). In France, under Articles L227, L230, and L236 of the Electoral Code (Code electoral, n.d.), 42,500 British nationals lost their right to vote (French Ministry of Interior 2020, ¶ 1.2) and to stand in local elections on 1 February 2020 (French Ministry of Interior 2020, ¶ 1.3). Interestingly, however, the 766 British local councillors (Fouchet 2020, 2) kept their seat until their term ended (in fact until 15 and 22 March, which were the dates of the next elections in that year) and were not decommissioned on Brexit day (French Ministry of Interior 2019, 2020, ¶ 1.4; *438696* 2020, ¶ 6). This disenfranchisement is quite problematic in the West and South of France, where some villages have a majority of British nationals (Wihtol de Wenden 2019, 38) and are thus now unable to be and feel part of the local community. In other words, they are completely disenfranchised from local elections in the EU Member State in which they reside. The fact that the overwhelming majority of the cases brought before the CJEU in relation to Brexit are linked to the loss of the right to vote (*Case C-673/20 E.P. v. Préfet du Gers* 2022b; *Case C-499/21 P Silver* 2023; *Case C-502/21 P Price* 2023; *Case C-501/21 P Shindler* 2023) is rather revealing of how disenfranchised UK nationals in the EU27 felt. Ferbrache, however, notes that though UK nationals have tried to reclaim this right as part of their EU citizenship, local voting rights "have not featured as distinctly within such efforts as, for example, claims for free movement rights and cross-border health care" (Ferbrache 2019b, 516).

[2] It should be noted that the estimated number of UK residents in Ireland was 115,000, but the situation of Irish nationals is caught by a different legal framework.

In summary, the analysis of the impact of Brexit on the right to vote and stand for elections, one of the key elements that gives EU citizenship its transformative value, reveals a mixed picture. The UK and the EU have, through the Withdrawal Agreement, removed this right from EU citizens in the UK and UK nationals in the EU27. Yet, whilst the UK has acknowledged its significance in *practice* by allowing long-term EU citizens the right to vote and to stand in elections, the EU has not extended this right to UK nationals in the EU27, as it has no powers to do so. Consequently, the "responsibility" fell on the Member States, some of which disenfranchised them and, accordingly, failed to recognise the importance of this *practice* and thus the transformative value of EU citizenship.

5.5 Conclusion

Over decades, the EU has "confer[red] upon [EU citizens] rights which [have] become part of their legal heritage" (*Case 26–62 van Gend & Loos* 1963, 12). Some of these rights, as the authors argued in Sect. 3.3, have led to the transformative value of the EU citizenship. An examination of the measures relating to Brexit demonstrates that these rights and the way they have been practised have largely been maintained, thus reinforcing the argument that EU citizenship is truly transformative. As Marrero Gonzalez explained already in 2016, "whilst EU citizenship is not autonomous from Member State nationality, certain rights associated to the residence in both the United Kingdom and the EU Member States can be frozen" (González 2016, 798) and in fact were, to some extent, frozen.

Regarding residence, its *right* has been retained in the Withdrawal Agreement and its *practice* in the UK too, as seen in the EU Settlement Scheme, which covers individuals who do not meet the strict legal requirements of the Agreement but are covered by CJEU jurisprudence. The sore point is that Brexit has remigranticised EU citizens in the UK and UK nationals in the EU27, both legally and mentally. The principle of non-discrimination as a *right* is solidly anchored in the Withdrawal Agreement, and its *practice* recognised in law. However, experience shows that post-Brexit, some forms of indirect discrimination are occurring. With regard to the right to vote and stand for local elections, although the Withdrawal Agreement does not retain this *right* and thus also its *practice*, the UK has recognised its *practice* by allowing EU citizens (albeit with some conditions) to vote and stand in local elections. In contrast, UK nationals in the EU27 have lost that *right* and *practice* unless EU Member States allow foreign nationals to vote and stand in elections, or their host State has signed an agreement with the UK regarding this matter.

A key point to note is the disparity in the level of recognition of the transformative value of EU citizenship between the UK and EU Member States. Espousing a broad approach in adopting a range of measures implementing the Withdrawal Agreement, the UK has kept for EU permanent residents not only the most important *rights* related to EU citizenship but also the *practice* of EU citizenship. In doing this, it has truly recognised the transformative value of EU citizenship. In contrast, by strictly adhering to the Withdrawal Agreement, EU Member States have acknowledged the *rights* related to EU citizenship, but in many instances not its *practice*. Indeed, UK nationals who experienced and enjoyed EU citizenship by living in another EU country but failed to meet the residence requirements set out in the Treaty and the Citizenship Directive have been unable to obtain the *right* to stay in their host States. In addition, UK nationals have been deprived of the right to vote and stand in elections (barring some exceptions). For UK nationals residing in an EU Member State, the most significant loss is certainly that of intra-European mobility as they are treated as third-country nationals and subject to the same limitations to free movement rights within the EU as this category of nationals (see More 2020, 469).

Using Brexit as a benchmark, this chapter has confirmed the transformative value of EU citizenship. This stands in contrast to other scholars who view Brexit as a return to a market citizenship conception of EU citizenship (see Juverdeanu 2025). For example, More contends that "Brexit underlines that market citizenship [...] remains indeed a fundamental aspect of EU citizenship" (More 2020, 481). Indeed, it might be contended that the Withdrawal Agreement, as such, reflects to some extent a market citizen approach; as O'Brien states, there is a "worrying signal that EU institutions do not consider the status of EU citizenship, acts of integration, or personal circumstances beyond the economic, to be relevant" (O'Brien 2021, 468). Yet, the measures adopted by the UK, as outlined in this chapter, prove that there is more to EU citizenship than that. The next chapter, which focuses on the emergence of pro-EU movements, attempts to establish an associate EU citizenship and naturalisation, further reinforces the claim about the transformative value of EU citizenship.

References

Acosta Arcarazo, Diego. 2015. Civic Citizenship Reintroduced? The Long-Term Residence Directive as a Post-National Form of Membership. *European Law Journal* 21 (2): 200–219. https://doi.org/10.1111/eulj.12112.

Agreement between the United Kingdom of Great Britain and Northern Ireland and the Grand Duchy of Luxembourg on the Participation in Certain Elections of Nationals of Each Country Resident in the Territory of the Other. 2019. https://assets.publishing.service.gov.uk/media/668e4063ab5fc5929851bd4c/TS_46.2024_UK_Luxembourg_Agreement_Participation_Certain_Elections_Nationals_Resident_Territory_Other.pdf.

Agreement between the United Kingdom of Great Britain and Northern Ireland and the Kingdom of Denmark on the Participation in Certain Elections of Nationals of Each Country Resident in the Territory of the Other. 2024. https://assets.publishing.service.gov.uk/media/6762c1d5ff2c870561bde792/TS_99.2024_UK_Denmark_Agreement_Elections_Nationals_Each_Country_Resident_Territory.pdf.

Agreement between the United Kingdom of Great Britain and Northern Ireland and the Kingdom of Spain on the Participation in Certain Elections of Nationals of Each Country Resident in the Territory of the Other. 2019. https://assets.publishing.service.gov.uk/media/6419b235d3bf7f7ff7d3b3c4/TS_12.2023_UK_Spain_Agreement_Certain_Elections_Each_Country_Residents_Territory.pdf.

Agreement between the United Kingdom of Great Britain and Northern Ireland and the Portuguese Republic Regarding the Participation in Local Elections of Nationals of Each State Resident in the Other's Territory. 2019. https://assets.publishing.service.gov.uk/media/667ebb8a97ea0c79abfe4d88/TS_44.2024_UK_Portugal_Agreement_Participation_Local_Elections_Nationals_Resident_Others_Territory.pdf.

Agreement between the United Kingdom of Great Britain and Northern Ireland and the Republic of Poland on the Participation in Certain Elections of Nationals of Each Country Resident in the Territory of the Other. 2020. https://assets.publishing.service.gov.uk/media/664c76eb993111924d9d38aa/TS_34.2024_UK_Poland_Agreement_Participation_Elections_Nationals_Resident_Territory.pdf.

Agreement on the Withdrawal of the United Kingdom of Great Britain and Northern Ireland from the European Union and the European Atomic Energy Community, OJ L 29/7. 2020. https://eur-lex.europa.eu/legal-content/EN/TXT/?uri=CELEX%3A02020W%2FTXT-20250430.

Anglmayer, Irmgard. 2021. Voting and Candidacy Rights of Mobile EU Citizens in Municipal Elections under Directive 94/80/EC. European Parliamentary Research Service. https://www.europarl.europa.eu/RegData/etudes/BRIE/2021/694233/EPRS_BRI(2021)694233_EN.pdf.

Antonucci, Lorenza, and Simone Varriale. 2020. Unequal Europe, Unequal Brexit: How Intra-European Inequalities Shape the Unfolding and Framing of Brexit. *Current Sociology* 68 (1): 41–59. https://doi.org/10.1177/0011392119863837.

Barnard, Catherine, Sarah Fraser Butlin, and Fiona Costello. 2022. The Changing Status of European Union Nationals in the United Kingdom Following Brexit: The Lived Experience of the European Union Settlement Scheme. *Social & Legal Studies* 31 (3): 365–388. https://doi.org/10.1177/09646639211032337.

Barnard, Catherine, Fiona Costello, and Fraser Butlin. 2024. *Low-Paid EU Migrant Workers: The House, the Street, the Town*, Bristol Studies in Law and Social Justice. Bristol University Press.

Becker, Michael A. 2004. Managing Diversity in the European Union: Inclusive European Citizenship and Third-Country Nationals. *Yale Human Rights & Development Law Journal* 7:132–183.

Benson, Michaela. 2019. Brexit and Rethinking the British in Europe. Discover Society, February 6. https://archive.discoversociety.org/2019/02/06/focus-brexit-and-rethinking-the-british-in-europe/.

Benson, Michaela. 2020. Brexit and the Classed Politics of Bordering: The British in France and European Belongings. *Sociology* 54 (3): 501–517. https://doi.org/10.1177/0038038519885300.

Benson, Michaela, and Chantelle Lewis. 2019. Brexit, British People of Colour in the EU-27 and Everyday Racism in Britain and Europe. *Ethnic and Racial Studies* 42 (13): 2211–2228. https://doi.org/10.1080/01419870.2019.1599134.

Benson, Michaela, Elena Zambelli, Catherine Craven, and Nando Sigona. 2022. British Citizens in the EU after Brexit. No. 1. MIGZEN Research Brief. https://migzen.net/site/assets/files/1402/benson_et_al__2022_british_citizens_in_the_eu_after_brexit.pdf.

Bernard, Nicolas. 2020. Union Citizens' Rights Against Their Own Member State after Brexit. *Maastricht Journal of European and Comparative Law* 27 (3): 302–324. https://doi.org/10.1177/1023263X20908761.

Blachnicka-Ciacek, Dominika, and Irma Budginaite-Mackine. 2022. The Ambiguous Lives of "the Other Whites": Class and Racialisation of Eastern European Migrants in the UK. *The Sociological Review* 70 (6): 1081–1099. https://doi.org/10.1177/00380261221121218.

Border Security, Asylum and Immigration Act 2025. n.d. Accessed 2 January 2026. https://www.legislation.gov.uk/ukpga/2025/31.

Botterill, Kate. 2018. Rethinking "Community" Relationally: Polish Communities in Scotland before and after Brexit. *Transactions of the Institute of British Geographers* 43 (4): 540–554. https://doi.org/10.1111/tran.12249.

Brahic, Benedicte, and Maxime Lallement. 2020. From "Expats" to "Migrants": Strategies of Resilience Among French Movers in Post-Brexit Manchester. *Migration and Development* 9 (1): 8–24. https://doi.org/10.1080/21632324.2018.1503486.

Brändle, Verena K., Charlotte Galpin, and Hans-Jörg Trenz. 2018. Marching for Europe? Enacting European Citizenship as Justice During Brexit. *Citizenship Studies* 22 (8): 810–828. https://doi.org/10.1080/13621025.2018.1531825.

Butler, Patrick, and Jennifer Rankin. 2019. Surge in EU Citizens Unfairly Refused Access to Universal Credit. Society. *The Guardian*, August 5. https://www.theguardian.com/society/2019/aug/05/surge-in-eu-citizens-unfairly-refused-access-to-universal-credit.

Cambien, Nathan. 2018. Residence Rights for EU Citizens and their Family Members: Navigating the New Normal. *European Papers – A Journal on Law and Integration* 3 (3): 1333–1352.

Carrera, Sergio, and Davide Colombi. 2025. Irregularising Human Mobility. *EU Migration Policies and the European Commission's Role.* SpringerBriefs in Law. Springer. https://i-claim.eu/project/irregularising-human-mobility/.

Case 26/62. 1963. N.V. Algemene Transport- En Expeditie Onderneming van Gend & Loos v. Netherlands Inland Revenue Administration, ECLI:EU:C:1963:1 (ECJ).

Case C-246/17. 2018. Ibrahima Diallo v. Belgium, ECLI:EU:C:2018:499 (CJEU).

Case C-325/09. 2011. Secretary of State for Work and Pensions v. Maria Dias, ECLI:EU:C:2011:498 (CJEU).

Case C-499/21 P. 2023. Joshua David Silver and Others vCouncil of the European Union, ECLI:EU:C:2023:479 (CJEU).

Case C-501/21 P. 2023. Harry Shindler and Others v. Council, ECLI:EU:C:2023:480 (CJEU).

Case C-502/21 P. 2023. David Price v. Council, ECLI:EU:C:2023:482 (CJEU).

Case C-673/20. 2022a. E.P. v. Préfet Du Gers and Institut National de La Statistique et Des Études Économiques (INSEE), ECLI:EU:C:2022:129 (Advocate General Collins).

Case C-673/20. 2022b. E.P. v. Préfet Du Gers and Institut National de La Statistique et Des Études Économiques (INSEE), ECLI:EU:C:2022:449 (CJEU).

Case C-709/20. 2021. C.G. v. The Department for Communities in Northern Ireland, ECLI:EU:C:2021:602 (CJEU).

Case Nr 438696, ECLI:FR:CEORD:2020:438696.20200221. 2020. (Conseil d'Etat, Juge des référés).

Charter of Fundamental Rights of the European Union, OJEU C326/391. 2012. http://data.europa.eu/eli/treaty/char_2012/oj/eng.

Cîrlig, Carmen-Cristina. 2020. EU and UK Citizens' Rights after Brexit: An Overview. PE 651.975. European Parliamentary Research Service. https://www.europarl.europa.eu/RegData/etudes/IDAN/2020/651975/EPRS_IDA(2020)651975_EN.pdf.

Code electoral. n.d. Accessed 3 January 2026. https://www.legifrance.gouv.fr/codes/texte_lc/LEGITEXT000006070239/.

Commission Implementing Decision on Documents to Be Issued by Member States Pursuant to Article 18(1) and (4) and Article 26 of the Agreement on the Withdrawal of the United Kingdom of Great Britain and Northern Ireland from the European Union and the European Atomic Energy Community, C(2020) 1114 final. 2020.

Consolidated Version of Treaty on the Functioning of the European Union (Lisbon). 2025. http://data.europa.eu/eli/treaty/tfeu_2016/2025-03-15.

Convention for the Protection of Human Rights and Fundamental Freedoms, CETS No. 213. 1950.

Council Directive 2003/109/EC of 25 November 2003 Concerning the Status of Third-Country Nationals Who Are Long-Term Residents, OJ L16/44. 2003.

Council Directive 94/80/EC of 19 December 1994 Laying Down Detailed Arrangements for the Exercise of the Right to Vote and to Stand as a Candidate in Municipal Elections by Citizens of the Union Residing in a Member State of Which They Are Not Nationals, OJ L368/38. 1994.

Cuibus, Mihnea. 2025. Voting Rights of EU Citizens Living in the UK after Brexit. Migration Observatory. https://migrationobservatory.ox.ac.uk/resources/briefings/voting-rights-of-eu-citizens-living-in-the-uk-after-brexit/.

D'Angelo, Alessio, and Eleonore Kofman. 2018. From Mobile Workers to Fellow Citizens and Back Again? The Future Status of EU Citizens in the UK. *Social Policy and Society* 17 (2): 331–343. https://doi.org/10.1017/S1474746417000495.

Dadomo, Christian, and Noëlle Quénivet. 2020. *European Union Law*. 3rd ed. Hall & Stott Publishing.

Davies, Katherine, and Adam Carter. 2025. Living with Brexit: Families, Relationships and the Temporalities of Everyday Personal Life in "Brexit Britain". *The Sociological Review* 73 (1): 156–174. https://doi.org/10.1177/00380261241260112.

Directive 2004/38/EC of the European Parliament and the of the Council of 29 April 2004 on the Rights of Citizens of the Union and Their Family Members to Move and Reside Freely within the Territory of the Member States Amending Regulation (EEC) No 1612/68 and Repealing Directives 64/221/EEC,

68/360/EEC, 72/194/EEC, 73/148/EEC, 75/34/EEC, 75/35/EEC, 90/364/EEC, 90/365/EEC, and 93/96/EEC, OJ L158/77. 2024.

Dougan, Michael. 2020. So Long, Farewell, Auf Wiedersehen, Goodbye: The UK's Withdrawal Package. *Common Market Law Review* 57:631–704. https://doi.org/10.54648/cola2020689.

Elections Act 2022, Explanatory Note. 2022. https://www.legislation.gov.uk/ukpga/2022/37/notes/division/7/index.htm.

Electoral Commission. n.d. Explore the Data: Who Is and Isn't Registered to Vote? Accessed 3 January 2026. https://www.electoralcommission.org.uk/research-reports-and-data/electoral-registration-research/explore-data-who-and-isnt-registered-vote.

EU Settlement Scheme: Person with a Zambrano Right to Reside, Version 8.0. 2023. https://assets.publishing.service.gov.uk/media/64dce0de3fde610013 4a53a8/EU_Settlement_Scheme_person_with_a_Zambrano_right_to_reside.pdf.

European Commission. 2017. *Decision on the Proposed Citizens' Initiative Entitled 'EU Citizenship for Europeans: United in Diversity in Spite of Jus Soli and Jus Sanguinis' C(2017) 2001.* [2017] OJEU C81/18.

European Commission. 2020. EU Citizenship Report 2020—Empowering Citizens and Protecting Their Rights. https://commission.europa.eu/document/download/691e7b42-fcac-4ebf-9327-dd50b36b1b66_en?filename=eu_citizenship_report_2020_-_empowering_citizens_and_protecting_their_rights_en.pdf.

European Parliament. 2020. Resolution on Implementing and Monitoring the Provisions on Citizens' Rights in the Withdrawal Agreement. January 15. https://www.europarl.europa.eu/doceo/document/TA-9-2020-0006_EN.html.

Ferbrache, Fiona. 2019a. Acts of European Citizenship: How Britons Resident in France Have Been Negotiating Post-Brexit Futures. *Geography* 104 (2): 81–88. https://doi.org/10.1080/00167487.2019.12094067.

Ferbrache, Fiona. 2019b. Local Electoral Rights for Non-French Residents? A Case-Study Analysis of British Candidates and Councillors in French Municipal Elections. *Citizenship Studies* 23 (5): 502–520. https://doi.org/10.1080/13621025.2019.1623864.

Fouchet, Julien. 2020. *Quand le Brexit s'invite aux élections municipales.* No. 2/2020. Blog Droit Européen. https://hal.science/hal-03468914v1/document.

French Ministry of Interior. 2019. Statute of British Local Councillors: Response to Question by Senator Goulet. Sénat, July 4. https://www.senat.fr/questions/base/2017/qSEQ170700312.html.

French Ministry of Interior. 2020. Letter to the Prefects and High Commissioners. INTA2001816J. January 23. https://www.haute-marne.gouv.fr/content/download/14454/96456/file/Instruction%20BREXIT%20INTA2001816J.pdf.

Garner, Oliver. 2016. After Brexit: Protecting European Citizens and Citizenship from Fragmentation. LAW 2016/22. EUI Working Papers. European University Institute—Department of Law.

Giner-Monfort, Jordi. 2018. End to Dream? British Retired Residents in Spain and Their Return Patterns. *Journal of Spatial and Organizational Dynamics* 6 (4): 360–374.

Giner-Monfort, Jordi, and Raquel Huete. 2021. Uncertain Sunset Lives: British Migrants Facing Brexit in Spain. *European Urban and Regional Studies* 28 (1): 74–79. https://doi.org/10.1177/0969776420972148.

Godin, Marie, and Nando Sigona. 2022. Intergenerational Narratives of Citizenship among EU Citizens in the UK after the Brexit Referendum. *Ethnic and Racial Studies* 45 (6): 1135–1154. https://doi.org/10.1080/01419870.2021.1981964.

González, Guayasén Marrero. 2016. "Brexit": Consequences for Citizenship of the Union and Residence Rights. *Maastricht Journal of European and Comparative Law* 23 (5): 796–811. https://doi.org/10.1177/1023263x1602300504.

GOV.UK. n.d. Implementation of Section 45 of the Border Security, Asylum and Immigration Act 2025. Accessed 2 January 2026. https://www.gov.uk/government/publications/border-security-asylum-and-immigration-act-2025-section-45/implementation-of-section-45-of-the-border-security-asylum-and-immigration-act-2025.

Gove, Michael. 2020. Citizens' Rights in the Withdrawal Agreement. May 14. https://assets.publishing.service.gov.uk/government/uploads/system/uploads/attachment_data/file/885252/200514_Letter_from_Rt_Hon_Michael_Gove_MP_to_VP_Sefcovic.pdf.

Griffiths, Melanie, and Colin Yeo. 2021. The UK's Hostile Environment: Deputising Immigration Control. *Critical Social Policy* 41 (4): 521–544. https://doi.org/10.1177/0261018320980653.

Guidance Note Relating to the Agreement on the Withdrawal of the United Kingdom of Great Britain and Northern Ireland from the European Union and the European Atomic Energy Community Part Two—Citizens' Rights, OJ 2020/C 173/01. 2020.

Guma, Taulant, and Rhys Dafydd Jones. 2019. "Where Are We Going to Go Now?" European Union Migrants' Experiences of Hostility, Anxiety, and (Non-)Belonging During Brexit. *Population, Space and Place* 25 (1): e2198. https://doi.org/10.1002/psp.2198.

Henley, Jon. 2023. 'Brexit: Thousands of Britons Expelled from EU Since End of Transition Period'. Politics. *The Guardian*, January 6. https://www.theguardian.com/politics/2023/jan/06/brexit-thousands-britons-expelled-eu.

Immigration Law Practitioners' Association. 2016. Written Evidence (AQR0004) to the House of Lords, European Union Committee, Brexit: Acquired Rights,

10th Report of Session 2016–17. http://data.parliament.uk/writtenevidence/committeeevidence.svc/evidencedocument/eu-justice-subcommittee/brexit-acquired-rights/written/39772.html.

Immigration Rules Appendix EU. 2025. https://www.gov.uk/guidance/immigration-rules/immigration-rules-appendix-eu.

Johnston, Neil. 2022. Who Can Vote in UK Elections? House of Commons Library. House of Commons. https://researchbriefings.files.parliament.uk/documents/CBP-8985/CBP-8985.pdf.

Joined Cases C-424/10 and C-425/10. 2011. Tomasz Ziolkowski and Others and Marlon Szeja v. Land Berlin, ECLI:EU:C:2011:866 (CJEU).

Juverdeanu, Cristina. 2025. Brexit and the EU Settlement Scheme: Continuity and Rupture with the European Union. *Journal of Contemporary European Studies* 33 (1): 278–293. https://doi.org/10.1080/14782804.2024.2372677.

Kochenov, Dimitry. 2013. The Essence of EU Citizenship Emerging from the Last Ten Years of Academic Debate: Beyond the Cherry Blossoms and the Moon? *International and Comparative Law Quarterly* 62 (1): 97–136. https://doi.org/10.1017/S0020589312000589.

Kochenov, Dimitry. 2016. *EU Citizenship and Withdrawals from the Union: How Inevitable Is the Radical Downgrading of Rights?* No. 111/2016. London School of Economics and Political Science Paper. London School of Economics and Political Science. https://aei.pitt.edu/93637/1/LEQSPaper111.pdf.

Kostakopoulou, Dora. 2018. Scala Civium: Citizenship Templates Post-Brexit and the European Union's Duty to Protect EU Citizens. *Journal of Common Market Studies* 56 (4): 854–869. https://doi.org/10.1111/jcms.12683.

Kulz, Christy. 2023. Spaces of the Local, Spaces of the Nation: Intersectional Bordering Practices in Post-Brexit Berlin. *European Urban and Regional Studies* 30 (3): 221–234. https://doi.org/10.1177/09697764221087644.

Lulle, Aija, Russell King, Veronika Dvorakova, and Aleksandra Szkudlarek. 2019. Between Disruptions and Connections: "New" European Union Migrants in the United Kingdom Before and after the Brexit. *Population, Space and Place* 25 (1): e2200. https://doi.org/10.1002/psp.2200.

Maas, Willem. 2021. European Citizenship in the Ongoing Brexit Process. *International Studies* 58 (2): 168–183. https://doi.org/10.1177/00208817211002008.

More, Gillian. 2020. From Union Citizen to Third-Country National: Brexit, the UK Withdrawal Agreement, No-Deal Preparations and Britons Living in the European Union. In *European Citizenship under Stress—Social Justice, Brexit and Other Challenges*, ed. Nathan Cambien, Dimitry Kochenov, and Elise Muir. Brill.

Mourão Permoser, Julia. 2017. Redefining Membership: Restrictive Rights and Categorisation in European Union Migration Policy. *Journal of Ethnic and Migration Studies* 43 (15): 2536–2555. https://doi.org/10.1080/1369183X.2017.1301202.

Neville, Ann. 2023. Update on the Implementation of the Citizens' Rights Provisions of the Withdrawal Agreement. PE 739.351. European Parliamentary Research Service. https://www.europarl.europa.eu/RegData/etudes/BRIE/2023/739351/EPRS_BRI(2023)739351_EN.pdf.

O'Brien, Charlotte. 2021. Between the Devil and the Deep Blue Sea: Vulnerable EU Citizens Cast Adrift in the UK Post-Brexit. *Common Market Law Review* 58 (2): 432–470. https://doi.org/10.54648/cola2021025.

O'Carroll, Lisa, and Michael Goodier. 2023. Fivefold Rise in Number of EU Citizens Fefused Entry to UK Since Brexit. *The Guardian*, November 25. https://www.theguardian.com/uk-news/2023/nov/25/fivefold-rise-number-eu-citizens-refused-entry-uk-since-brexit.

Olorunfunmilayo Oluwaseun Akinsanya & Naomi Anin-Adjei. 2024. (On the Application Of) v. Secretary of State for the Home Department, EWHC 469 (Admin) (UK High Court).

Olorunfunmilayo Oluwaseun Akinsanya and Secretary of State for the Home Department. 2022. EWCA Civ 37 (UK Court of Appeal (Civil Division).

Peers, Steve. 2021. The End - or a New Beginning? The EU/UK Withdrawal Agreement. *Yearbook of European Law* 39 (March): 122–198. https://doi.org/10.1093/yel/yeaa010.

Porchia, Ornella. 2019. Citizens' Rights in the Post Brexit Scenario. *ERA Forum* 19 (4): 585–595. https://doi.org/10.1007/s12027-018-0545-0.

Ranta, Ronald, and Nevena Nancheva. 2019. Unsettled: Brexit and European Union Nationals' Sense of Belonging. *Population, Space and Place* 25 (1): e2199. https://doi.org/10.1002/psp.2199.

Regulation (EU) No 492/2011 of the European Parliament and of the Council of 5 April 2011 on Freedom of Movement for Workers within the Union, OJ L141/1. 2011.

Representation of the People Act 1983. 1983. https://www.legislation.gov.uk/ukpga/1983/2/introduction.

Shuibhne, Niamh Nic. 2023. Protecting the Legal Heritage of Former Union Citizens: EP v Préfet Du Gers. *Common Market Law Review* 60 (2): 475–516. https://doi.org/10.54648/cola2023028.

Siklodi, Nora. 2023. (Br)Exit Citizenship: Belonging, Rights and Participation. *Journal of Contemporary European Studies*, December 26, 1–17. https://doi.org/10.1080/14782804.2023.2298330.

Smismans, Stijn. 2018. EU Citizens' Rights Post Brexit: Why Direct Effect Beyond the EU Is Not Enough. *European Constitutional Law Review* 14 (3): 443–474. https://doi.org/10.1017/S1574019618000317.

Spaventa, Eleanor. 2017. *The Impact of Brexit in Relation to the Right to Petition and on the Competences, Responsibilities and Activities of the Committee on Petitions*. Research Paper for the European Parliament. European Parliament, Policy Department for Citizens' Rights and Constitutional Affairs, Directorate

General for Internal Policies of the Union. https://www.europarl.europa.eu/RegData/etudes/STUD/2017/583154/IPOL_STU(2017)583154_EN.pdf.

Spaventa, Eleanor. 2019. Mice or Horses?: British Citizens in the EU 27 after Brexit as "Former EU Citizens". *European Law Review* 44 (5): 589–604.

Specialised Committee on Citizens' Rights. 2021a. Joint Statement Following the Eighth Meeting of the Specialised Committee on Citizens' Rights. https://commission.europa.eu/publications/joint-statement-following-meeting-specialised-committee-citizens-rights-0_en.

Specialised Committee on Citizens' Rights. 2021b. Joint Statement Following the Meeting of the Specialised Committee on Citizens' Rights Between the European Commission and the UK Government Via Video Conference. https://commission.europa.eu/publications/joint-statement-following-meeting-specialised-committee-citizens-rights-between-european-commission-0_en.

Specialised Committee on Citizens' Rights. 2021c. Joint Statement Following the Seventh Meeting of the Specialised Committee on Citizens' Rights. https://commission.europa.eu/publications/joint-statement-following-meeting-specialised-committee-citizens-rights_en.

Specialised Committee on Citizens' Rights. 2022a. Joint Statement Following the Ninth Meeting of the Specialised Committee on Citizens' Rights. https://commission.europa.eu/system/files/2022-03/9th_joint_statement_en.pdf.

Specialised Committee on Citizens' Rights. 2022b. Joint Statement Following the Tenth Meeting of the Specialised Committee on Citizens' Rights. https://commission.europa.eu/document/download/ef15113a-f3f8-4262-895a-17c16ef3f2f6_en?filename=20.06.2022_joint_statement_sc_citizens_rights_en.pdf.

Specialised Committee on Citizens' Rights. 2022c. Sixth Joint Report on the Implementation of Residence Rights under Part Two of the Withdrawal Agreement. https://commission.europa.eu/document/download/545c8561-214d-4082-a60b-e5e242436370_en?filename=final_sixth_joint_report_on_residence_rights.pdf.

Specialised Committee on Citizens' Rights. 2023a. Joint Statement Following the Eleventh Meeting of the Specialised Committee on Citizens' Rights. https://commission.europa.eu/document/download/5c36ef69-02f3-4b0b-ac60-10b8ac085d92_en?filename=joint-statement-following-the-meeting-of-the-Specialised-Committee-on-Citizens-Rights-13012023.pdf.

Specialised Committee on Citizens' Rights. 2023b. Joint Statement Following the Thirteenth Meeting of the Specialised Committee on Citizens' Rights. https://commission.europa.eu/document/download/dcff3b9d-f29f-4cec-b9ab-a489b8e33033_en?filename=13th-SCCR-draft-joint-statement.pdf.

Specialised Committee on Citizens' Rights. 2023c. Joint Statement Following the Twelfth Meeting of the Specialised Committee on Citizens' Rights. https://commission.europa.eu/document/download/e6f3d70d-959b-497d-9351-983a2fffcd7a_en?filename=2023-05-25-joint-statement.pdf.

Specialised Committee on Citizens' Rights. 2024a. Joint Statement Following the Fifteenth Meeting of the Specialised Committee on Citizens' Rights. https://commission.europa.eu/document/download/1509ec4c-2dc7-42e2-9908-90ffc9140e2a_en?filename=15th-SCCR-joint-statement-en.pdf.

Specialised Committee on Citizens' Rights. 2024b. Joint Statement Following the Fourteenth Meeting of the Specialised Committee on Citizens' Rights. https://commission.europa.eu/document/download/998fa9d2-8737-4be6-b315-10a73e8363ef_en?filename=2024-06-18-Updated-joint-statement.pdf.

Specialised Committee on Citizens' Rights. 2025a. Joint Statement Following the Seventeenth Meeting of the Specialised Committee on Citizens' Rights. https://commission.europa.eu/document/download/bccd9296-97a3-4eb5-ae32-9492e4dacc9f_en?filename=joint-statement-following-the-seventeenth-meeting-of-the-specialised-committee-on-citizens-rights.pdf.

Specialised Committee on Citizens' Rights. 2025b. Joint Statement Following the Sixteenth Meeting of the Specialised Committee on Citizens' Rights. https://commission.europa.eu/document/download/061e9d78-64f2-4f44-b9b7-5f99302f2e2b_en?filename=16th_sccr_joint_statement_en.pdf.

Sredanovic, Djordje. 2021. Brexit as a Trigger and an Obstacle to Onwards and Return Migration. *International Migration* 59 (6): 93–108. https://doi.org/10.1111/imig.12712.

Sredanovic, Djordje. 2022. The Tactics and Strategies of Naturalisation: UK and EU27 Citizens in the Context of Brexit. *Journal of Ethnic and Migration Studies* 48 (13): 3095–3112. https://doi.org/10.1080/1369183X.2020.1844003.

Sredanovic, Djordje, and Francesco Della Puppa. 2023. Brexit and the Stratified Uses of National and European Union Citizenship. *Current Sociology* 71 (5): 725–742. https://doi.org/10.1177/00113921211048523.

'Statement by Chloe Smith, Minister of State for the Constitution and Devolution; Statement UIN HCWS99'. 2021. June 17. https://questions-statements.parliament.uk/written-statements/detail/2021-06-17/hcws99.

Sumption, Madeleine, and Zovanga Kone. 2018. Unsettled Status? Which EU Citizens Are at Risk of Failing to Secure Their Rights after Brexit? Migration Observatory. https://migrationobservatory.ox.ac.uk/wp-content/uploads/2018/04/Report-Unsettled_Status-1.pdf.

Tilindyte, L. 2017. *EU Citizenship Rights.* European Parliamentary Research Service. https://www.europarl.europa.eu/RegData/etudes/BRIE/2017/599361/EPRS_BRI(2017)599361_EN.pdf

Tomlinson, Joe, and Alice Welsh. n.d. *Digital Immigration Status: A Monitoring Framework*. Public Law Project. Accessed 8 March 2025. https://publiclawproject.org.uk/resources/digital-only-status/.

UK Government. 2021. Local Voting Rights for EU Citizens in the UK. https://www.gov.uk/government/publications/local-voting-rights-for-eu-citizens-living-in-the-uk/local-voting-rights-for-eu-citizens-living-in-the-uk.

UK Home Office. 2024. How Many People Have Been Granted Settlement via the EU Settlement Scheme? https://www.gov.uk/government/statistics/immigration-system-statistics-year-ending-june-2024/how-many-people-have-been-granted-settlement-via-the-eu-settlement-scheme.

Valcu, Elise-Nicoleta. 2022. The Statute of the British Citizens on the Territory of Romania in the Context of Brexit—Union Legislative and Transposition Mechanisms. *AGORA International Journal of Juridical Sciences* 1:17–24.

Wihtol de Wenden, Catherine. 2019. Le Brexit et l'immigration européenne à Londres. Translated by Vanessa Kientz. *Hommes & Migrations* 1326 (July): 37–41. https://doi.org/10.4000/hommesmigrations.9602.

Zambelli, Elena, Michaela Benson, and Nando Sigona. 2022. *British-European Families after Brexit*. No. 3. MIGZEN Research Brief.

CHAPTER 6

The "Triumph" of European Union Citizenship

Abstract The chapter examines three key reactions of EU citizens in the wake of Brexit: the rise of pro-EU movements, proposals for associate citizenship, and naturalisation trends among EU citizens in the UK and UK nationals in the EU27. Grassroots activism, exemplified by groups such as *the3million* and British in Europe, framed EU citizenship as a shared identity and mobilised around the "right to have rights," though these movements remained limited in scope and impact. Academic and political initiatives to decouple EU citizenship from the nationality of EU Member States or create an associate EU citizenship underscored its perceived significance but failed to gain traction. Naturalisation as well as (re)gaining EU citizenship emerged as a pragmatic response, driven by both strategic considerations and deeper processes of embeddedness, revealing the transformative potential of EU citizenship in everyday life. Ultimately, Brexit heightened awareness of the transformative value of EU citizenship.

Keywords EU citizenship • Brexit • Naturalisation • Integration • Associate EU citizenship • Pro-EU movements

C. Dadomo, N. Quénivet, *The Transformative Value of EU Citizenship after Brexit*,
https://doi.org/10.1007/978-3-032-20595-7_6

6.1 Introduction

The withdrawal of the United Kingdom from the European Union represents a critical juncture in the evolution of EU citizenship, exposing its fragility and the tensions inherent in its nature as a legal *status*, a set of *rights* and a *practice* in the form of a lived experience. The referendum urged individuals, both EU citizens in the UK and UK nationals in the EU27, to reassess the normative and practical value of EU citizenship. After all, "citizenship is a mode of action and not of being" (Tassin 1994, 109).

This chapter thus interrogates the strategies adopted in response to the loss of EU citizenship legal *status*, which entails a loss of *rights*, aligning with the legal-participatory view of EU citizenship that emphasises the status and rights of EU citizens, to which the authors have added the *practice* of EU citizenship (see Chap. 1). It argues that Brexit acted as a stress test, exposing the transformative value of EU citizenship: EU citizens in the UK and UK nationals in the EU27 recognised its fundamental status and the associated rights. It shows how Brexit triggered major shifts in the understanding of the value of EU citizenship. However, it is not the aim of this chapter to explore the deeper meaning of EU citizenship, to discuss whether Brexit resulted in a supranational understanding of EU citizenship, or to examine the specific issues faced by EU citizens in the UK and UK nationals in the EU27 when applying for another nationality.

The chapter begins by examining the emergence and development of pro-EU movements, emphasising their role in redefining EU citizenship as a shared identity and a focus of political mobilisation. It argues that the value of EU citizenship as a bundle of rights has been recognised by those who exercise[d] it. It then considers proposals to maintain some form of EU citizenship after Brexit, placing these initiatives within a discourse of preserving not only the rights and practice of EU citizenship but also some form of legal status. Finally, the chapter explores naturalisation practices among EU citizens in the UK and UK nationals in the EU27, analysing whether these choices are driven by strategic considerations or represent deeper processes of practice and embeddedness. It reveals that the transformative value of EU citizenship has been acknowledged not only by those who have exercised it but also by UK nationals who have never exercised their freedom of movement.

6.2 Pro-EU Movements in the UK and in the EU

Following the referendum results, there was a surge of activism amongst EU nationals in the UK and UK nationals in the EU27. Realising that their *rights* were at risk, they presented a rather unified front against Brexit, mostly over EU citizenship. From recipients of a citizenship they had *practised* but not necessarily fully and consciously embraced, they seemed to have become ardent defenders of its value. The reality, however, paints a slightly more nuanced picture, especially nearly ten years after the referendum.

Owing to the lack of formal channels, they first gathered online, often on Facebook and then formed local grassroots organisations, which formed umbrella organisations (Brändle et al. 2018, 810; van Kessel and Fagan 2023, 975) as well as cross-national networks, often concentrated in certain countries (van Kessel and Fagan 2023). In the UK, *the3million* movement was formed after the 2016 referendum (the3million 2022) and was (and still is) the most established and vocal not-for-profit organisation working on behalf of EU citizens living in the UK. In France, various campaign groups emerged (Expat Citizens Rights in the EU and Remain in France Together (RIFT, n.d.)) (see Ferbrache 2019a, 86), and eventually UK nationals in the EU27 founded under French law in early 2017 "British in Europe", a coalition of UK citizens in Europe to "give UK citizens living, working and studying across the EU a voice in the Brexit negotiations" ('About BiE | British in Europe', n.d.) These movements emerged from the bottom up, driven by citizens without formal political leadership. Other new groups included Forever Europeans-Remain in the EU (Facebook, n.d.-b), the 48 and Beyond (Facebook, n.d.-c), Britain for Europe (Facebook, n.d.-a), and older groups, such as the New Europeans, set up in 2013, and the European Movement, formed in 1949 (European Movement, n.d.), gained momentum. All contributed to increased dialogue among people of different nationalities, driven by the same purpose (Vathi and Trandafoiu 2022, 757).

In that short time, the movements accomplished, though not always successfully, a wide range of activities lobbying for the rights of those directly impacted by Brexit. First, before the beginning of the transition period, as the Withdrawal Agreement excluded the applicability of the European Citizens' Initiative during that time (Withdrawal Agreement 2020, art. 127(1)(b)), they presented two initiatives: "STOP Brexit" (European Commission 2017a) and "British Friends – stay with us in EU"

(European Commission 2018a). The former's request is self-explanatory, and the latter aimed to create a platform enabling all EU citizens to take part in the initiative. The Commission rejected the registration of both initiatives on similar grounds: there was no legal basis in the Treaties to prevent the UK from withdrawing from the EU, and thus the proposals fell outside the Commission's competences (European Commission 2017a, 2018a; see Athanasiadou 2020, 403).

Second, they organised the largest pro-EU march in history, advocating for a second referendum (Siklodi 2023, 1–2). The march, organised by Unite for Europe, is estimated to have attracted between 25,000 and 100,000 participants (Brändle et al. 2018, 810), the vast majority of whom were British citizens (Brändle et al. 2018, 815).

Third, they launched the largest petition in UK history titled "Revoke Article 50 and remain in the EU" with over six million signatures by the end of March 2019 (Siklodi 2023, 2).

Fourth, they lobbied for specific rights to be included in the Withdrawal Agreement (see, e.g., 'About BiE | British in Europe', n.d.). They were invited to committees to discuss the campaign and engaged with various political actors at the national and European levels (Jablonowski 2017; Ferbrache 2019a, 87). *The3million*'s success was probably due to its political neutrality vis-à-vis Brexit (Jablonowski 2017), which, however, caused some issues with Remainer grassroots groups (Aouanes-Perriere 2025).

Essentially, these groups highlighted how EU citizens could raise their voices, whilst concomitantly pointing out that democracy at both the EU and UK levels had failed to meet their needs. Undoubtedly, there was a rise in interest in the EU and the Brexit process (Brahic and Lallement 2020, 16) as well as in informal political participation, which some scholars saw as the creation of an EU diaspora (Siklodi 2023, 4) or "acts of European citizenship" (Siklodi 2023, 4). A 2021–2022 survey supported such academic research (Benson, Craven, et al. 2022a, 7). These movements went against the grain. Indeed, writing in 1996, Herzog bemoaned the lack of a civic link in the European Union, explaining that there was no transnational public relation (Herzog 1996, 39). For those impacted by Brexit, EU citizenship rose as *practice*.

The benefits and potential loss of EU citizenship were the focal points of these movements. They centred on the "right to have rights" as EU citizens, as Brexit was felt to shatter the life expectations of those affected by it (Brändle et al. 2018, 811). It was a first in history as "EU citizenship had become a shared value and identity around which grassroots organisations mobilised" (Benson, Craven, et al. 2022a, 1; Jablonowski 2017). EU citizenship became, to use Maduro's words, "a political relationship [that] unite[d] the peoples of Europe" (*Case C-135/08 Rottman (A.G.)* 2009, ¶ 23). The lived experience of EU citizenship had brought these individuals together with a view to defending that status, its associated rights, and the practice. The *3million* emerged as an EU-citizen constituency that was accepted at the negotiating table on the basis that they "represent[ed] EU citizens' common interests post-Referendum." At the time, concerns about citizens' rights fostered a sense of identification, belonging, and attachment to the EU (Benson, Craven, et al. 2022a, 1) or Europeanness (Ranta and Nancheva 2019, 2 and 8). For many EU citizens in the UK, the EU was "a united political space that is a source of common rights, such as mobility, but also a modern-day family whose ties are based on shared interests" (Vathi and Trandafoiu 2022, 756). Even for Eurosceptics, "the European imaginary remain[ed] a stable feature in [their] identity" (Vathi and Trandafoiu 2022, 761). Likewise, British groups in France centred on "rights, justice and citizenship, with a particular focus on issues such as health care, pensions, free movement, exchange rates, voting rights and employment" (Ferbrache 2019a, 86).

Whilst these movements showed that a shared EU citizenship could serve as a bonding link, deeper research into them revealed that it was, however, neither a movement about the EU nor EU citizens at large. First, these movements to keep the rights of EU citizens in the UK and UK nationals in the EU27 did not gather support elsewhere in the EU. This interest in EU citizenship was limited to those directly affected by Brexit. The insufficient number of signatures on the European Citizens' Initiatives is testimony to this. As Athanasiadou explains, "they gained certain popularity in essence only in the UK and did not manage to create a transnational movement" (Athanasiadou 2020, 408). The European Union was not the public space where the Brexit debate was held. Second, whilst at the "institutional level", *the3million* and the British in Europe campaigned and worked together, especially concerning the negotiations relating to the Withdrawal Agreement (Jablonowski 2017), there were very few links between EU citizens in the UK and UK nationals in the EU27. The lack of solidarity among these two groups of EU citizens fundamentally questioned their commitment to EU citizenship and the broader EU, beyond just defending specific segments of the EU population. Third, Brexit activism among the EU diaspora in the UK aimed to distinguish itself from its British counterparts. Although UK nationals were losing their EU citizenship, EU nationals in the UK did not feel they could relate to them. On the contrary, as one EU national put it, Brexit "act[ed] as a bonding thing for the rest of the Europeans versus the English" (Vathi and Trandafoiu 2022, 757). Brexit repositioned them "away from the British and closer to fellow Europeans" (Vathi and Trandafoiu 2022, 760). And yet, the majority of those surveyed who took part in the March for Europe were British nationals who described the loss of EU citizenship as bereavement, heartbreak, and similar terms (Brändle et al. 2018, 821). Fourth, some EU citizens preferred to strengthen their ties with fellow nationals (Blachnicka-Ciacek and Budginaite-Mackine 2022, 1085) either in online groups or by taking part in events organised by embassies and consulates (Vathi and Trandafoiu 2022, 757). Fifth, whilst on the surface these were large movements, many EU citizens did not engage with organisations lobbying for the UK to stay in the EU or for upholding the rights of EU citizens in the UK (Brahic and Lallement 2020, 20); it was, to some extent, a limited mass movement. Sixth, many campaigns centred on EU citizens' rights and the need for a second referendum; they lacked a positive pro-European message (van Kessel and Fagan 2023, 983–84). In conclusion, it is accurate to state that, for these movements, "the EU [did] not represent a shared public realm in any meaningful sense of the term" (Vasiljević 2006, 128).

Another significant issue with these movements was that they reproduced an EU that is essentially male and culturally white. As noted by Siklodi, "a large portion of ethnic minorities and EU migrants have been found to be absent from pro-EU debates and citizen groups" (Siklodi 2023, 4). Interviews conducted with activists show that they bemoaned the lack of engagement of minorities, not just during anti-Brexit mobilisations but also more generally in the EU activist sector (Siklodi 2023, 7).

The muted response of EU citizens from Central and Eastern Europe was also noted. In interviews carried out at the end of 2020, very few participants from Central and Eastern European States reported being active in Brexit politics (Siklodi 2023, 12). Their engagement was, to say the least, marginal. A 2023 survey conducted on behalf of the European Commission confirmed that EU citizens from countries that had joined the EU later were much less interested in European affairs and had a less positive image of the EU (Kantar Public 2023, 5). As Vathi and Trandafoiu surmise, this political apathy and inaction might stem from the fact that some individuals, because of the tone of the campaign, felt excluded (Vathi and Trandafoiu 2022, 575) or from the fact that they saw no meaning in engaging in the political process because of prior negative experiences in countries affected by a painful post-communist transition (Vathi and Trandafoiu 2022, 762).

All those activities certainly demonstrate that EU citizens in the UK and UK nationals in the EU27 understood the consequences of losing their status and, consequently, their rights and practice of EU citizenship (Vathi and Trandafoiu 2022, 763; Brändle et al. 2018, 812). But the ultimate question remains whether these movements are still relevant today in shaping the discourse around EU citizenship and whether this has led to any long-term change in how individuals perceive their status, rights, and the practice of EU citizenship.

Undoubtedly, "[t]he anti-Brexit movement lost its drive after the crucial 2019 general election that secured the UK's departure from the EU" (van Kessel and Fagan 2023, 972). Yet *the3million* and the British in Europe still exist, having established themselves as the key organisations representing EU citizens living in the UK (for the3million, see Aouanes-Perriere 2025). Most importantly, they have access to UK and EU institutions, notably the Specialised Committee on Citizens' Rights, where they can present the concerns of EU citizens in the UK and UK nationals in the EU27 regarding the implementation and application of Part Two of the Withdrawal Agreement (see Sect. 4.3.3). Both also work as platforms to support and advocate for EU citizens. As Aouanes-Perriere explains, in 2025, *the3million* "remains a powerful mediator in terms of legalising residency status in the UK" (Aouanes-Perriere 2025). In contrast, the British in Europe, owing to a lack of funding, seems to be much less active. Altogether, it is not clear whether they can still shape the discourse on EU citizenship beyond their access to relevant institutions.

However, it is possible to determine whether the population's support was short-lived and based on economic and personal grounds or revealed true political adherence to European norms and values on which a European *civitas* should be founded. In 2023, the European Parliament published a study on EU citizens living in the United Kingdom, to investigate their attitudes regarding the EU and EU citizenship. The results showed that EU citizens living in the UK are, on average, more interested in and more positive about the EU than the general EU population (Kantar Public 2023, 5). This positive view is also reflected in a strong sense of EU citizenship, as 83% of respondents say they consider themselves EU citizens, compared with 74% of the general EU population (Kantar Public 2023, 6). A survey conducted in 2021–2022 by academics had revealed similar findings: Brexit had heightened EU citizens in the UK's sense of being European. This had led to a "shift in their involvement and engagement with issues relating to the EU and a better understanding of its values" (Benson, Craven, et al. 2022a, 4). For UK nationals in the EU27, the 2021–2022 survey showed that they had a strong emotional attachment to the EU and the UK (Benson, Zambelli, et al. 2022, 11). Nevertheless, they found themselves a bit left aside. For example, they expressed the feeling that Brexit "ha[d] left [them] with a pervasive sense of embarrassment about being British and a reinvigoration of their sense of being European" (Benson, Craven, et al. 2022a, 4). A minority of respondents felt that the EU had let them down; they expected more of the EU. Their negative feelings towards the EU stemmed from the fact that they had fewer rights than before (Benson, Craven, et al. 2022a, 5). In a 2020 survey conducted by the European Union on about 30 non-EU citizens (mostly UK nationals) "the majority of them stated their frustration with the results of the Brexit referendum and the deprivation of their EU citizenship rights" (European Commission 2020, 59).

Overall, Brexit was a political awakening for some; for others, those who had been politically active before, their attention shifted to Brexit and related issues (Benson, Craven, et al. 2022a, 7). It was all because politics had a direct impact on their lived experience of EU citizenship, on their EU citizens' rights. Political engagement decreased or stopped because individuals could no longer participate formally, felt their actions had little effect, or experienced changes in personal circumstances (Benson, Craven, et al. 2022a, 7). Brexit led EU citizens to become more aware of their rights and the value of the EU citizenship they had often practised, without realising it. As Blumann wrote in 1991, "European identity cannot be decreed; it is gradually proven through movement and action" (Blumann 1991, 290). Yet, these were no pro-EU movements but rather pro-EU citizenship rights movements.

6.3 Retaining Some Form of EU Citizenship

As the prospect of losing EU citizenship became increasingly imminent, not only did UK nationals turn to national courts and the Court of Justice of the European Union (see Sect. 4.2.2) and the European Citizens' Initiative mechanism (see Sect. 6.2) to oppose the potential loss of EU citizenship, but academics and policymakers also began to consider various alternatives. Chief among these was the idea of some form of associate citizenship. Proposals varied, but fundamentally, they all showed that academics and policymakers involved regarded EU citizenship as a status of fundamental value. The point was that the *status* of EU citizenship should be kept in one form or another, as it was the status that gave the *rights* and enabled the *practice*. None of these proposals was accepted. Given the lack of success of such proposals, this section does not delve into their details and their counterarguments; rather, it explores how Brexit, more profoundly, sparked a debate over the value of EU citizenship.

Formally, through the European Citizens' Initiatives, EU citizens lobbied for keeping EU citizenship. Four such initiatives were registered in the wake of Brexit (see Athanasiadou 2020, 404–6): the first initiative, entitled "European Free Movement Instrument" (also known as the "Choose Freedom Initiative") aimed at giving "all Europeans of good standing" a unified document of laissez-passer (*European Free Movement Instrument* 2017; European Commission 2016); the second at retaining European Citizenship (European Commission 2017b); the third at decoupling EU citizenship from the nationality of a Member State (*Commission Decision on CI 'United in Diversity'* 2017); and the fourth at supporting a permanent European Union citizenship "to avoid risk of collective loss of EU citizenship and rights" (European Commission 2018b). None of them collected enough signatures to be examined by the European Commission. Yet, they signified a profound understanding of the value of EU citizenship or better said, its loss for UK nationals.

Members of the European Parliament were the first to suggest the possibility of associate citizenship which, however, differs from EU citizenship (see Walker and Robinson 2018, 3–5; van den Brink and Kochenov 2019, 1369–70; Cambien 2018, 1345). Guy Verhostadt, the European Parliament's Brexit coordinator, suggested in December 2016 a form of associate citizenship that would allow individuals to "keep free movement to live and work across the EU, as well as a vote in European Parliament elections" (Stone 2019). However, no concrete proposals were made by the European Parliament. The closest was a draft motion for a resolution to wind up the debate on negotiations with the United Kingdom that, after mentioning that UK nationals had "expressed strong opposition to losing the rights they currently enjoy pursuant to Article 20 TFEU", proposed "that the EU-27 examine how to mitigate this within the limits of Union primary law whilst fully respecting the principles of reciprocity, equity, symmetry and non-discrimination" (Draft Motion for Resolution on Wind Up Debate on Negotiations 2017). In brief, this would have been a new status encompassing some of the most important EU citizenship rights, though the contour of these proposals remained unclear (see van der Mei 2020, 453–55). As Shaw bluntly stated at the time, "[t]his plea seems utopian as well as impractical in a legal sense" (Shaw 2019, 449), a feeling echoed by van den Brink and Kochenov (van den Brink and Kochenov 2019). Yet, this proposal highlights the concerns at the time about the loss of EU citizenship for UK nationals and the rush to find solutions.

Barring Kostakopoulou, who early on also expressed her support for an associate citizenship status (Kostakopoulou 2018, 866), and then joined the more mainstream scholarship (Kostakopoulou 2019), the vast majority of academic proposals relied on delinking EU citizenship from the nationality of an EU Member State and on the idea that the European Union could independently declare that a person is an EU citizen (Kostakopoulou 2019).

The point was made that European citizenship, much like the European Union, is constantly evolving and has reached a point at which it can sever the umbilical cord between nationality and EU citizenship. Indeed, as noted by the Spanish delegation in 1990, EU citizenship is intimately linked to the Union's final objective, whose progress "will simultaneously add substance to the status of European citizenship" (Note of the Spanish delegation SN 3940/90 'The Road to European Citizenship' of 24 September 1990, as reproduced in Laursen and Vanhoonacker 1992, 329). Along these lines, as Kostakopoulou explains, "European citizenship constitutes a unique experiment for stretching social and political bonds beyond national boundaries and for creating a political community in which diverse peoples become associates in a collective experience and institutional designers" (Kostakopoulou 2007, 624). Originally, the idea of EU citizenship was to go beyond formal bonds, usually reflected in rights offered to EU citizens, between the EU citizen and the EU. It was about creating a psychological sense of attachment. Yet, as Barber points out, it is difficult to instil such a psychological sense of attachment owing to differences in language, culture, and tradition (Barber 2002, 247). People struggle to conceptualise themselves as a united group. Weiler also makes the point that there is a need for a "resonant fiction of relatedness" for a real sense of attachment to exist (Weiler 1999, 345). This proposal, therefore, lacked significant practical backing.

The evolution of the EU legal order was also used to support the view that EU citizenship creates a direct relationship between the individual and the EU. After all, the basic pattern of citizenship is about this direct relationship between the individual and the entity, polity or community (Vasiljević 2006, 117). The combination of the *Costa v. E.N.E.L.* jurisprudence that established the principle of supremacy of EU law, clearly referring to the existence of supranational laws establishing rights and duties between nationals of EU Member States and the European Union (*Case 6–64 Costa* 1964), and that of *Van Gend en Loos*, specifying that these rights and obligations have become part of the legal heritage of such nationals (*Case 26–62 van Gend & Loos* 1963), indicates that the birth of EU citizenship can be traced back to these first seminal cases of the CJEU (Pertek 2013, 429). Moreover, if "the defining and primordial element of citizenship is the enjoyment of political rights" (Closa 1992, 1139) and bearing in mind that political rights (or special rights) are given by the EU directly to EU citizens then, accordingly, the bond or genuine link between the EU and the individuals should enable the EU to be autonomous in its decision to grant EU citizenship (see Christopoulos 2019). An independent EU citizenship would eliminate the barriers of being a national of an EU Member State, enabling third-country nationals to seek EU citizenship (de Waele 2010, 332–33). Yet, from a legal point of view, this proposal makes little sense. As explained in Sect. 3.2, EU citizenship, as defined in Article 20 TFEU, is currently inextricably linked to the nationality of an EU Member State (see commentary in van den Brink and Kochenov 2019, 1373).

A wide array of scholars has mooted that lawful residence in the territory of the European Union should be the key criterion for obtaining EU citizenship (Garner 2018, 141; Kostakopoulou 2019; Lepoutre 2019). After all, much of the CJEU case-law on free movement of persons stresses the importance of being a lawful resident and having a genuine link with the country of residence (*Case C-209/03 Bidar* 2005; *Case C-138/02 Collins (A.G.)* 2003; *Case C-456/02 Trojani* 2004; *Case C-393/13 Dano and Dano* 2014). Moreover, in this context, EU citizenship is conceived as inclusionary, in contradistinction to its current definition as exclusionary, that is, against the other, the third-country national (Barnard 2016, 326), as it is based on domicile rather than nationality. Kostakopoulou strongly argues in favour of a "domicile paradigm which features at the top of the normative agenda for the development of EU citizenship" (Kostakopoulou 2018, 856). Such an EU citizenship would be based on "a genuinely postnational model of citizenship reflecting the complex interconnections that individuals have by virtue of living, working and participating in the socio-economic and political life of their place of residence" (Kostakopoulou 2018, 858). Such a proposal would no doubt be in line with the lived experience of those EU citizens who used their freedom of movement to reside in another EU Member State. On a theoretical level, it falls squarely within Schachar's work, who envisaged a citizenship based on an "actual, real, everyday, and meaningful web of relations and human interactions" (Shachar 2009, 167). Indeed, such a proposal is not new, neither in discussion relating to nationality and citizenship generally (as a flurry of academics have suggested models based on domicile, affected interests, post-national citizenship, or *jus nexi* (see Ferbrache 2019b, 507)) nor in relation to EU citizenship more specifically. Already in 2004, Becker suggested that "a non-derivative European citizenship based on a uniform residency requirement could improve the capacity of EU institutions and national governments to integrate TCN populations more successfully into national and European societies" (Becker 2004, 138). This proposal is still under discussion in the academic circle but has yet to be taken up by EU Member States, as it would require a treaty amendment.

As More noted, "Brexit has paradoxically brought the concept of EU citizenship alive!" (More 2020, 461). Yet, under pressure, none of the proposals was solid enough to warrant closer examination by the parties to the negotiations. Whilst the European Parliament demonstrated the EU's willingness to protect its citizens, thereby signalling the importance of the *status* of EU citizenship as more than just a mere aspiration, it was unable to "protect" those whose EU citizenship was robbed from them by democratic choice. The fate of UK nationals losing their EU citizenship was being decided through treaty interpretation (see Sect. 4.2) and the negotiations of the Withdrawal Agreement (see Sect. 4.3), which retained many of the *rights* of EU citizenship. It was a decision of the EU and the UK, at a level far away from the lived experience and *practice* of EU citizens in the UK and UK nationals in the EU27 whose lives were anchored on the national and local levels.

6.4 Naturalisation and Acquisition of EU Citizenship

For some EU citizens in the UK and UK nationals in the EU27, a key question was whether the rights conferred under the Withdrawal Agreement were sufficient. For others, Brexit questioned their legal relationship with their host State and, more generally, with EU citizenship, a choice often framed in terms of settlement or (further) migration. This section investigates naturalisation processes for EU citizens in the UK and UK nationals in the EU27, examining whether these decisions are motivated by strategic reasons or reflect deeper practices and integration.

6.4.1 Lounes: *Naturalisation as the Pinnacle of Integration*

In Kostakopoulou's words, naturalisation "is the process whereby a person is transformed from an alien guest to a citizen invested with the rights and privileges pertaining to indigenous subjects" (Kostakopoulou 2003, 88). Also, it shows that the person intends to stay permanently (Kostakopoulou 2003, 88–89). It turns the foreigner, the stranger, into a fellow citizen, a member of the same community. "[C]itizenship is a means of social closure of great significance" (White 2002, 289). It is a double process: one of identification, in which an individual declares their loyalty and allegiance to the "new" community and the individual thus becomes a full participant in the community's governance (Kostakopoulou 2003, 92), and one that enables an individual to participate in, and gain access to, the community's socioeconomic and political life and goods (Sredanovic and Della Puppa 2023, 726). This, in particular, explains why States have set out naturalisation requirements; it is to ensure that the new citizens fulfil expectations associated with the State's traditions and representations (see Kostakopoulou 2003, 94–97 on models of justifications for naturalisation requirements).

EU citizenship obviates the need for naturalisation in EU Member States (Shaw 2007, 2553), as it provides for appropriate integration and protection in the country of residence, barring the right to vote in national elections (Shuibhne 2023, 498). In particular, the principle of non-discrimination in EU Law was meant to avoid foreigners applying for nationality (Thym 2016, 314). It accords a privilege that other "foreigners", that is, non-EU citizens, do not have (Ferbrache 2019a, 83). Data show that EU citizens are reluctant to change their nationality, even in circumstances when it is relatively easy to do so, and this is because permanent residency status as an EU citizen has "in practice the same scope of social rights as [national] citizen status" (Fanning et al. 2021, 264; see Barwick 2021, 3). As White puts it, "citizenship of the EU is really a mass reciprocal naturalisation without renunciation of previous citizenship or prior residence" (White 2002, 312).

Accordingly, the Commission explained that "promoting naturalisation in the host country as a means of increasing political rights would be at odds with the role of EU citizenship as the primary vehicle for promoting respect for national identity and diversity, and ensuring equality of treatment irrespective of nationality" (European Commission 2014, sect. 5.1). Yet, naturalisation should not come as a surprise. After all, as explained in Chap. 3, the transformative value of EU citizenship resides in its ability to embed EU citizens within the local community; the experiential aspect of EU citizenship means it is fundamentally grounded in personal, lived experience. If "[n]aturalisation [...] encapsulates a politics of becoming" (Kostakopoulou 2003, 89), then the "end road" of EU citizenship is naturalisation. In *Lounes* the CJEU explains that "the rights conferred on a Union citizen by Article 21(1) TFEU [...] are intended, amongst other things, to promote the gradual integration of the Union citizen concerned in the society of the host Member State" (*Case C-165/16 Lounes* 2017b, ¶ 56). Advocate General Bot made it even more obvious, explaining that naturalisation is the "logical conclusion" of integration that is the aim pursued by Article 21(1) TFEU and the Citizenship Directive as permanent residence is a "genuine vehicle for integration" (Citizenship Directive 2024, ¶ 18 of preamble; *Case C-165/16 Lounes (A.G.)* 2017a, ¶ 58). In other words, naturalisation is the process by which an EU citizen seeks "to become more deeply integrated in the host Member State" (*Case C-165/16 Lounes (A.G.)* 2017a, ¶ 86), an expression reiterated by the CJEU in *J.Y.* (*Case C-118/20 J.Y.* 2022, ¶ 43). Accordingly, Réveillère states that "[n]aturalization is seen as the prolongation of EU citizens' integration in the host Member State, which is itself seen as the prolongation of free movement rights" (Réveillère 2018; see 2022, 2). Likewise, Coutts argues that "[t]he culmination of the integration envisaged by Union citizenship law is ***naturalisation,*** i.e. full membership of the national community of the host Member State; it is integration into the national community of the host Member State that is aimed at and [...] is facilitated by the residence guaranteed by Union law" (Coutts 2019, 330; see Shuibhne 2023, 499).

In this light, naturalisation is the expression of an EU citizen's intention "to become permanently integrated in that State" (*Case C-165/16 Lounes* 2017a, ¶ 57) after "having exercised their freedom of movement" (*Case C-165/16 Lounes* 2017a, ¶ 58). In the EU context, naturalisation is often viewed as a choice, an opportunity or a privilege, rather than an obligation or a necessity. In *Préfet du Gers,* A.G. Collins noted that the claimant had "chosen not to acquire French nationality" in spite of "her long residence in France and her marriage to a French national" (*Case C-673/20 EP v. Préfet du Gers (A.G.)* 2022, ¶ 33). It is often only once EU citizenship is taken away (from UK nationals in the EU27) or rendered inapplicable (for EU citizens in the UK) that naturalisation appears to many as a more attractive option.

Naturalisation unquestionably carries a range of specific benefits. Naturalisation can be seen as a "positive signalling device", avoiding discrimination (Peters et al. 2020, 514); it is a question of being accepted as equal to the nationals. Concrete examples are inter alia avoiding the hassle of the employer having to check whether the migrant can work (Peters et al. 2020, 514), and being able to apply for jobs reserved for nationals only, such as posts in the public sector, the legal professions, or military roles (Peters et al. 2020, 514). Moreover, a study based in the Netherlands demonstrated that naturalisation provides only benefits in earnings for migrants from poorer countries of origin; hence, naturalisation helps those at the lower end of the wage scale in the labour market (Peters et al. 2020, 533). It gives the individual the right to vote in all elections, including national elections ('Statement by Chloe Smith, Minister of State for the Constitution and Devolution; Statement UIN HCWS99' 2021). More generally, naturalisation is a way of getting rid of the intricacies, complexities and inconveniences of dealing with administrative requirements for entry and residence, as it removes the individual from immigration control and deportation (Sredanovic and Della Puppa 2023, 726).

6.4.2 Naturalisation of EU Citizens in the UK and UK Nationals in the EU27

With the coat of EU citizenship removed, EU citizens in the UK and UK nationals in the EU27 rely on the good application of the Withdrawal Agreement which does not cover all the rights they had as EU citizens and still does not give them access to rights that only nationals have (see Chap. 5.). Therefore, some EU citizens in the UK and UK nationals in the EU27 chose to naturalise; some UK nationals in the EU27 and in the UK decided to apply for EU citizenship, while the overwhelming majority of those affected by Brexit decided not to apply.

6.4.2.1 Attitude of EU Citizens in the UK Towards Naturalisation

The effect of Brexit on the naturalisation of EU citizens in the UK is well-documented (Pataut 2021, 3). Following the referendum, the Home Office saw a significant surge in applications for British citizenship. In November 2025, a Home Office report on citizenship explained that "the number of grants to EU nationals remains high compared with pre-2016 levels" (Home Office 2025a) and clearly linked it to the UK's departure from the EU. The number of EU citizens naturalising had more than tripled since 2016 (EEAS 2025). Most applications surged straight after the referendum and then after the introduction of the EU Settlement Scheme (Home Office 2025a) though there has been a constant stream of applications (Home Office 2025a, Fig. 7). A total of 471,771 EU citizens applied for British citizenship between 2016 and September 2025 (Home Office 2025b). As of September 2025, Italians, Romanians, and Poles "form the top 3 European nationalities granted British citizenship and these 3 have accounted for over 40% of all grants of citizenship to EU nationals since 2012" (GOV.UK 2025). Compared to the overall population of EU citizens in the UK, the number of naturalisations is very small as recent research by the Migration Observatory shows. Only 17% of EU-born people held a UK passport in 2021 (Migration Observatory 2025). The Migration Observatory, however, expects an increasing number of EU citizens to apply after engaging with the EU Settlement Scheme (Migration Observatory 2025).

However, naturalisation was not easy for some EU citizens. Aware that their status as EU citizens would no longer be valid in the UK after Brexit, that their rights could vanish entirely, and that the practice of their rights might be severely hindered by a lack of recognition, EU citizens had to choose which path to take. Some toyed with the possibility of leaving (Godin and Sigona 2022, 1149–50), especially higher-skilled individuals (Lulle et al. 2019, 9) or young people (Lulle et al. 2018, 8) who were more prone to leave. Yet, it was not an option because they were too embedded in the UK. British partners and non-transferable professional skills limited opportunities to leave (Sredanovic 2021, 97). Having children in the UK was another anchoring factor (Sredanovic 2021, 101; Godin and Sigona 2022, 1142). There was no "Brexodus"; the mobility of EU citizens in the UK had been overestimated (Sredanovic 2021, 97).

Some, overwhelmed by a sense of powerlessness or disempowerment, shifted their perspective, considering naturalisation and deeper embedding in British society (Vathi and Trandafoiu 2022, 757). As Shaw explained, "[t]he irony is that many are seeking UK citizenship not because they feel more integrated in the UK, but precisely because they face more hostility than ever before" (Shaw 2019, 453; see Nancheva and Ranta 2022, 1992). Indeed, in the wake of the referendum, "[t]he UK [felt] less like home [...] and so the form of security offered by formal citizenship seem[ed] more desirable"(Shaw 2019, 453). For example, Poles, feeling insecure after the referendum, were more likely to state that they would seek naturalisation than previously (Fanning et al. 2021, 269; see Guma and Dafydd Jones 2019, 7), but, it was largely an intention which did not necessarily materialise (see below) (Fanning et al. 2021, 271; see Lulle et al. 2018, 8). Furthermore, some EU citizens in the UK were driven by the fact that they could vote in the general elections (Sredanovic and Della Puppa 2023, 732). Research also shows that those Poles who intended to apply for citizenship had voted in local elections more and so were more politically motivated (Fanning et al. 2021, 272).

Others applied for the sake of the paper. It was a "shotgun citizenship" with no emotional resonance for its holders (Siklodi 2023, 9), with the aim of maintaining the rights they had enjoyed before and wanted their children to enjoy too (Godin and Sigona 2022, 1143). Often, it was because family considerations were at stake (Godin and Sigona 2022, 1150). That being said, this is not necessarily specific to Brexit, as research shows that individuals tend to make an instrumental use of citizenship and view naturalisation as opportunistic (Della Puppa et al. 2021, 22; Sredanovic 2023, 110).

Finally, some could not resolve themselves to apply for British nationality (Brahic and Lallement 2020, 19). They felt betrayed (Godin and Sigona 2022, 1142) or perceived it as unfair to be asked to prove one's right to stay after having contributed to UK society (Godin and Sigona 2022, 1148).

Legal and administrative issues also impeded the intention and process of naturalisation. For some EU citizens, gaining UK nationality meant losing their EU citizenship as their State of nationality did not allow for dual nationality (e.g., Lithuania, Austria, Poland, Bulgaria) (Barnard et al. 2022, 376; Godin and Sigona 2022, 1148). Multiple nationalities are not yet recognised across the EU Member States (Kostakopoulou 2018, 861), and there are limits to the accumulation of Member State nationalities (Kochenov 2016, 19). However, this issue was limited to a small group (Sredanovic 2022, 3103), all the more so as some EU Member States following Brexit allowed for dual nationality. The administrative burden and financial cost of applying for naturalisation further hindered EU citizens from seeking naturalisation (see Fanning et al. 2021, 274; Nancheva and Ranta 2022, 1991–92; Sredanovic 2022, 3103; Barnard et al. 2022, 375; Burrell and Schweyher 2019, 197; Godin and Sigona 2022, 1136 and 1147). For example, prior to the Withdrawal Agreement, EU citizens from Central and Eastern Europe realised that they did not meet the eligibility criteria for British citizenship (Fanning et al. 2021, 274) or lacked sufficient financial resources to apply for it (Siklodi 2023, 9). They accordingly applied for mandatory residency, but then realised it was difficult to complete too (Siklodi 2023, 9). As the EU Settlement Scheme was introduced, they accepted their new status under it (Siklodi 2023, 3). In contrast to EU-15 citizens, considerable expenses and numerous bureaucratic hurdles prevented many EU citizens from Central and Eastern Europe from naturalising (Siklodi 2023, 3). More than half of the naturalisations between 2016 and September 2025 (258,364) are from the citizens of the EU14 (Home Office 2025b), which is disproportionate to their overall number. "For example, around 60% of German-born residents of England and Wales held a British passport, while the figure was much lower for people born in Poland (8%), Romania (6%), or Lithuania (3%), the average percentage of EU citizens holding a UK passport being 17%" (Migration Observatory 2025).

Although the CJEU describes naturalisation as the pinnacle of integration, many individuals chose not to apply for British nationality before Brexit. One might have expected that Brexit would compel them to make this choice. However, very few people applied, and naturalisation did not occur "naturally". It is unclear why as several factors might be at play. One explanation for this lack of urgency to rush to obtain British passports is the EU Settlement Scheme, which functions well and, as discussed in Chap. 5, has largely preserved the *rights* of EU citizens and the *practice* of exercising those rights. For those who applied, the naturalisation process was not one relating to embeddedness, an accomplishment of the transformative value of EU citizenship; rather, it was a defensive or protective reaction (see Godin and Sigona 2022, 1143–47), but not a feeling of embeddedness.

6.4.2.2 *Attitude of UK Nationals in the EU27 Towards EU Citizenship*

UK citizens in the EU27 also opted to acquire a nationality giving them EU citizenship. Over 123,000 British nationals acquired citizenship in the EU between 2016 and 2023 (Vink 2025). There was a clear peak in 2019

(Vink 2025). Vink clearly demonstrates that "British citizens acquired the citizenship of another European country *and likely would not have done so, had it not been for Brexit*" (Vink 2025). Fifty-five per cent of all naturalisations occurred in three countries: Germany, France, and Sweden, with Germany well ahead of the other two (Vink 2025). Perhaps this was because, in addition to the fact that most British nationals were in France and Germany, all three countries, unlike others, allow dual nationality.

Whilst pointing out that UK nationals applied for a nationality giving them EU citizenship might offer an easy way to gauge the transformative value of EU citizenship by pointing out that UK citizens value a *status* that carries *rights* (i.e., the right to residence, the principle of non-discrimination, and the right to vote) that are then *practised* in everyday life, it is marred by issues. Indeed, one might question why UK nationals acquired the nationality of an EU Member State. Vink argues that this rush to acquire citizenship of another EU or associate State highlights the perceived value of EU citizenship (Vink 2025). This is disputable and certainly needs more nuance.

First, it is possible that UK nationals in the EU27 applied for citizenship in their State of residence because it gave them access to the same rights as nationals. In other words, it was a "simple" naturalisation process, as described earlier (see Sect. 6.4.1), that is, turning the foreigner into a national citizen. After all, such an act would eliminate the risk of being viewed and classed as a "foreigner", a rather precarious status, as the individual is in the hands of national legislation that can be amended and repealed at any time. Following Brexit, a group of Britons surveyed in France who had originally in 2003–2005 no intention of applying for French citizenship applied for nationality, transforming their "citizen-like" status into full citizenship as they had a high localised sense of belonging (Benson 2020, 508–9). The fact that this nationality came with EU citizenship rights might be incidental. It should be remembered that in research carried out pre-referendum, in a sample of Britons interviewed in France, barely any of them acknowledged their rights as EU citizens (Ferbrache and Yarwood 2015, 76; see Ferbrache 2019a, 85; Drake and Collard 2008, 227). Yet, this would fit with the discourse projected by the CJEU in the *Lounes* case, in which naturalisation is the logical conclusion of integration as an EU citizen and naturalisation becomes a reflection of the embeddedness and *practice* of EU citizenship. Naturalisation in this context can also demonstrate the very value of EU citizenship, which has unconsciously permeated the lives of those who have experienced life in another country. EU citizenship has created a "vécu", a "lived experience", that people do not want to renounce as they have established personal, sociological, and cultural ties in their country of choice.

Academic studies carried out in various countries, however, paint a more elaborate picture. Ferbrache's research in France in 2019 establishes that Britons acquired citizenship with three aims: to retain the ability to move within the EU, to stay in the country, and to access health care and social security benefits (Ferbrache 2019a, 85). To freedom of movement, Harzoune adds the possibility of keeping a post in the public sector or an electoral mandate (Harzoune 2019, 200). A survey by Benson et al. in 2021–2022 also refers to retaining the right to vote in the EU Parliament elections as a key factor (Benson, Craven, et al. 2022a, 6). Sredanovic and Della Puppa's research identifies retention of EU citizenship status as more important than naturalisation for Britons in Belgium (Sredanovic and Della Puppa 2023, 730), as they emphasise the value of the right for them and their children to move to and work in another EU Member State (Sredanovic and Della Puppa 2023, 730; see Sredanovic 2023, 121). Moreover, whereas studies show that in Germany "migrants with a secure status do not even bother to apply for nationality even though they would fulfil the requirements for naturalisation" (Thym 2019), statistics reveal that Germany is the number one (and by far ahead) country where UK nationals naturalised (Vink 2025; see Barwick 2021, 8). Barwick's study reveals that naturalisation in Germany was not about acquiring German nationality but about retaining EU citizenship (Barwick 2021, 11) and identifying as European (Barwick 2021, 2 and 12–13). But for Brexit they would not have naturalised (Barwick 2021, 8–9). What seems clear is that EU citizenship increases one's capacity not only for settlement but also for mobility and that it is probably the latter that UK nationals in the EU27 have understood to be the key advantage of EU citizenship (Sredanovic 2023, 112).

Second, and relatedly, some UK nationals in the EU27 chose a different nationality from that of their country of residence, yet from another EU State, thus granting them EU citizenship. Again, one could infer that UK nationals were interested in acquiring EU citizenship but found it easier to obtain another EU nationality. For example, becoming Irish seemed to be a simpler route for those with Irish ancestry than applying for the nationality of their country of residence (Sredanovic 2023, 113; Ferbrache 2019a, 85; Sredanovic 2022, 3100–3101). Some considered applying for Italian citizenship by descent (Sredanovic 2023, 113). Others purchased EU citizenship through Malta or Portugal, or passports from

States (e.g., St Lucia and St Kitts & Nevis) that offer residency rights and visa-free travel to the EU (Cruise 2020). This pathway, which was available to a limited number of UK nationals, was taken to access EU citizens' rights, to stay in the country of residence and continue to enjoy free movement rights (Ferbrache 2019a, 86). Ultimately, UK nationals aimed to shield themselves from the effects of Brexit, specifically the loss of their EU citizenship and related rights, regardless of which nationality provided them with EU citizenship. It was less about integration and embeddedness in the country of residence and more about the *status* of and the *rights* relating to EU citizenship. And it was also about the opportunity of onward migration (Sredanovic 2021, 102 and 104; Neville 2023, 6), especially for mixed-status families (Aradau et al. 2010, 6–7). In this context, Vink brings to the fore the concept of "global citizenship hierarchy" (see Sredanovic 2022, 3096) in which EU citizenship is highly valuable, for it brings with it mobility rights within Europe (Vink 2025). It is a strategic use of EU citizenship.

Third, some UK nationals did not apply for another nationality, which means that their *rights* are entirely determined by the Withdrawal Agreement and thus linked to them obtaining national status (see Chap. 5.). Some did not apply because it was too expensive or because they did not fulfil the eligibility requirements, notably those related to language acquisition (Benson 2020, 510); others feared that they would lose their British nationality (Barwick 2021, 9). Lack of financial and cultural capital prevented them from doing so. Whilst the Withdrawal Agreement retains the overwhelming majority of their EU citizens' rights, one of the sore points of the agreement is that UK nationals do not enjoy the right of freedom of movement within the EU. They are stuck in their country of residence. Yet, this might not necessarily be considered as opposing the transformative value of EU citizenship; they might have chosen to integrate into that society and, with the Withdrawal Agreement in mind, like many EU citizens in the UK, do not see the point of applying for naturalisation as they believe that the Withdrawal Agreement guarantees their *rights* and *practice* of EU citizenship. In fact, it might be their behaviour that best reveals the transformative, that is, integration, value of EU citizenship. A survey conducted in 2021–2022 nevertheless reveals that some UK nationals in the EU27 sensed the "removal of free movement as become more immobile, stuck in place" (Benson, Zambelli, et al. 2022, 7), and as "involuntary sedentarisation" (Zambelli et al. 2022, 7). In other words, free movement within the EU was a crucial aspect of EU citizenship for them and this was particularly the case for people with mixed-status relationships, that is, where within a family and across generations members had different nationalities (Benson, Zambelli, et al. 2022b, 8).

Fourth, and this might certainly be more revealing of the value of EU citizenship, is the number of UK nationals who applied for another EU Member State's nationality without actually living outside the UK. This seems to stand in stark contrast to decades of UK nationals refusing to identify as Europeans (Carl et al. 2019, 286). One of the ironic results of Brexit is this interest in an EU citizenship (Sredanovic 2023, 125), as the UK was the only Member State where, since 2012, the public supported leaving the EU (Hobolt 2016, 1271). Yet, it does not because even those who voted to remain in the UK did so because they feared a negative effect on the economy, jobs, and prices. The least important reason was a strong attachment to the EU (Lord Ashcroft 2016). "Ordinary Britons understood immediately that Brexit means a severe degradation of their rights" (van den Brink and Kochenov 2019, 1367). Straight after the vote, Ireland registered an increased interest in Irish passports (EUI Global Citizenship Observatory 2016) as UK nationals were "[s]eeking or reactivating a second 'backstop' citizenship (e.g. by ancestry or family ties)" (Shaw 2019, 449) to keep their rights. Sredanovic's research shows that, for those seeking Irish citizenship, whether UK nationals in Belgium or in the UK, it was the practical advantages and even the identity of being an EU citizen that were significant rather than Irish identity (Sredanovic 2023, 125). It is striking that many who took part in the March for Europe defended not only their own rights but also their children's European futures (Brändle et al. 2018, 821). It was somehow the imagined potential use of the rights granted by the EU citizenship for their children that triggered them (Sredanovic 2023, 121). It was the concrete fears of a loss of opportunity (Brändle et al. 2018, 823). As Preuß explains, EU citizenship is "a bundle of options within a physically broadened and functionally more differentiated space" (Preuß 1995, 280). To some extent, the rush of UK nationals in the UK, who had not even enjoyed the right to residence, the principle of non-discrimination, and the right to vote as they had not exercised their freedom of movement, to apply for Irish citizenship to retain their EU citizenship can be understood under this angle of the potential loss of opportunities.

Taken as a whole, the reaction of UK nationals, whether in the EU27 or in the UK, reveals that, as Sredanovic explains, there is an "EU bonus" in having a nationality of an EU Member State, and for some Britons, it was important to keep EU citizenship, its *status*, to maintain their *rights* (Sredanovic 2023, 112; see 2022, 3103). The vision of European citizenship as one that is legal-participatory is clearly reflected in this situation. The fact that some UK nationals living in the EU27 applied for the nationality of an EU Member State (though not necessarily for that of their country of residence at the time), and that UK nationals in the UK who had never exercised their freedom of movement rights also applied for the nationality of another Member State (such as Ireland) suggests that, for them, EU citizenship was largely disconnected from *practice*. Instead, it raises questions as to whether the transformative value of EU citizenship lies in embeddedness or whether it is more about the loss of rights and opportunities, the key right and opportunity being that of freedom of movement.

6.5 Conclusion

Brexit exposed the derived nature of EU citizenship, grounded in the nationality of the Member States, and thus challenged assumptions about its fundamental status. The responses of those affected, mobilising through grassroots movements or resorting to naturalisation, as well as those involved politicians and academics advocating for alternative forms of citizenship, reveal both the resilience and the limitations of EU citizenship as an additional status (layer) that can be removed once a Member State decides to leave the EU. Whilst activist campaigns and legal initiatives underscored the symbolic and normative significance of EU citizenship, their limited success highlighted the absence of a truly transnational public sphere and the enduring primacy of national frameworks. At the core were not so much the European Union as a political space or the EU citizenship as a legal *status* but more the *rights* associated with it and the *practice* of EU citizenship which had embedded these citizens in the fabric of their country of residence.

Undoubtedly, Brexit increased awareness of the value of EU citizenship, as many EU citizens in the UK and UK nationals (both in the UK and in the EU27) realised that losing this status meant a loss of rights, whether exercised or potential. Consequently, it might be argued that Brexit facilitated the emergence of a certain type of European *civitas*, the benefits of EU citizenship becoming clearer. In 2002, Davis already suggested that the EU "could [...] draw Union members' attention to the rights they would not have had but for their membership of the Union, to which rights their duties vis-à-vis the Union would correlate" (Davis 2002, 136).

Naturalisation trends, however, complicate the picture because "naturalisation involves personal and collective reckoning with a sense of loss of status and imagined future" (Godin and Sigona 2022, 1150). For some, acquiring a new nationality was an instrumental strategy to preserve their *rights* as EU citizens. "Brexit has been a strong stimulus for defensive naturalisations, that is, naturalisations that are enacted in response to a loss or potential loss of rights, in order to safeguard such rights" (Sredanovic 2023, 111). For others, it reflected deeper processes of embeddedness, largely grounded in *practice*. Others did not even consider naturalising, thereby refusing to bring embeddedness and the transformative value of EU citizenship to their logical conclusions under the *Lounes* jurisprudence. For UK nationals who lost their *status*, it was particularly the exercise (actual or potential) of free movement (which is the first step towards the transformative value of EU citizenship) that seemed significant in their decision to acquire EU citizenship.

To some extent, one can claim that Brexit has enabled the triumph of the transformative value of EU citizenship, as a greater number of EU citizens have come to understand what it means in terms of *rights* and *practice*. However, the loss of momentum of pro-EU movements, the failure of proposals for associate citizenship, and the reliance on national naturalisation underscore the paradox at the heart of EU citizenship: while conceived as an additional status, it remains tethered to Member State sovereignty.

References

'About BiE | British in Europe'. n.d. Accessed 24 November 2025. https://www.britishineurope.org/page/1016446-about-bie.

Agreement on the Withdrawal of the United Kingdom of Great Britain and Northern Ireland from the European Union and the European Atomic Energy Community, OJ L 29/7. 2020. https://eur-lex.europa.eu/legal-content/EN/TXT/?uri=CELEX%3A02020W%2FTXT-20250430.

Aouanes-Perriere, Marie. 2025. EU Citizens' Residence Rights after Brexit: The CSI Justice Campaign, a Grassroots Initiative by The3million. *Mémoire(s), Identité(s), Marginalité(s) Dans Le Monde Occidental Contemporain* 31. https://doi.org/10.4000/1406w.

Aradau, Claudia, Jef Huysmans, and Vicki Squire. 2010. Acts of European Citizenship: A Political Sociology of Mobility. *Journal of Common Market Studies* 48 (4): 945–965. https://doi.org/10.1111/j.1468-5965.2010.02081.x.

Athanasiadou, Natassa. 2020. The European Citizens' Initiative in Times of Brexit. In *European Citizenship under Stress—Social Justice, Brexit and Other Challenges*, ed. Nathan Cambien, Dimitry Kochenov, and Elise Muir. Brill.

Barber, N. W. 2002. Citizenship, Nationalism and the European Union. *European Law Review* 27 (3): 241–259.

Barnard, Catherine. 2016. *The Substantive Law of the EU—The Four Freedoms*. 5th ed. Oxford University Press.

Barnard, Catherine, Sarah Fraser Butlin, and Fiona Costello. 2022. The Changing Status of European Union Nationals in the United Kingdom Following Brexit: The Lived Experience of the European Union Settlement Scheme. *Social & Legal Studies* 31 (3): 365–388. https://doi.org/10.1177/09646639211032337.

Barwick, Christine. 2021. Legal Integration and the Reconfiguration of Identifications: Material and Symbolic Effects of Brexit on British Nationals in Berlin. *Innovation: The European Journal of Social Science Research* August 18:1–17. https://doi.org/10.1080/13511610.2021.1966297.

Becker, Michael A. 2004. Managing Diversity in the European Union: Inclusive European Citizenship and Third-Country Nationals. *Yale Human Rights & Development Law Journal* 7:132–183.

Benson, Michaela. 2020. Brexit and the Classed Politics of Bordering: The British in France and European Belongings. *Sociology* 54 (3): 501–517. https://doi.org/10.1177/0038038519885300.

Benson, Michaela, Catherine Craven, and Nando Sigona. 2022a. *European Belongings and Political Participation beyond Brexit*. MIGZEN Research Brief No. 4. https://zenodo.org/records/7070702.

Benson, Michaela, Elena Zambelli, Catherine Craven, and Nando Sigona. 2022b. *British Citizens in the EU after Brexit*. Vol. No. 1. MIGZEN Research Brief. https://migzen.net/site/assets/files/1402/benson_et_al__2022_british_citizens_in_the_eu_after_brexit.pdf.

Blachnicka-Ciacek, Dominika, and Irma Budginaite-Mackine. 2022. The Ambiguous Lives of "The Other Whites": Class and Racialisation of Eastern European Migrants in the UK. *The Sociological Review* 70 (6): 1081–1099. https://doi.org/10.1177/00380261221121218.

Blumann, Claude. 1991. L'Europe des citoyens. *Revue de l'Union Européenne* 346 (April): 283–292.

Brahic, Benedicte, and Maxime Lallement. 2020. From "Expats" to "Migrants": Strategies of Resilience Among French Movers in Post-Brexit Manchester.

Migration and Development 9 (1): 8–24. https://doi.org/10.1080/21632324.2018.1503486.
Brändle, Verena K., Charlotte Galpin, and Hans-Jörg Trenz. 2018. Marching for Europe? Enacting European Citizenship as Justice During Brexit. *Citizenship Studies* 22 (8): 810–828. https://doi.org/10.1080/13621025.2018.1531825.
Burrell, Kathy, and Mateus Schweyher. 2019. Conditional Citizens and Hostile Environments: Polish Migrants in Pre-Brexit Britain. *Geoforum* 106 (November): 193–201. https://doi.org/10.1016/j.geoforum.2019.08.014.
Cambien, Nathan. 2018. Residence Rights for EU Citizens and their Family Members: Navigating the New Normal. *European Papers—A Journal on Law and Integration* 3 (3): 1333–1352.
Carl, Noah, James Dennison, and Geoffrey Evans. 2019. European but Not European Enough: An Explanation for Brexit. *European Union Politics* 20 (2): 282–304. https://doi.org/10.1177/1465116518802361.
Case 26/62. 1963. N.V. Algemene Transport- En Expeditie Onderneming van Gend & Loos v. Netherlands Inland Revenue Administration, ECLI:EU:C:1963:1 (ECJ).
Case 6/64. 1964. Flaminio Costa v. E.N.E.L., ECLI:EU:C:1964:66 (ECJ).
Case C-118/20. 2022. J.Y. v. Wiener Landesregierung, ECLI:EU:C:2022:34 (CJEU).
Case C-135/08. 2009. Janko Rottman v. Freistaat Bayern, ECLI:EU:C:2009:588 (Advocate General Maduro).
Case C-138/02. 2003. Brian Francis Collins v. Secretary of State for Work and Pensions, ECLI:EU:C:2003:409 (Advocate General Colomer).
Case C-165/16. 2017a. Toufik Lounes v. Secretary of State for the Home Department, ECLI:EU:C:2017:407 (Advocate General Bot).
Case C-165/16. 2017b. Toufik Lounes v. Secretary of State for the Home Department, ECLI:EU:C:2017:862 (CJEU).
Case C-209/03. 2005. The Queen, on the Application of Dany Bidar v. London Borough of Ealing and Secretary of State for Education and Skills, ECLI:EU:C:2005:169 (ECJ).
Case C-393/13. 2014. Elisabeta Dano and Florin Dano v. Jobcenter Leipzig, ECLI:EU:C:2014:2358 (CJEU).
Case C-456/02. 2004. Michel Trojani v. Centre Public d'Aide Sociale de Bruxelles (CPAS), ECLI:EU:C:2004:488 (ECJ).
Case C-673/20. 2022. E.P. v. Préfet Du Gers and Institut National de La Statistique et Des Études Économiques (INSEE), ECLI:EU:C:2022:129 (Advocate General Collins).
Christopoulos, Dimitris. 2019. A Relative Dissociation of Union Citizenship from Member States Nationality Needs to Mean Something More than Long Term Residence Status. *Verfassungsblog*, January 17. https://verfassungsblog.de/a-relative-dissociation-of-union-citizenship-from-member-states-nationality-needs-to-mean-something-more-than-long-term-residence-status/.

Closa, Carlos. 1992. The Concept of Citizenship in the Treaty on European Union. *Common Market Law Review* 29 (6): 1137–1169. https://doi.org/10.54648/cola1992065.

Commission Decision on the Proposed Citizens' Initiative Entitled 'EU Citizenship for Europeans: United in Diversity in Spite of Jus Soli and Jus Sanguinis'. 2017. OJ L81/18. European Commission. https://eur-lex.europa.eu/legal-content/EN/TXT/?uri=CELEX:32017D0599.

Coutts, Stephen. 2019. The Shifting Geometry of Union Citizenship: A Supranational Status from Transnational Rights. *Cambridge Yearbook of European Legal Studies* 21:318–341. https://doi.org/10.1017/cel.2019.19.

Cruise, Sinead. 2020. 'Wealthy Britons Step up Citizenship Shopping to Thwart Brexit'. *Reuters*, September 26. https://www.reuters.com/business/finance/wealthy-britons-step-up-citizenship-shopping-thwart-brexit-2020-09-26/.

Davis, Roy W. 2002. Citizenship of the Union ... Rights for All? *European Law Review* 27 (2): 121–137.

de Waele, Henri. 2010. EU Citizenship: Revisiting Its Meaning, Place and Potential. *European Journal of Migration and Law* 12 (3): 319–336. https://doi.org/10.1163/157181610X520391.

Della Puppa, Francesco, Nicola Montagna, and Eleonore Kofman. 2021. Onward Migration and Intra-European Mobilities: A Critical and Theoretical Overview. *International Migration* 59 (6): 16–28. https://doi.org/10.1111/imig.12815.

Directive 2004/38/EC of the European Parliament and the of the Council of 29 April 2004 on the Rights of Citizens of the Union and Their Family Members to Move and Reside Freely within the Territory of the Member States Amending Regulation (EEC) No 1612/68 and Repealing Directives 64/221/EEC, 68/360/EEC, 72/194/EEC, 73/148/EEC, 75/34/EEC, 75/35/EEC, 90/364/EEC, 90/365/EEC, and 93/96/EEC, OJ L158/77. 2024.

Draft Motion for a Resolution to Wind Up the Debate on Negotiations with the United Kingdom Following Its Notification That It Intends to Withdraw from the European Union, B8-000/2017. 2017. https://www.europarl.europa.eu/resources/library/media/20170329RES69090/20170329RES69090.pdf.

Drake, Helen, and Susan Collard. 2008. A Case Study of Intra-EU Migration: 20 Years of "Brits" in the Pays d'Auge, Normandy, France. *French Politics* 6 (3): 214–233. https://doi.org/10.1057/fp.2008.11.

EEAS. 2025. New Research Reveals Insights into the Lives of EU Citizens Living in the UK. https://www.eeas.europa.eu/delegations/united-kingdom/new-research-reveals-insights-lives-eu-citizens-living-uk_en?s=3225.

EUI Global Citizenship Observatory. 2016. Increase in Requests for Irish Passports after Brexit. Globalcit, July 29. https://globalcit.eu/increase-in-requests-for-irish-passports-after-brexit/.

European Commission. 2014. *Report of the Commission to the European Parliament, the Council, the European Economic and Social Committee and the Committee of Regions Addressing the Consequences of Disenfranchisement of Union Citizens Exercising Their Right to Free Movement.* COM/2014/033 final. European Commission. https://eur-lex.europa.eu/legal-content/EN/TXT/?uri=celex%3A52014DC0033.

European Commission. 2016. Your Request of 11 November 2016 for Registration of a Proposed Citizens' Initiative Entitled 'European Free Movement Instrument'. C(2016) 8900 final. European Commission. https://register.eci.ec.europa.eu/core/api/register/document/17674144382724.

European Commission. 2017a. *Commission Decision on the Proposed Citizens' Initiative Entitled 'Stop Brexit'.* C(2017) 2000 final. https://register.eci.ec.europa.eu/core/api/register/document/24271214280452.

European Commission. 2017b. *Decision on the Proposed Citizens' Initiative Entitled 'Retaining European Citizenship'.* C(2007) 2002 final.

European Commission. 2018a. *Commission Decision on the Proposed Citizens' Initiative Entitled 'British Friends—Stay with Us in EU'.* C(2018) 1730. European Commission. https://eur-lex.europa.eu/legal-content/EN/TXT/?uri=CELEX:32018D0517.

European Commission. 2018b. *Decision on the Proposed Citizens' Initiative Entitled 'Permanent European Union Citizenship'.* OJEU C264/4. European Commission. https://eur-lex.europa.eu/legal-content/EN/TXT/?uri=CELEX:32018D0726(01).

European Commission. 2020. EU Citizenship 2020—Results of the Public Consultation on EU Citizenship Rights 2020. https://commission.europa.eu/document/download/567dd687-43eb-4efc-b706-188df9906084_en?filename=report_on_the_public_consultation_on_eu_citizenship_rights_2020_en.pdf.

European Free Movement Instrument. 2017. ECI(2017)000001. https://citizens-initiative.europa.eu/initiatives/details/2017/000001_en.

European Movement. n.d. About the European Movement. European Movement. Accessed 3 January 2026. https://www.europeanmovement.co.uk/about.

Facebook. n.d.-a. 'Britain for Europe'. Accessed 3 January 2026. https://www.facebook.com/Britain4Europe/?locale=en_GB.

Facebook. n.d.-b. Forever Europeans (Remain in the European Union). Accessed 3 January 2026. https://www.facebook.com/groups/RemainInTheEuropeanUnion/?locale=en_GB.

Facebook. n.d.-c. The 48 & Beyond. Accessed 3 January 2026. https://www.facebook.com/48AndBeyond/.

Fanning, Bryan, Weronika Kloc-Nowak, and Magdalena Lesińska. 2021. Polish Migrant Settlement Without Political Integration in the United Kingdom and Ireland: A Comparative Analysis in the Context of Brexit and Thin European

Citizenship. *International Migration* 59 (1): 263–280. https://doi.org/10.1111/imig.12758.

Ferbrache, Fiona. 2019a. Acts of European Citizenship: How Britons Resident in France Have Been Negotiating Post-Brexit Futures. *Geography* 104 (2): 81–88. https://doi.org/10.1080/00167487.2019.12094067.

Ferbrache, Fiona. 2019b. Local Electoral Rights for Non-French Residents? A Case-Study Analysis of British Candidates and Councillors in French Municipal Elections. *Citizenship Studies* 23 (5): 502–520. https://doi.org/10.1080/13621025.2019.1623864.

Ferbrache, Fiona, and Richard Yarwood. 2015. Britons Abroad or European Citizens? The Negotiation of (Trans)National Space and Citizenship by British Migrants in France. *Geoforum* 62 (June): 73–83. https://doi.org/10.1016/j.geoforum.2015.03.021.

Garner, Oliver. 2018. The Existential Crisis of Citizenship of the European Union: *The Argument for an Autonomous Status. Cambridge Yearbook of European Legal Studies* 20:116–146. https://doi.org/10.1017/cel.2018.6.

Godin, Marie, and Nando Sigona. 2022. Intergenerational Narratives of Citizenship among EU Citizens in the UK after the Brexit Referendum. *Ethnic and Racial Studies* 45 (6): 1135–1154. https://doi.org/10.1080/01419870.2021.1981964.

GOV.UK. 2025. How Many Indefinite Leave (Settlement and EUSS Settled Status) and Citizenship Grants Have Been Issued in the UK? November 27. https://www.gov.uk/government/statistics/immigration-system-statistics-year-ending-september-2025/how-many-indefinite-leave-settlement-and-euss-settled-status-and-citizenship-grants-have-been-issued-in-the-uk.

Guma, Taulant, and Rhys Dafydd Jones. 2019. "Where Are We Going to Go Now?" European Union Migrants' Experiences of Hostility, Anxiety, and (Non-)Belonging During Brexit. *Population, Space and Place* 25 (1): e2198. https://doi.org/10.1002/psp.2198.

Harzoune, Mustapha. 2019. Les bonnes clôtures font-elles les bons voisins? *Hommes & Migrations* 1325 (April): 199–202. https://doi.org/10.4000/hommesmigrations.9406.

Herzog, Philippe. 1996. L'Europe peut-elle devenir l'affaire des citoyens? *Esprit* 224 (8/9): 32–53.

Hobolt, Sara B. 2016. The Brexit Vote: A Divided Nation, a Divided Continent. *Journal of European Public Policy* 23 (9): 1259–1277. https://doi.org/10.1080/13501763.2016.1225785.

Home Office. 2025a. How Many Indefinite Leave (Settlement and EUSS Settled Status) and Citizenship Grants Have Been Issued in the UK? https://www.gov.uk/government/statistics/immigration-system-statistics-year-ending-september-2025/how-many-indefinite-leave-settlement-and-euss-settled-status-and-citizenship-grants-have-been-issued-in-the-uk.

Home Office. 2025b. Immigration System Statistics. November 27. https://assets.publishing.service.gov.uk/media/691adb26493305b49ce6e844/citizenship-datasets-sep-2025.xlsx.

Jablonowski, Kuba. 2017. You Don't Have Rights, You Use Them: Brexit and European Citizenship. *The Sociological Review Magazine*, July 13. https://thesociologicalreview.org/collections/sociology-of-brexit/you-dont-have-rights-you-use-them-brexit-and-european-citizenship/.

Kantar Public. 2023. European Union Citizens Living in the United Kingdom. European Commission. https://www.europarl.europa.eu/at-your-service/files/be-heard/eurobarometer/2023/eu-citizens-in-uk-2023-report-en.pdf.

Kochenov, Dimitry. 2016. *EU Citizenship and Withdrawals from the Union: How Inevitable Is the Radical Downgrading of Rights?* No. 111/2016. London School of Economics and Political Science Paper. London School of Economics and Political Science. https://aei.pitt.edu/93637/1/LEQSPaper111.pdf.

Kostakopoulou, Dora. 2003. Why Naturalisation? *Perspectives on European Politics and Society* 4 (1): 85–115. https://doi.org/10.1080/15705850308438854.

Kostakopoulou, Dora. 2007. European Union Citizenship: Writing the Future. *European Law Journal* 13 (5): 623–646. https://doi.org/10.1111/j.1468-0386.2007.00387.x.

Kostakopoulou, Dora. 2018. Scala Civium: Citizenship Templates Post-Brexit and the European Union's Duty to Protect EU Citizens. *Journal of Common Market Studies* 56 (4): 854–869. https://doi.org/10.1111/jcms.12683.

Kostakopoulou, Theodora. 2019. Who Should Be a Citizen of the Union? Toward an Autonomous European Union Citizenship. *Verfassungsblog*, January 16.

Laursen, Finn, and Sophie Vanhoonacker, eds. 1992. *The Intergovernmental Conference on Political Union: Institutional Reforms, New Policies, and International Identity of the European Community.* Professional Research Paper. Intergovernmental Conference on Political Union, Dordrecht. Martinus Nijhoff.

Lepoutre, Jules. 2019. A Dysfunctional Eurozenship? The Question of Free Movement. *Verfassungsblog*, January 23. https://verfassungsblog.de/a-dysfunctional-eurozenship-the-question-of-free-movement/.

Lord Ashcroft. 2016. How the United Kingdom Voted on Thursday... and Why. *Lord Ashcroft Polls*, June 24. https://lordashcroftpolls.com/2016/06/how-the-united-kingdom-voted-and-why/.

Lulle, Aija, Laura Moroşanu, and Russell King. 2018. And Then Came Brexit: Experiences and Future Plans of Young EU Migrants in the London Region. *Population, Space and Place* 24 (1): e2122. https://doi.org/10.1002/psp.2122.

Lulle, Aija, Russell King, Veronika Dvorakova, and Aleksandra Szkudlarek. 2019. Between Disruptions and Connections: "New" European Union Migrants in the United Kingdom Before and after the Brexit. *Population, Space and Place* 25 (1): e2200. https://doi.org/10.1002/psp.2200.

Migration Observatory. 2025. Characteristics of EU Citizens Living in the UK. Briefing. Migration Observatory. https://migrationobservatory.ox.ac.uk/resources/briefings/characteristics-of-eu-citizens-living-in-the-uk/.

More, Gillian. 2020. From Union Citizen to Third-Country National: Brexit, the UK Withdrawal Agreement, No-Deal Preparations and Britons Living in the European Union. In *European Citizenship under Stress—Social Justice, Brexit and Other Challenges*, ed. Nathan Cambien, Dimitry Kochenov, and Elise Muir. Brill.

Nancheva, Nevena, and Ronald Ranta. 2022. Do They Need to Integrate? The Place of EU Citizens in the UK and the Problem of Integration. *Ethnic and Racial Studies* 45 (10): 1983–2003. https://doi.org/10.1080/01419870.2021.1977363.

Neville, Ann. 2023. Update on the Implementation of the Citizens' Rights Provisions of the Withdrawal Agreement. PE 739.351. European Parliamentary Research Service. https://www.europarl.europa.eu/RegData/etudes/BRIE/2023/739351/EPRS_BRI(2023)739351_EN.pdf.

Pataut, Étienne. 2021. Être ou ne pas être (européen). *Revue Trimestrielle de Droit Européen* 3:517–520.

Pertek, Jacques. 2013. *Droit des institutions de l'Union européenne*. 4th ed. Presses Universitaires de France.

Peters, Floris, Hans Schmeets, and Maarten Vink. 2020. Naturalisation and Immigrant Earnings: Why and to Whom Citizenship Matters. *European Journal of Population* 36 (3): 511–545. https://doi.org/10.1007/s10680-019-09540-1.

Preuß, Ulrich K. 1995. Problems of a Concept of European Citizenship. *European Law Journal* 1 (3): 267–281. https://doi.org/10.1111/j.1468-0386.1995.tb00032.x.

Ranta, Ronald, and Nevena Nancheva. 2019. Unsettled: Brexit and European Union Nationals' Sense of Belonging. *Population, Space and Place* 25 (1): e2199. https://doi.org/10.1002/psp.2199.

Réveillère, Vincent. 2018. Family Rights for Naturalized EU Citizens: Lounes. *Common Market Law Review* 55 (6): 1855–1878. https://doi.org/10.54648/cola2018147.

Réveillère, Vincent. 2022. Chronique Citoyenneté de l'UE – Perte du statut de citoyen de l'Union et refus de naturaliser. *Revue Trimestrielle de Droit Européen* 03 (October): 570.

RIFT. n.d. RIFT—Remain In France Together / UK Citizens in France'. Accessed 3 January 2026. https://www.remaininfrance.fr.

Shachar, Ayelet. 2009. *The Birthright Lottery: Citizenship and Global Inequality*. Harvard University Press.

Shaw, Jo. 2007. E.U. Citizenship and Political Rights in an Evolving European Union. *Fordham Law Review* 75 (5): 2549–2578.

Shaw, Jo. 2019. "Shunning" and "Seeking" Membership: Rethinking Citizenship Regimes in the European Constitutional Space. *Global Constitutionalism* 8 (3): 425–469. https://doi.org/10.1017/S2045381719000133.

Shuibhne, Niamh Nic. 2023. Protecting the Legal Heritage of Former Union Citizens: EP v Préfet Du Gers. *Common Market Law Review* 60 (2): 475–516. https://doi.org/10.54648/cola2023028.

Siklodi, Nora. 2023. (Br)Exit Citizenship: Belonging, Rights and Participation. *Journal of Contemporary European Studies*, December 26, 1–17. https://doi.org/10.1080/14782804.2023.2298330.

Sredanovic, Djordje. 2021. Brexit as a Trigger and an Obstacle to Onwards and Return Migration. *International Migration* 59 (6): 93–108. https://doi.org/10.1111/imig.12712.

Sredanovic, Djordje. 2022. The Tactics and Strategies of Naturalisation: UK and EU27 Citizens in the Context of Brexit. *Journal of Ethnic and Migration Studies* 48 (13): 3095–3112. https://doi.org/10.1080/1369183X.2020.1844003.

Sredanovic, Djordje. 2023. Brexit and Citizenship by Descent: A Relational Understanding of Defensive Pragmatism and of the Rediscovery of Belonging. *Revue Européenne Des Migrations Internationales* 39 (2–3): 109–129. https://doi.org/10.4000/remi.23035.

Sredanovic, Djordje, and Francesco Della Puppa. 2023. Brexit and the Stratified Uses of National and European Union Citizenship. *Current Sociology* 71 (5): 725–742. https://doi.org/10.1177/00113921211048523.

'Statement by Chloe Smith, Minister of State for the Constitution and Devolution; Statement UIN HCWS99'. 2021. June 17. https://questions-statements.parliament.uk/written-statements/detail/2021-06-17/hcws99.

Stone, Jon. 2019. EU Negotiators Will Offer Brits an Individual Opt-in to Remain EU Citizens, Chief Negotiator Confirms. *The Independent*, December 15. https://www.independent.co.uk/news/uk/politics/brexit-eu-citizenship-keep-freedom-of-movement-guy-verhofstadt-chief-negotiator-opt-in-passports-live-move-abroad-a7465271.html.

Tassin, Etienne. 1994. Identités nationales et citoyenneté politique. *Esprit* 198 (1): 97–111.

the3million. 2022. Our Story. February 28. https://the3million.org.uk/our-story.

Thym, Daniel. 2016. "Citizens" and "Foreigners" in EU Law. Migration Law and its Cosmopolitan Outlook. *European Law Journal* 22 (3): 296–316. https://doi.org/10.1111/eulj.12164.

Thym, Daniel. 2019. The Case Against an Autonomous "EU Rump Citizenship". *Verfassungsblog*, ahead of print, January 18. https://doi.org/10.17176/20190211-221659-0.

van den Brink, Martijn, and Dimitry Kochenov. 2019. Against Associate EU Citizenship. *Journal of Common Market Studies* 57 (6): 1366–1382. https://doi.org/10.1111/jcms.12898.

van der Mei. 2020. Member State Nationality, EU Citizenship and Associate European Citizenship. In *European Citizenship under Stress—Social Justice, Brexit and Other Challenges*, ed. Nathan Cambien, Dimitry Kochenov, and Elise Muir. Brill.

van Kessel, Stijn, and Adam Fagan. 2023. Defending Europe from Below: Pro-European Activism in Germany and the UK and Its Contribution to the Politicisation of Europe. *Journal of European Integration* 45 (7): 971–993. https://doi.org/10.1080/07036337.2023.2220073.

Vasiljević, Snježana. 2006. The Concept of European Citizenship. In *Croatian Accession to the European Union (Volume 4)—Challenges of Participation*, ed. K. Ott. Institute of Public Finance and Friedrich Ebert Stiftung. https://d-nb.info/1191058271/34.

Vathi, Zana, and Ruxandra Trandafoiu. 2022. A Post-National EU Diaspora? Political Mobilization of EU Citizens in the UK Post-Brexit. *Global Networks* 22 (4): 752–765. https://doi.org/10.1111/glob.12373.

Vink, Maarten. 2025. The Brexit Naturalisation Effect: An Update Eight Years After the Referendum. Globalcit, March 6. https://globalcit.eu/the-brexit-naturalisation-effect-an-update-eight-years-after-the-referendum/.

Walker, Nigel, and Tim Robinson. 2018. European Union Citizenship. CDP-2018/0061. House of Commons Library. https://researchbriefings.files.parliament.uk/documents/CDP-2018-0061/CDP-2018-0061.pdf.

Weiler, J. 1999. To Be a European Citizen: Eros and Civilisation. In *The Constitution of Europe*, ed. J. Weiler. Cambridge University Press.

White, Robin M. 2002. Nationality, Citizenship and the Meaning of Naturalisation: Brubaker, the United Kingdom, EU Citizens, Third-Country Nationals and the European Union. *Northern Ireland Legal Quarterly* 53 (3): 288–317.

Zambelli, Elena, Michaela Benson, and Nando Sigona. 2022. *British-European Families after Brexit*. No. 3. MIGZEN Research Brief.

CHAPTER 7

Conclusion

Abstract This chapter concludes the book that explores how Brexit transformed the lived experiences of EU citizenship for EU citizens in the UK and UK nationals in the EU27, highlighting its transformative value. While EU citizenship is traditionally understood as a *status* conferring *rights*, the authors' analysis demonstrates its transformative value through *practices* rooted in free movement, expressed through the right to residence, the principle of non-discrimination, and the right to vote and stand as a candidate in local elections. Brexit revealed the fragility of a status derived from Member State nationality; yet the Withdrawal Agreement and domestic measures preserved substantial rights and practices for permanent residents, underscoring that EU citizenship is more than just a legal status. The authors' findings reveal asymmetries: the UK broadly protected rights and practices, whereas many EU Member States adhered strictly to the legal provisions of the Withdrawal Agreement, limiting continuity for UK nationals. Brexit reconfigured the sense of belonging for previously settled residents, but also encouraged mobilisation, litigation, and naturalisation strategies, highlighting the experiential dimension of EU citizenship. Despite losses, such as intra-EU mobility and local voting rights for UK nationals in the EU27, the resilience of rights and practices demonstrates that EU citizenship has transformative value. Ultimately, Brexit illustrates that EU citizenship is shaped by experience and identity,

C. Dadomo, N. Quénivet, *The Transformative Value of EU Citizenship after Brexit*,
https://doi.org/10.1007/978-3-032-20595-7_7

reaffirming its value beyond market integration and its role in fostering belonging and connectedness.

Keywords EU citizenship • Brexit • Integration • Withdrawal Agreement • Free movement • Right to residence • Principle of non-discrimination • Right to vote

This book aimed to explore how Brexit changed the lived experiences of EU citizenship for EU citizens in the UK and UK nationals in the EU27, as well as what these changes reveal about the essence of EU citizenship itself. The authors' hypothesis was that EU citizenship had transformative value, and they tested it within the context of Brexit. Indeed, rather than focusing on what is gained through EU citizenship, as many previous studies have done, this book examines what has remained post-Brexit.

The authors' conceptual framework views EU citizenship not only as a legal *status* that serves as a gateway to a bundle of *rights* but also as having a transformative value that emerges through *practices* rooted in the exercise of free movement (Chap. 3). The rights that enable this *practice* and thus confer this transformative value are the right to reside, the principle of non-discrimination, and the right to vote in local elections. These three elements ensure that EU citizens, especially permanent residents, are embedded in the national and local fabric of the society they live in and are exercising their right to free movement. Put simply, EU citizenship is experiential, beginning with free movement and deepening through the three rights of residence, non-discrimination, and political participation, as well as everyday interaction with the institutions and people of the host State. It is through *practice* (i.e., working, studying, voting locally, accessing services, forming social and cultural ties) that individuals come to perceive themselves as EU citizens, beyond the original market function they were supposed to operate in. In this way, EU citizenship fuses legal strictures (*status* and *rights*) with *practice*. This is particularly significant for permanent residents (who are the focus of this enquiry) as it turns them from foreigners into quasi-nationals. It is through the triad of *status*, *rights*, and *practice* that the authors examined the value of EU citizenship.

The 2016 referendum and the United Kingdom's subsequent decision to leave the European Union sent a shockwave through the population of EU citizens in the UK and UK nationals in the EU27, as they realised that their lives would be different from then on. Brexit exposed the fragility of a status derived from Member State nationality. A conventional reading presents EU citizenship as a status that opens the gateway to rights; by withdrawing, the UK removed that gateway for UK nationals and, within its jurisdiction, divorced EU citizens' rights from EU law. After all, the CJEU was very clear in *E.P. v Préfet du Gers:* EU citizenship is derived from the nationality of an EU Member State, and so the withdrawal of a Member State from the EU means that its nationals lose EU citizenship (Sect. 4.2). Accordingly, Brexit would confirm a minimalist approach to EU citizenship, where status is the most important, before rights, and practice is contingent on status and rights. Brexit posed a challenge to the fundamental status of EU citizenship.

Yet, the authors' analysis shows that this account is largely incorrect. The negotiations on the Withdrawal Agreement, the Withdrawal Agreement itself, and citizens' movements, amongst others, have exposed the transformative value of EU citizenship despite the loss of EU citizenship for UK nationals and the UK's loss of recognition of that status. All have shown a willingness to preserve substantial elements of that practice for permanent residents. In short, the integrity of EU citizenship as a concept and its experiential, embedding, and transformative character have not collapsed in the wake of Brexit; on the contrary, EU citizenship has revealed itself as a powerful concept with transformative value.

Negotiators placed citizens' rights at the heart of the Withdrawal Agreement, establishing an international legal framework to keep residence and associated rights for those who had exercised free movement before the end of the transition period. The fact that citizens' rights were prioritised in the negotiations reveals that both the EU and the UK recognised their fundamental importance (Sect. 4.3).

This new legal architecture preserved a significant part of the rights and, overall, translated the pre-Brexit legal framework (*rights*) and *practice* into a post-Brexit legal regime rather well (Chap. 5). The legal provisions demonstrate recognition at an institutional level by the UK and the EU that the value of EU citizenship is not limited to its status; it is a combination of rights and practices.

The record of the Withdrawal Agreement across the three elements of the transformative value of EU citizenship is instructive (see Chap. 5). For

EU citizens in the UK who qualified under the Settlement Scheme, residence remained secure. For UK nationals in the EU27, continuity depended on meeting the criteria set out in the Citizenship Directive and/or national transposition measures; those who did not meet them faced loss or precariousness. The Withdrawal Agreement anchored the principle of non-discrimination. Yet post-Brexit practice revealed instances of indirect discrimination or administrative hurdles (e.g., digital-only proofs, hostile environment), which reframed EU citizens as "migrants". The Agreement did not retain local voting rights. In practice, the UK allows many EU citizens to continue voting and standing in local elections, subject to conditions, but for UK nationals in the EU27 this is patchier. Some Member States extend such rights to third-country residents (including UK nationals) or have bilateral arrangements with the UK, but many do not allow UK nationals to vote in local elections. Taken together, these outcomes show that where the rights and practice were enshrined in the Withdrawal Agreement and supported or even furthered by legislative and administrative measures, permanent residents could sustain their embeddedness; where they were not, it was left to the UK and the Member States to determine whether the rights and practice warranted legal protection.

The authors' findings on the preservation of rights and practice reveal a notable asymmetry (Chap. 5). The UK adopted a broad approach, often implementing measures that recognised not only rights but also the practical exercise of EU citizenship by permanent residents. Its domestic provisions, in some respects, went beyond the terms of the Agreement, such as capturing individuals protected by CJEU jurisprudence under the EU Settlement Scheme even where they did not squarely fit its formal categories, and providing long-term resident EU citizens with the right to vote and eligibility in local elections. EU Member States, by contrast, generally adhered more strictly to the provisions of the Withdrawal Agreement, acknowledging rights where applicable yet often declining to reconstruct their *practice* for UK nationals who fell outside treaty-based residence criteria. As a result, many UK nationals struggled to secure continued residence if they had not previously met the Directive's thresholds. They were also more likely to fall victim to the complexities and differences among national administrative systems as each State implemented its own procedures. Moreover, their loss of intra-EU mobility could not be remedied by EU Member States and their right to local elections was lost, save in States that extend such rights to third-country nationals or where bilateral arrangements with the UK could be forged. This divergence underscores how States can either narrow EU citizenship to the *rights* enshrined in the Withdrawal Agreement or widen it to encompass the *practices* residents have built over time, thereby aligning with the idea that EU citizenship has transformative value.

Brexit could be read as a reversion to "market citizenship", treating EU citizenship as ancillary to economic integration, with rights primarily framed around the mobility of economically-active persons (see Chap. 2). Somehow, there is a kernel of truth here: aspects of the Withdrawal Agreement reflect the market origins of free movement, focusing on residence rights and the principle of non-discrimination. Yet, Brexit's post-Agreement landscape in the UK demonstrates a broader recognition that long-term residents had built lives anchored in EU-citizenship practices. The UK's willingness to secure those practices suggests its acknowledgement of the non-market dimensions. Conversely, the tighter formalism in several EU Member States highlights the limits of an EU citizenship that lacks autonomous status; where the EU cannot (e.g., right to vote in local elections) or chooses not to oblige recognition of certain rights and practice (e.g., intra-EU mobility), Member States may choose not to or cannot recreate such rights and practice. Overall, the Brexit experience tilts the balance towards acknowledging the transformative value of EU citizenship.

One of Brexit's most salient effects was to remigranticise EU citizens in the UK and UK nationals in the EU27 (see Sect. 5.2.2). This was done legally, by requiring documentary confirmation of their continued residence, and psychologically, by casting previously settled residents as migrants again. For all of them, the shift from automatic EU Law-based rights to nationally processed schemes altered the phenomenology of belonging: practice became conditional upon proving eligibility, obtaining new statuses, or meeting documentary thresholds. While residence was largely retained for those covered by the Withdrawal Agreement or domestic schemes, the emotional and symbolic reclassification was significant for them because it highlighted that EU citizenship is an additional layer dependent on and derived from Member State nationality, and thus removable for the nationals of the Member State leaving the EU. Yet, precisely because people had woven EU-citizenship practices into their daily lives, this remigration effect did not translate into total disengagement; instead, it generated community action, (political) mobilisation, legal action, and, in some instances, naturalisation strategies to restore or safeguard that practice.

Indeed, when the referendum result threatened these rights and practices, individuals responded in two major ways (see Chap. 6). First, grassroots and institutional mobilisation, ranging from activist campaigns to litigation and scholarly proposals for associate or alternative citizenship models, emerged. Although they had mixed results, in the long run, they brought EU citizenship to prominence. Indeed, Brexit increased public awareness of what EU citizenship entails. The mere prospect of losing rights proved educative as individuals realised that it was EU citizenship that had structured their rights and practice. This consciousness contributed to a nascent European *civitas*, a diffuse sense of shared citizenship and calls by politicians and scholars for the creation of a new or revised EU citizenship, often one that is autonomous from the nationality of the Member States. Yet, momentum waned as pro-EU citizenship movements lost steam and proposals for associate citizenship failed to achieve traction.

Second, some EU citizens in the UK sought to preserve their rights via naturalisation; some UK nationals in the EU27 sought to preserve their EU citizens' rights (residence and mobility) by applying for the nationality of an EU Member State (see Sect. 6.4). This research shows that naturalisation patterns are more than tactical moves; they are existential reckonings with loss of status, imagined futures and opportunities, and ease of mobility. For many who applied for another Member State's nationality, it was instrumental: a means to retain residence, welfare access, or intra-EU movement. For others, it expressed embeddedness forged through years of practice that had turned them into local citizens in all but name. Others resisted the implication that EU citizenship's embeddedness should culminate in naturalisation under the *Lounes* jurisprudence. The difference of these choices underscores the authors' central point: EU citizenship's transformative value is felt in practice, not merely in status or rights, and individuals respond to disruptions by balancing pragmatic preservation of rights with normative commitments to identity and belonging. Moreover, the fact that UK nationals who had not exercised their right to free movement also applied for another Member State's nationality in order to keep EU citizenship reveals how central free movement (at least as an opportunity) is to EU citizenship.

The mixed success of these efforts to cling to some link to the EU citizenship is instructive. It confirmed both the resilience of EU citizenship, where practice could be legally safeguarded, and the enduring primacy of national frameworks, which is linked to the lack of an autonomous concept of EU citizenship.

So, what does this all reveal about EU citizenship? It is tempting to narrate Brexit as a story of loss (and mourning): the UK nationals' loss of EU citizenship, EU citizens' loss of status in the UK, the loss of intra-EU mobility for UK nationals in the EU27, the loss of local voting rights in many EU Member States. But another narrative emerges, that of recognition of the rights and practice of EU citizenship. Through the Withdrawal Agreement and domestic measures (particularly in the UK), the rights and practice of EU citizenship for permanent residents have been substantially preserved. First, through the Withdrawal Agreement and UK domestic measures, EU citizens in the UK retained residence and related rights. Their everyday practice of EU citizenship continues, albeit reframed under international and national law. This is the clearest case of continuity. Second, despite the inclusion of the principle of non-discrimination in the Agreement, its practical application faces some hurdles. Practice survives but is more contestable, and residents feel more like migrants than integrated locals. Third, the intra-EU mobility for UK nationals and local electoral rights in most EU27 jurisdictions represent losses of significant rights. Where EU Member States do not unilaterally extend voting rights to third-country nationals or bilateral arrangements have not been agreed upon, practice has not been reconstructed. Brexit has therefore showcased both the fragility and resilience of EU citizenship.

The book begins by noting that most scholarship highlights the benefits of EU citizenship, while fewer studies consider what is lost when it disappears. Brexit prompted an examination of these losses, leading to a deeper understanding of the essence and purpose of EU citizenship. It goes beyond facilitating movement; it fosters a sense of belonging and transforms rights into routines, thereby shaping identities. And the book concludes that, ultimately, the "*Dasein*" of EU citizenship is experiential and transformative, centred on how individuals enjoy their status as Union citizens in everydayness. Overall, the conceptual integrity of EU citizenship, as experiential and transformative, remains despite Brexit.

Index[1]

[1] Note: Page numbers followed by 'n' refer to notes.

C. Dadomo, N. Quénivet, *The Transformative Value of EU Citizenship after Brexit*,
https://doi.org/10.1007/978-3-032-20595-7

The manufacturer's authorised representative in the EU is Springer Nature Customer Service Centre GmbH, Europaplatz 3, 69115 Heidelberg, Germany. If you have any concerns regarding our products, please contact ProductSafety@springernature.com

Printed and bound by CPI Group (UK) Ltd, Croydon, CR0 4YY
21/09/2026
02219945-0002